In January 1995, Azim Khamisa's 20-year-old son, Tariq, was shot and killed by a 14-year-old gang member in a pizza delivery gone awry. At the time, a devastated father had to relearn how to live, saying, "I had to find a way to climb out of my grief just as I had climbed out of my son's grave." Nine months after the tragedy, Azim started the Tariq Khamisa Foundation (TKF) in his son's memory with the purpose of stopping kids from killing kids. For the past twelve years, he and the murderer's grandfather, Ples Felix, have been standing side by side as brothers in the work of teaching children and adults alike the ways of nonviolence and forgiveness.

Beginning with the Violence Impact Forum (VIF) and expanding over the years into several distinct programs, the foundation has positively impacted hundreds of thousands of students with its key message of peace. Azim's message of forgiveness is also internationally shared through lectures at conferences and other venues and through his public workshop, where his audiences come to the self-empowering realization that they always have choice.

"When I lost my son, my heart blew up into a million bits, and I did not know if I would ever recover," he says. "But I have found fulfillment again, and that it comes from the ongoing act of forgiveness."

From Forgiveness to Fulfillment - a sequel to his first book, *Azim's Bardo: From Murder to Forgiveness* - beautifully illustrates how Azim has found fulfillment through forgiveness, detailing the evolution of a father dedicated to healing not only his heart but also the wounds of our society.

ANK Publishing, Inc.
La Jolla, California

Other Works by
Azim Khamisa

Books

From Murder to Forgiveness

Secrets of a Bullet-proof Spirit
How to Take a Hard Knock and Come out on Top
(from Random House Publishing, Spring 2009)

CDs

Achieving Fulfillment through Spiritual Activism

Conversations with the Dalai Lama

Forgiveness - The Crown Jewel of Personal Freedom
(3 Disk Series and Workbook)

DVDs

Garden of Life

Collective Wisdom & Spiritual Activism

See complete and updated list at:
www.AzimKhamisa.com

From Forgiveness
to Fulfillment

Peace + Many blessings

[signature]

8189 Via Mallorca
La Jolla, CA 92037
Tel: (858) 452-2541
Azim@AzimKhamisa.com
www.AzimKhamisa.com

From Forgiveness to Fulfillment

by **Azim Khamisa**

ANK Publishing, Inc.
La Jolla, California

To my son, Tariq, for connecting me with my heart and soul.

To my daughter, Tasreen, and grandchildren, Shahin & Khalil, for keeping that connection alive.

And to the countless kids who have been touched and who continue to be touched by Tariq's spirit.

This book could not have seen completion without the help of the following people to whom I offer my most heartfelt thanks.

To my daughter, Tasreen; every father should have the gift of a daughter like her, and for the immense joy I receive in my life from my two grandsons, Shahin and Khalil.

To Tariq's mother, Almas, for her friendship and support, and for giving birth to two amazing souls, Tasreen and Tariq.

To my son-in-love (as he likes to be called), Mehrdad, for being a great husband and an awesome father.

To my family, for their love and support:

- Dad, Mum
- My sister, Neyleen
- My brother, Nazir, his wife Shelina, and their daughter Soraiya
- My deceased sister, Yasmin (may her soul rest in eternal peace), her husband Tony, and their sons Karim, Nazim, and Salim

To Ples Felix, for being my brother and friend, first in grief and now in love, and for his unwavering commitment and partnership in stopping violence among our children and youth.

To Tony Hicks, without whom this story would be incomplete, and for his significant contribution to TKF.

To Dan Pearson, for his love, friendship, and guidance, and for always being there for me.

To Kit Goldman, for her friendship and contribution to the work and mission of TKF.

To Mark Fackler—the President of TKF—for his exemplary leadership and generous contribution of time and treasure, and for his commitment to the work of TKF.

To TKF's current Board of Trustees: Harriett Carter, Peter Deddeh, Dianne McKay, Lou Adamo, Richard Taylor, Martin Shapiro, Derek Myron, Cheryl Rhodes, Johan Oeyen, Laura Angel-Zavala, and to all the past board members for giving generously of their time and treasure to TKF.

To the TKF current staff: Lisa Grogan, Suzanne Beacon, Megan Thomas Westcott, Katie Bowles, Betsy Frank, Mayra Nunez, Jenifer Finkelstein, Niki Kosteck, Donna Pinto, and the many past staff members, all who so significantly contribute their hearts and souls on a daily basis to fulfill the mission of TKF.

To Sal Giacolone, Javier Ortega, Mayra Nunez, and others for serving as passionate facilitators and panelists for TKF's signature program, the Violence Impact Forum Assembly.

To TKF and its many volunteers, who in so many ways offer support to carry forward the important mission of our work.

To Brian Klemmer, Founder of Klemmer & Associates, Inc., for his friendship, support, and "adoption" of TKF, inspiring so many wonderful people to become Seeds of Hope Society members.

To all those who have supported the foundation's work by generously donating their time, treasure and other resources.

To the current and past CANEI staff, all who so significantly contribute their hearts and souls on a daily basis to fulfill our mission, and especially to Nola LaWarre, who has provided administrative support to me since CANEI was established. My work with CANEI would not be possible without the support she always offers with a smile.

To DeAnna LoCoco, for her friendship and generous spirit, and for her significant contribution of time and treasure.

To Wendy Craig-Purcell, for her love and support, and for inspiring me to create a workshop to teach forgiveness to adults.

To the ANK team: Jullya Conklin, Jim Ellis, Jennifer Geronimo, JD Mumma, and Adam Pearson, who help and support me in my work of creating peace, love, and unity around the world.

To Mubarak Awad and Marvena Twigg for their love, support, and friendship, for their tireless commitment and passion for our children and youth, and for their support of the CANEI program.

To Marian Wright Edelman, Founder and President of the Children's Defense Fund, for her tireless work and unwavering commitment to improving the lives and conditions of our children.

To Arun Gandhi, Co-Founder of the M. K. Gandhi Institute for Nonviolence, for his love and support of my work, and for his passion and commitment to teach the Gandhian principles of Ahimsa and Satyagraha.

To Marianne Williamson, for her love and friendship, for her passionate commitment and ministry to creating peace on our planet, and for contributing the foreword for my book.

To Michael Beckwith, for his love and friendship, for his amazing ministry to teach Agape— universal love—which he accomplishes with such grace, impact, and passion, and for contributing the afterword for my book.

To Ted Lewis, Judy Strnad, Scott Timmerman, Marvena Twigg, and Professor Mark Umbreit for their expertise and help with ensuring the manuscript's accuracy.

To my friends and readers: Joan Adamo, Suzanne Bacon, Beth Bell, Katie Bowles, Bernice Burg, Sylvia Clute, Bill Gladstone, Sara Granby, Lisa Grogan, Upasana Grugan, DeAnna LoCoco, Dianne McKay, Mayra Nunez, Dan Pearson, Donna Pinto, Jillian Quinn, Robin Stark, Megan Thomas Wescott, Colby White, and Kim Wilson for their heartfelt support and valuable input.

To Andrea Cagan, for her immensely valuable and skillful editorial review of the manuscript.

To Steve Hardin and Amanda Moss for their passionate work in designing the cover and interior of my book.

To Jim Ellis for his dedicated passion and diligence to get this book through the production process.

To Dianne McKay, for generously and meticulously proof-reading the manuscript . . . twice.

And, finally, a special and well deserved, profound acknowledgement to my research and writing partner, Karen J. Gordon, for her passionate pursuit and brilliant research and writing of my book—this could not have been achieved without her. Thank you, Karen, from the bottom of my heart.

To anyone I may have forgotten to acknowledge, I offer you my deepest apology and expression of love.

Contents

Foreword

Forgiveness.

Why? And most importantly, how?

If love creates miracles, and to withhold forgiveness is to withhold love, then to refuse to forgive someone is to refuse a miracle.

The fact that that is easy to intellectually understand does not mean forgiveness is always easy to practice. If it were, we would have all forgiven a lot more than we have, and the world would be more full of miracles.

In fact, forgiveness is often difficult. We nurse our grievances, as though to let them go would be to condone wrong action and minimize our own pain. We feel we don't want to let the perpetrator "get away with it." We find perverse comfort in being perceived by others as a victim, or an aggrieved party. Yet while such emotions are perfectly natural, and might make sense for a time, there comes a point at which they block the healing that would remove our suffering. Ultimately, the choice to forgive is not something you do for someone else; it is something you do for yourself.

One of the best ways to achieve anything is to find someone else who has achieved it already, and emulate him or her. I have been blessed in my life by knowing people who have truly, genuinely forgiven things I know in my heart I would have an extremely difficult time forgiving. Foremost among them is Azim Khamisa, who has turned the tragedy of his only son's murder into not only a paragon of forgiveness, but also a paragon of hope for all of us.

Why is Azim's demonstration of profound forgiveness not only an example for all of us personally, but also a hope for our world? Because forgiveness alone can do what no amount of external power can do: it can transform our thoughts about the past and free the future to new possibilities. Azim has more than healed his own heart by his capacity to find forgiveness in the midst of a cruel fate: he has brought the sweet healing of forgiveness to his family, his friends, and even to his son's murderer. He has taught hundreds, even thousands more people how they too can achieve the spiritual medicine of forgiveness. And with this book, he applies his understanding of the ultimate wisdom of forgiveness to the conundrum of global violence and terror.

Who among us is not yearning for the antidote to violence, both in our hearts and in our world? Forgiveness is that antidote, and learning how to practice it is the greatest thing any of us can do to help turn our world in a more peaceful direction. This book is one man's story and one man's teaching. It is the strange and sad and ultimately miraculous tale of the transformation of a human heart. It is the description not only of a path which one man tread, but the description of a path which all of us can tread, to bring fulfillment to our own lives and greater peace to our precious world.

Azim makes it clear that although his son has died, he did not die in vain. Not only his life, but the way his family responded to his death, has created more light and love and peace in the world around them. And that is just the beginning. With this book, I hope the mission of Azim Khamisa, and the foundation which he began, will extend even further and wider to bring the balm of forgiveness to all hearts that suffer.

Nothing matters more than forgiveness, and no one understands forgiveness better than my friend and hero Azim Khamisa. What he has learned, he now teaches. And what he teaches, may all of us learn.

Marianne Williamson
July 2007

Lord, make me an instrument of Thy peace.
Where there is hatred let me sow love;
Where there is injury, pardon;
Where there is doubt, faith;
Where there is despair, hope;
Where there is darkness, light;
Where there is sadness, joy.
O Divine Master,
Grant that I may seek not so much to be consoled,
As to console;
Not so much to be understood,
As to understand;
Not so much to be loved,
As to love.
For it is in giving that we receive.
It is in pardoning that we are pardoned.
It is in dying that we awaken to eternal life.

— St. Francis of Assisi

Introduction

When I received the news on the morning of January 22, 1995, that my only son had been shot and killed, I felt like a nuclear bomb had gone off in my heart. As the blinding moment of tragedy crushed me, any vision I'd once held of a fulfilled life had been destroyed. I felt my own life force draining out of me from my head to my toes. And with the pain too great to bear, I had the spiritual experience of leaving my body.

In this altered state of consciousness, I felt held and comforted in the arms of my God. There, in that state of peace, I realized a profound truth—an idea so far removed from a normal reaction to my son's murder that to others it would seem inconceivable. What was this knowledge that I instantaneously embraced? Simply this:

There were victims at both ends of the gun.

From Murder To Forgiveness

In my first book, *From Murder to Forgiveness*, I described in detail the tragedy that set me on my spiritual path. I introduced my only son, Tariq, a twenty-year-old university student, who was tragically murdered while delivering pizzas to a bogus address. I wrote about Tony Hicks, the fourteen-year-old gang member, who in one moment of blinding and irreversible unconsciousness shot and killed my son and threw his own life away. And I introduced a man named Ples Felix, Tony's

When Azim Khamisa heard the news of the murder of his only son, it was like a nuclear bomb had gone off in his heart.

grandfather, who raised him from the age of nine as if he were his own son. In one tragic moment on the night of January 21, 1995, all of our lives were changed forever.

Most parents would agree with the sentiment that it's a parent's job to keep his or her child safe. I felt like I'd failed. If only I could have prevented Tariq from being there that night.

If only I had been there to take that bullet for him. So many thoughts, yet no resolution. I felt tremendously guilty for the death of my son.

And what about anger? Did I not feel hatred for the boy who'd killed Tariq? Did I not want revenge? I was angry, yes, but never at Tony directly. After having awakened to the true meaning of victimhood, I was angry at a society and a culture that had promoted a violent atmosphere in which children were killing children. That was a defining moment in my life. I understood that I could allow anger and guilt to fester and grow into an ugly and self-abusive mass of negativity . . . or I could make another choice.

Nine months after my son died, I established the Tariq Khamisa Foundation (TKF) in his memory. I reached out to Ples, letting him know I held no ill will toward him, his grandson, or their family. Aware that there were victims at both ends of the gun—Tariq, a victim of his grandson; his grandson, a victim of society—I invited Ples to join the foundation and assist me in teaching kids to choose forgiveness and nonviolence as a way of life. He instantly agreed, and we have been working together as colleagues and as brothers—first as brothers-in-grief and now as brothers-in-love—for twelve years.

A few years after TKF's inception, my daughter, Tasreen, joined us. She had graduated from the University of Washington with a degree in Sociology and a specialization in working with juvenile delinquents—just like the boy who had killed her brother. In 1988, Tasreen came to the foundation as assistant executive director, and about a year later the board promoted her to executive director. For six years she did a stellar job, and after she left TKF to start a family, my daughter blessed me with two beautiful grandchildren. We still contact her from time to time, as she continues to wisely advise me, board members, and staff.

As we at the Tariq Khamisa Foundation continue to see the many wonderful results from the implementation of our prevention programs, we gain inspiration. Our broader vision to help more children choose lives of peace and nonviolence is always being newly created. Since its inception in 1995, TKF has expanded into the following six distinct programs, which I will describe in this book:

- The Violence Impact Forum Assembly (VIF)
- Circle of Peace
- Ending the Cycle of Violence
- Substitute Teacher Program
- In-School Suspension Program
- Parent Peace Coalition

TKF is a successful prevention program. But what about the kids who are already on the slippery slope? CANEI (Constant and Never Ending Improvement), a program I developed under the auspices of the National Youth Advocate Program (NYAP), improves the lives of troubled at-risk youth through a caring and holistic approach to treatment. This approach emphasizes the model of restorative justice, as discussed in my first book.

Supportive of my work with children through TKF and CANEI, my friend, Reverend Wendy Craig-Purcell, encouraged me to take my message of forgiveness to the adult population. From discussions with her, and with a perspective gained over time, I was able to distill my process of embracing forgiveness as a way of life into three basic steps. I present my workshop, *Forgiveness, The Crown Jewel of Personal Freedom*, at various domestic and international venues, and it is also offered as a

CD series. The following three steps of forgiveness, which I teach in my workshop, are covered in detail in this book:

1. Acknowledge you have been wronged.
2. Give up all resulting resentment.
3. Reach out.

FORGIVENESS

As I travel the country and the world talking about peace and nonviolence, I emphasize that forgiveness is something we do for ourselves. When we choose to forgive another person— or ourselves—we release the resentment, anger, and guilt we've held so close. We are then able to allow the natural flow of love back into our hearts. Through forgiveness we can create a culture of peace in this world. We are all One. We all emanate from the same source. Unless we learn to create brotherhood and sisterhood from conflict, the human race will surely perish.

When asked how I could forgive the murderer of my son, I answer by saying that forgiveness is a process, not an event, and I forgive Tony every day. I have dedicated this book to help others find the courage and stamina to forgive their aggressors, or themselves, just as I did and just as Tony is trying to do. When people learn to forgive and move out into the world with open and compassionate hearts, goodwill spreads like a ripple effect. The goal is to find and establish in our current society the grace of forgiveness, fulfillment, and world peace, one healed heart at a time.

FULFILLMENT

When I lost my son, I thought my life was over. How could I go on? How would I ever feel joy and happiness again? I turned to the teachings of my Ismaili faith and was reminded that we could fill the first forty days of Tariq's journey in the next world with mourning, but excessive grieving would impede his soul's journey.

My faith directed me to turn my grief into good deeds for the living, deeds that would fuel Tariq's soul's journey, not hinder it. One of my spiritual teachers reminded me that the quality of the rest of my life depended on my reaction to my son's murder. I knew that for a life to have quality, it must have purpose. My faith renewed me and gave me a reason for living. I decided that I would help Tariq's soul on its journey. I would turn my grief into the good deed of stopping children from killing each other. I would become a foe, not of my son's killer, whom I believed was a victim himself, but rather of the forces that put a young boy like Tony Hicks on a dark street, holding a handgun, about to shoot and kill someone he didn't even know.

When I lost my son, my heart blew up into a million bits, and I did not know if I would ever recover. But I can sincerely tell you that I have found fulfillment again and that it comes from the ongoing act of forgiveness. As I travel the world speaking about forgiveness and telling the story of Tariq and Tony, of Azim and Ples, over and over again, I ask myself, "Was this event a tragedy, or was it mystically meaningful?"

I can see now that both are true. That my son died is most certainly a tragedy. My family and I miss him deeply, and this dark night in our family's life did not end with my son's death. It extended to Tariq's fiancée, Jennifer, who suffered so greatly with her loss that she eventually took her own life. Indeed, this event was tragic with rippling repercussions. But at the same time, Tariq's death set me on my spiritual path.

This has been a blessing. So it is both. It is a tragedy, and it is mystically meaningful. With grace, I have moved from murder to forgiveness and from forgiveness to fulfillment. I have found peace again and so can you, no matter how devastated and broken you feel.

The Tariq Khamisa Foundation is now twelve years old. It started with one act of forgiveness — an act which saved my life from utter devastation. But there has also been a ripple effect. CANEI is greatly improving the lives of troubled at-risk youth in several states. Through my forgiveness workshops and talks to organizations and corporations, and through our in-school programs, multi-media presentations, and media broadcasts, millions of children and adults are being exposed to new ways of dealing with the difficulties, anger, and guilt in their own lives. Instead of seeking revenge or retaliation, they now seek understanding, compassion, forgiveness, and peace. And with each and every soul that is touched by our vision, my heart grows deeper into love.

I offer this book to you now, to implement your own understanding of the choices that you and your family can make between violence and nonviolence. I have come to understand that we are all on the same path, and we are all doing the best we can. Please know that no matter which step of the path you are on, I honor the place in you in which the entire Universe dwells. I honor the place in you that is of love, of truth, of light, and of peace. When you are in that place and I am in that place, we are One.

Namaste.

Azim Khamisa
July 2007

*I will lead my life; they can say what they will. The
ones who really care will be with me at the end...
For I am what I am and that's all I will be.*

— Tariq Khamisa
Tariq's Journal, October 24, 1994

Tariq's Philosophy of Life

(Written in 1992 for a high school assignment at age eighteen)

These are six of the aphorisms that I base my life on. It means a lot to me to follow these aphorisms, and I try my utmost to.

1) **"Hang in there when the odds are against you."**

I feel that this quote has helped me a lot in all the things I do, especially in school and in sports. In wrestling, this quote has helped me out a lot. Especially when you're matched up against that really good wrestler who's pinned everyone. This quote lets you know to tough it out even though the odds aren't in your favor, and a lot of the times when you do this you do end up coming out ahead when you were sure you weren't going to succeed.

2) **"Treat people the way you would want to be treated."**

This is very important to me. I feel you should treat everyone with respect, and in return you will be treated with it. I feel that you should be kind to people and, in general, treat them the way you know you would want to be treated.

3) **"Give life your best effort."**

I feel this is so important to me because if you always give life your best effort, in your mind you'll never be a failure. If

Tariq Khamisa
1974 – 1995

you always give your 110 percent, you know you're trying your hardest, and that gives you a good feeling of satisfaction even if you don't always come out ahead.

4) "Use your time wisely."

I feel time not spent doing useful things is time wasted. I live by this quote because I feel time is the most precious commodity known to man; because once it's gone, it's gone forever. Time is one thing you can never get back once it's gone, so you should always spend your time wisely.

5) "It is all right to be disappointed but a winner can never allow himself to be discouraged."

This quote allows you to face the trials and tribulations of life, and still be able to walk with your head up. Failure is unavoidable, but you have to be able to move on, and getting discouraged won't help you at all!

6) "Living by giving."

I feel it is much better to give than to receive. It makes you feel so good to be able to give things to people; not only material things, but also special things. Perhaps a warm smile to that person who's having a bad day or some good advice to a person with a problem. Giving is a wonderful thing and I urge all of you to try it. It doesn't take much and it will give you a wonderful feeling of satisfaction.

*Out beyond the ideas of wrong-doing and right-doing
there is a field; I'll meet you there.*

— Rumi

Meeting Tony Hicks

Chapter One

On January 1, 1995, just a few weeks before fourteen-year-old Tony Hicks shot and killed my son, Tariq, the state of California passed a law that fourteen-year-olds could be tried as adults. Tony was the first youth to be sentenced under that new law, and he received twenty-five- years-to-life.

Tony's Sentencing Speech
(April 1996 at age fifteen)

Good morning Judge,

On January 21, 1995, I shot and killed Tariq Khamisa, a person I didn't even know and who didn't do anything wrong to me. On April 11, 1996, I pled guilty to first-degree murder because I am guilty. I wanted to save the Khamisa family and my family from further pain.

From my grandfather I have learned about the Khamisa family and their only son, Tariq. I have learned about the love they have for him. Through my grandfather and Mr. Reynolds, they have tried to explain to me the compassion the Khamisa family has for me.

I have had a lot of problems in my life. Over the last year, while I have been in Juvenile Hall, I have thought about my problems. I wish I didn't have the type of life I had. I wish I had a relationship with my father. I think about the warmth

1

Tariq age 5   *Tony age 6*

Innocence is immortal.

*that my grandfather gave me. I wonder why I didn't listen to
my grandfather.*

*At night, when I'm alone, I cry and beg God to let me
out of here. I promise Him that I will be a better person —
I won't mess up. When I see my mom, I want to hold her as
tight as I can and beg her, "Take me out of jail!"*

*However, I don't want to use my problems as an excuse
for my actions. I think I would have gone to jail sometime,
but I honestly don't think getting busted for a robbery or
something like that would have changed me. I was too mad
at everyone: my mom, my dad, my grandfather. When I first
came to the Hall, I was mad at the District Attorney and the*

people at the Hall for keeping me here. Now, I'm just scared and mad at myself.

I'm alone at Juvenile Hall. I often think about the night I shot Tariq, especially when I'm alone in my cell. When it's dark and quiet, I wonder what it's like to die. I wonder why I'm still alive. Sometimes when I roll over in bed and I lay next to the cold wall, I feel as far away from everything as possible. I wonder if that's what dying feels like.

I still don't know why I shot Tariq. I didn't really want to hurt him or anyone else. I'm sorry. I'm sorry for killing Tariq and hurting his family. I'm sorry for the pain I caused for Tariq's father, Mr. Khamisa. I pray to God every day that Mr. Khamisa will forgive me for what I have done, and for as long as I live I will continue to pray to God to give him strength to deal with his loss.

My grandfather promised me that he will be Mr. Khamisa's friend and help him in any way he can for the rest of his life. I am very sorry for what I have done. Thank you for giving me the chance to speak.

IN PRISON

Tony made this emotional speech when he was fifteen years old, just fifteen months after the terrible tragedy. He is now twenty-six and is serving his sentence in an adult prison with no possibility of parole until 2025. Tony is as remorseful today as he was when he so poignantly spoke to the judge at his sentencing hearing that day in 1996. He knew the moment he pulled the trigger that he had done something so wrong that it could never be made right again. But it was too late. His decision to follow his gang leader Antoine's order to "Bust him,

Bone!" could not be reversed. Tariq was dead. And Tony was responsible.

In prison, Tony has had a lot of time to think over that fateful night and the hours before that led up to the tragic shooting. Here are his words from a written interview conducted in October 2006 by my research and writing partner, Karen Gordon. Some of Tony's recollections vary from what was written in my first book. I attribute this both to the traumatic state he was in at the time of his first interviews and also to the passage of time.

"I don't know if I've told this to anyone before, but things were moving extremely fast in those hours between the time I ran away from home and the time I was arrested. The truth is my mind was somewhat in a fog at that time. I want to say it was a drug-induced fog, but that was only part of it. I've only recently begun to feel like I was [now] thinking with some clarity.

"I remember the main parts about what happened that night, but a lot of the details were filled in during the court process. I don't really know what my feelings were at that moment [when I shot Tariq]. The Tony Hicks then seems like a totally different person than the one sitting here struggling to express himself.

"I can tell you that I was angry. I'd just run away from home. I imagine I was confused and frustrated. Also feeling a little powerless at fourteen. But these weren't feelings that manifested themselves at the moment of the shooting, but long-standing feelings that were brought to a head that night.

"I don't recall any vacillation when I was told to shoot Tariq. I also didn't consider my choices. I didn't know what my choices really were at that moment. The shooting wasn't reflexive, though. I do remember a pause on my part. Why? I don't recall. And I don't want to make up an answer or make myself sound sympathetic.

"I don't believe that I had time to think or feel directly after the shooting. Again, things were moving pretty fast. I didn't gain perspective on what I had done until I was given time to think about everything in jail."

Tony was referring to the juvenile facility where he was held until his sentencing hearing. Since his 1996 imprisonment in Sacramento's New Folsom California State Prison at the age of sixteen, he's been moved several times. In June 2000, he was transferred to the state prison in Calipatria (California's Imperial Valley), and then in December 2001 to the California Correctional Institution (CCI) in Tehachapi.

In 2002 there was an altercation between Tony, another prisoner, and a guard. Due to this event, Tony's sentence was increased by ten years (of which he will serve eight). Sometime after the altercation, he was transferred to Corcoran State Prison north of Bakersfield, and then he was moved once more, this time to Pelican Bay State Prison in Crescent City. Here Tony was placed in solitary confinement for five years, and in March of 2006 he was moved back into the general population.

I was sad to hear about this confrontation with the guard. I obviously had hoped that the love and support Ples and I were giving Tony would help to keep him out of further trouble. Nonetheless, he *was* involved and took responsibility, and he had to suffer the consequences of the extended sentence.

In Tony's words: "The confrontation that I had with staff was ultimately an argument that got way out of hand, although I understand that the staff and their peers don't see it that way.

One of their own was hurt, so for them it was more personal. I don't want to go into much detail [about it] here, because the situation involved another inmate, and I don't want to tell his story.

"I was twenty-one at the time, I believe, and struggling with reconciling my beliefs that I had formed over the years [since the shooting] with my environment, and [I was] having a lot of difficulty doing it. How does one not fall into the muck of the situation when that's all you have to look forward to? Another big thing that I was weighing was the definition of [that] which is more than likely what allowed an argument to get out of hand. I know that all of this isn't saying much, but it's hard to explain how something like that goes wrong.

"My attitude has matured some, but I still have trouble with belief vs. environment. But I'm at a level of peace with it. I know that it may be something that I struggle [with] for the whole of my life."

The personal beliefs Tony's talking about grew out of the seed of compassion that was planted in his heart by my forgiveness and which continues to be nurtured by the love of both me and his grandfather. He spends most of his prison day thinking and reading, and he has had a lot of time to mull over all the events of his life. He wrote to Karen about what a day in prison is like for him.

"A day in my life is brief, because the days in here are so short. I get up around six in the morning. I read for an hour or until breakfast comes. After I eat I work out for an hour or an hour and a half. After that I do some more reading. I'm taking a college course through the mail, so a large part of my time is taken up by that. If I'm done taking notes and doing my assignments by two, I watch some TV or catch up on some writing. This all depends on [whether] or not we're given yard that day and at what time.

"I think I'm more on track now on my journey of self-discovery than ever before. I have a better sense of who I am as a person. There are even a few things about myself that I'm proud of. The personal healing is less fluent. It's still difficult to reconcile who I am and what I believe with taking Tariq's life."

A TROUBLED YOUTH

As Tony said in his letter to the judge, he had a lot of problems in his life. He had an absent father and a mother who did what she could; but at fifteen years old, she was only a baby herself. Most of his immediate family members were involved with gangs and violence, and at a young age he was sexually molested by one of his mother's partners. The anger from all of these experiences sat deep inside, and there was no safe place for him to shed the festering emotions.

Tony's absent father showed up on three separate occasions, but he physically abused the boy on each visit. Realizing she needed help raising her son, Tony's mother went to live with her grandmother and periodically stayed with her own father, Ples. When Tony was nine, his favorite cousin was killed in a storm of automatic gunfire in a drive-by shooting, and Tony witnessed his cousin's remains being removed by the coroner's staff. This incident permanently scarred Tony, and a few months later it was decided that he should leave Los Angeles and go to live full time with his grandfather in the San Diego area.

The transition to his grandfather's loving but strict environment was not an easy one. Ples tried to teach Tony that he could be a can-do person instead of a can't-do kid. When he began fourth grade, Tony could not read, write, or function at that grade level. But with the support and assistance of his grandfather and the teachers at his elementary school, Tony grew determined to succeed. After repeating the first half of fifth grade, he was moved up to the sixth grade so that he could complete his studies and graduate with his own class.

Ples remembers that Tony was a kind-hearted, polite, and well-spoken kid. But he also had anger issues. Ples engaged a therapist to help him with anger management, and after a year of therapy Tony seemed to be coping better. However, Ples noticed that by his fourteenth birthday his grandson was requesting to spend more time out after sundown to be with his friends. Tony enjoyed playing basketball at the local park, but Ples didn't think that hanging out at night with a group of his friends was a good idea and insisted that he only participate in adult-supervised activities.

Tony was required to bring home a teacher-signed sheet at the end of every week noting what assignments had been completed. He wasn't used to this kind of discipline, and he rebelled against the authority and pressure to accomplish all that Ples felt he needed to do in order to achieve success and gain confidence in his life. Tony became angry with his grandfather's restrictions. Though they were the type any reasonable parent would make concerning school work, house chores, and after-school activities, Tony began to rebel against them.

On Friday, January 20, 1995, Ples received one of the teacher-signed assignment sheets showing that Tony hadn't done any of his class work for that week—none of it at all. His grandfather was reasonably upset, and Tony was grounded from seeing his friends the next day, Saturday, until all his work was completed.

Ples spoke with his grandson that evening about the importance of protecting his future by focusing on his education rather than getting high with his friends. Tony grew angrier still. Ples pointed out that he would soon be tested and that someone would put a gun in his hands and tell him to shoot someone.

"Daddy, I would never do that," Tony replied.

"That's what you tell me," Ples said. "But will you be strong enough to say no to your homies?"

The next morning, Ples got up with Tony and gave him a list of chores to do that day. He told his grandson that when the chores were completed, he could go play ball with his friends. Tony was still angry when his grandfather left, and when Ples returned around 5:00 p.m., the house was dark. He went to his room and saw a note on his dresser that said, "Daddy, I have run away. Love, Tony." Ples's heart sank. Where had his grandson gone?

It was late evening of January 21, 1995, when Tony gave in to deadly peer pressure. In a gang activity called "jack the pizza guy," he tragically shot and killed a pizza delivery man. It wasn't premeditated. He didn't go out that night to deliberately kill someone. But Tony is the person responsible for the death of my son, and he will live with his action and with his remorse for the rest of his life.

Tony loved his grandfather. He even signed his run-away note, "Love, Tony." But this love was not enough to keep him from his friends who reinforced his anger—and gave him an outlet for it. It was this festering emotion of anger erupting inside Tony that influenced his decision to listen to his gang leader, Antoine (street name Q-Tip), who ordered him to pull the trigger. In the single moment of a bad decision, two lives abruptly came to an end. Tariq, my only son, lay dead. And Tony, the only son Ples ever knew, was lost to the California state prison system.

The Seed Of Compassion

I knew I needed to see Tony Hicks face-to-face, since part of my healing could only come after I met the person who'd taken Tariq's life. There were some things I needed to complete, some holes that needed to be filled. It took me five years to prepare for this meeting, and six months after I'd made my request through Ples to visit Tony, he was also ready. When Ples had first told his grandson that I'd like to come to prison for a visit someday, Tony had told him that he was not yet ready to meet me.

Tony wrote, "My grandfather told me that Azim may be interested in meeting me face-to-face one day early on. I don't recall if it was before or after I was already sentenced. I didn't understand why, though. And I had hoped to myself that it was something that would pass.

"It wasn't easy for me to face the reality of what I had done. I didn't feel inside me like I could face Azim. When he finally came to visit me some years later, I was in Folsom and struggling with a host of other issues like the fact that I was the youngest inmate in the prison at the time. [I was] getting some understanding for the first time of what my sentence meant. Plus [I was] beginning the slow process of addressing some of my past issues. (The process was slow because I spent the first few years in denial about my situation and my life up to that point.)"

I can still remember traveling to New Folsom Prison, which is north of Sacramento. I had a lot of anguish, because I really did not know how I would react when I came eyeball to eyeball with my son's killer. I remember also that I'd been meditating for months before—several thousand hours of meditation—and trying to gather up the strength that I would need to finally meet Tony.

Once at the prison, the process of going through the very high fences with barbed wire on the top was scary for me. I don't know how many gates we had to go through to finally get to a room where Ples and Tony were already seated. There were little coffee tables around, and others in the room were visiting with prisoners. As soon as I walked in, Ples raised his hand. I walked over to them and hugged Ples, as we always do, and then shook hands with Tony before we all sat down.

We talked a little about Tony's life in prison, what it was like during the day. I had told Ples that I wanted some alone time with Tony because I felt he might share more openly without his grandfather being there. I wanted to collect the stories Tony might tell me about the night that Tariq died. I wanted to know the last words Tariq spoke, but Tony kept telling me that Tariq never said anything back to him. Perhaps in the shock of the moment, he had simply blanked it out.

"When I did meet Azim, I felt uncomfortable," Tony wrote. "I didn't know what to say or what to expect. I agreed to the visit because I thought it was the least that I could do to provide some closure [for him]. After visiting with Azim I felt extremely sad. I didn't feel like I deserved the forgiveness that

Azim showed. I had trouble reconciling my taking Tariq's life with Azim embracing me.

"That feeling of not deserving lasted for some time. It still lingers to this day. Azim is a good man with compassion and great spiritual strength. Knowing him has been a learning experience. It's also been difficult for me, because I don't know if I will live long [enough] to feel like I finally deserve his forgiveness.

"Azim's ability to forgive me did allow me the space to begin working on forgiving myself. Both my grandfather and Azim tell me that forgiving myself is going to be important to my own growth. But that's been a struggle as well. I don't know if most people can imagine having a reason to not like yourself every day.

"I do see the benefits of forgiving someone who has hurt you. I also agree with the idea of nonviolence as an alternative. [These are] concepts that I had heard before but weren't real to me until I was brought into Azim's life."

A White Light

While we were visiting in the prison that day, Tony told me that when he pulled the trigger, he saw a white light that came from the sky. This bright light illuminated both him and Tariq. He also told me that after he shot Tariq, he knew that he had done the worst thing he possibly could have done. He knew that he had taken the life of an unarmed innocent person just trying to do his job delivering pizzas. Tony said he'd gotten an order from Q-Tip to "Bust him, Bone," and he did. He shot Tariq. One bullet, but it was fatal.

When I think back to that first meeting, I remember how surprised I was that Tony, at nineteen years old, did not display a typical nineteen-year-old street-smart attitude of youth in our society. On the contrary, Tony was soft spoken, extremely well mannered, gentle, kind, and polite. I could tell right away that he was remorseful. He asked for my forgiveness, and I granted it to him. I told him that I do not feel any animosity toward him and that I feel he too was a victim of this tragedy. I said that I have the privilege of working closely with his grandfather, and that Ples and I have become like brothers.

I know that it is still hard for Tony to forgive himself, but on that day I could see that Tony's consciousness had shifted in an immense way. I was deeply touched by how forgiveness had helped this young man come back to feeling love and compassion in his own life in spite of the difficult conditions he had to deal with on a day-to-day basis in prison. The following story is a good example of how caring Tony is.

Ples paid for a docket of Polaroid photographs of the three of us standing against a wall: one for Ples, one for me, and one for Tony—a memoir of our first meeting. Tony was holding all three photos, and I could see that he was deep in thought.

"Tony," I said. "I noticed that you are contemplating something very deeply. Do you want to share what that is?"

"Yes, I was just wondering something," he said. "There are three photographs. I would like to keep two, because I'd like to keep one and send one to my mother for a Mother's Day present."

I was touched to see that this boy had so much love and compassion for his mother. I was simply unable to look at him and see a bitter nineteen-year-old with attitude. When I looked

13

deeply into Tony's eyes, I did not see a murderer. What I saw was another soul just like me. He had been so touched by this action of forgiveness that you could see his spirit in a moment of awakening. I could see how powerful Tony will be one day when he is on stage with me and Ples, talking to kids, affecting them with his presence and his words, saving so many children from the choices he made.

I forgave Tony Hicks. I forgave him with all my heart. I chose forgiveness so that I could begin to heal the gaping wound left in my soul when my son was killed. This gift of forgiveness put Tony on his own path toward compassion and healing, and by offering him a job with the Tariq Khamisa Foundation upon his release, I have also given Tony the opportunity to redeem himself.

He was a fourteen-year-old boy when he shot Tariq. He is now a young man who has had much time for reflection during these years of his confinement. Tony's maturity and self-awareness has come slowly and painfully as he searches to find meaning in his own life. He is trying to reconcile the boy he once was—a boy who made a tragic life-shattering decision— with the man he is today, a man who would never, ever do such a thing.

In Tony's letter to Karen, he wrote, "The shift to take a plea was not my idea but my lawyer's. I believe that he spoke with my grandfather about it first, but I'm not sure. [When the plea was presented to me] I agreed that I should at least save Tariq's family from the pain of a trial. I also felt a need to answer for what I had done even though it was difficult to do.

"[You asked me about] forgiving others? I'm way ahead of where I would have thought I'd be. That falls under that belief vs. environment thing I wrote about. I'm not at the level of Azim, but I do see the benefit of being there at some point.

"My hope is to get a degree in something and one day be able to express myself in a way that helps young people work through their issues. My plan is to keep working on bettering myself in every way I can."

Through my forgiving heart, I have come to care deeply for Tony. Over the years we have stayed in touch, and he knows that I am here to support him in any way I can. He wrote a letter to me in August of 2006 where he said, "I'm doing well, Azim. As well as one can and a lot better than a number of people. I still struggle with things I feel I should have a handle on by now, reconciling the beliefs that I'm cultivating with the imprisonment that I'm in and my response to my environment. I guess [the fact] that I still struggle with these issues is a good sign that I'm at least doing some of the work to better myself.

"So the journey continues . . . ."

Yes, Tony. So the journey continues.

Forgiveness is not the misguided act of condoning irresponsible, hurtful behavior. Nor is it a superficial turning of the other cheek that leaves us feeling victimized and martyred. Rather it is the finishing of old business that allows us to experience the present free of contamination from the past.

— Joan Borysenko

Why Forgiveness?

Chapter Two

"Why?" you ask. "Why should I forgive?"

It is a reasonable question. There are many reasons why we choose to hold onto anger, hatred, revenge, and resentment. There are many circumstances where we feel hurt by other people's actions. We have axes to grind. Doesn't the person who did this thing deserve your animosity? Doesn't he or she deserve your anger and hatred? Don't you have the right for revenge and retaliation? Why should you forgive?

Well, I have an answer for you. And my answer is very simple. You see, it really doesn't have anything to do with the other person. It doesn't matter who they are or what they have done. You forgive for one reason. That reason is to become whole, to awaken to peace and freedom. When you forgive, it is a gift to yourself. You forgive so that you can feel better and move on with your life. When you choose forgiveness, the difficult emotions you've been holding onto will begin to fall away. When you are no longer holding onto those emotions that cause you pain and suffering, you will find that your heart once again has room for love and joy.

An Ongoing Process

There are many people in our lives who we feel have done us wrong. In families it is typical to have issues between

In April 2000, Azim went along with Ples Felix to visit Tony Hicks in prison. Tony wanted two copies of this photo, one for him and one he could send his mother on Mother's Day.

mothers and daughters, fathers and sons. The problem might be with a sibling, ex-spouse, co-worker, or business associate. Perhaps the conflict is with someone even further removed, such as a clerk in a store or a teller in a bank. Maybe the person is a total stranger. This was the case for me.

It's likely that I would never have crossed paths with Tony Hicks had he not made that fateful choice on the night of January 21, 1995, and killed my son. Tony was a complete stranger to both me and Tariq. Had my son survived the shooting, it would have been up to him to forgive Tony. It would have been Tariq's decision to give up his own anger and resentment. But Tariq is not here to make that choice. I am. And my choice is to forgive Tony.

In fact, I wake up and forgive Tony every day. It is an ongoing process. I do this for me. I do this so that my heart will continue to open. I do this because really I have no other choice. Without forgiveness, I could not go on.

When I heard the news that Tariq had been killed, it was like a bomb exploded in my heart. I was broken into a million little pieces, and it felt like I would never be whole again. The pain was excruciating and I literally collapsed into the arms of my maker, my God, my Source. It was in the safety and love of that experience that I knew the truth: There were victims at both ends of the gun.

I was angry. Not at the boy who'd shot and killed my son, but at the societal flaws that allowed for such a thing to take place. Kids killing kids. It was beyond my comprehension, and it made me angry and terribly sad. My son was dead. And a fourteen-year-old was lost to the penal system.

If it was true that both Tariq and Tony were victims, and I felt with all my heart that it was, then I knew I must forgive this stranger—this fourteen-year-old boy who had murdered my son. I knew that if I was ever going to be whole again, my healing had to begin with forgiveness. Had I not reached out to Tony and his grandfather, Ples, I would have continued to be consumed with anger and pain. I was suicidal. I was like a zombie . . . not eating, not sleeping. I had no quality of life as a victim, and I knew that if I held onto the darkness I would never recover.

FORGIVING YOURSELF

Now this is an extreme case. Many of you who are reading this book will have lesser conflicts to deal with. But the act of forgiveness and the reasons to forgive are the same. Forgiveness is for you. It is a selfish thing to do. You forgive so that you can let go of your own pain and bitterness and move on with your life. Because the longer you hold on, the longer you will keep your own heart closed to love. As long as you keep living your life from a place of anger and resentment, you will not know true peace, contentment, and fulfillment.

It is one thing to talk about forgiving someone else. That person is usually easy to identify, and you can understand the concept of reaching out to him or her in forgiveness. But what if the person you need to forgive is yourself? Maybe there was a time when you knowingly took action against someone else. Or maybe a circumstance or event left you feeling responsible, whether or not you were actually at fault. Perhaps you have been eaten up with guilt for years. Please understand that guilt is self-inflicted hatred and is just as potent as anger directed at you from someone else. In fact, it can be more harmful because there is a continuously running tape of guilt in your mind, and you are hating yourself behind the scenes twenty-four hours a day.

Tony made a poor choice, one which he will regret every day for the rest of his life. He was a child when he pulled the trigger, but he is a twenty-six-year-old adult now. Even though Ples shared with Tony within just a few months after the shooting that I had reached out my hand to him in forgiveness, it took me five years before I was ready to meet Tony face-to-face.

20

Was Tony able to accept my heartfelt gesture? At the age of fifteen, was he ready to forgive himself? No, he was not. It has taken Tony years of self-reflection, along with the support of both Ples and me, to even begin to open his heart to forgiveness. As you read in the preceding chapter, Tony struggles every day with trying to reconcile who he is today with who he was when he killed Tariq. When he heard from his grandfather that his victim's father had forgiven him, he didn't know what to do with that. Even after our first meeting, he had trouble reconciling my forgiving embrace with the fact that he had taken my son's life.

Tony simply did not feel that he deserved my compassion. That feeling still lingers to this day. My reaching out to him did have one immediate effect, though. Through my act of forgiveness, Tony was able to begin the process of forgiving himself. Even though he couldn't fully accept my forgiveness, he did hear me. The very knowledge that I had made this choice allowed him to begin the work of his own self-healing. This will be a lifelong process for Tony, just like my lifelong process is to forgive him every day.

MAINTAINING FORGIVENESS

After I had my spiritual experience and understood there were victims at both ends of the gun, it was obvious to me that I had to forgive my son's killer. It was less obvious to me that I had to forgive myself. In the process of self-forgiveness it would take longer for me to see results. Like every parent, I believed it was my job to keep my child safe from harm, and when Tariq died I believed I had failed. I felt that I had let him and my family down. I felt tremendously guilty.

So every day when I wake up I meditate, I pray, and I forgive. I forgive Tony, and I also forgive myself. It is through these acts of forgiveness that I find peace in my heart. I think of it as my forgiveness muscle. Every day it grows stronger, and my capacity for compassion, love, and goodness grows larger. I will always love and miss Tariq. I think of my son every day. The hole I have in my heart will never be completely healed. But through the forgiveness of my son's killer and through self-forgiveness, I have been able to find a way back to the light of my soul.

I want you to understand that this process of forgiveness really does work. It worked for me, and it will also work for you. By choosing to forgive, you have a chance to find peace again. By letting go of your resentment and anger, you will find that your capacity to love will grow. You will also find that your relationships with others, and with yourself, will heal and be more open, more loving, and more joyful.

But how do you forgive? Can simply saying the words make a difference in your life? Taking time to look back at my journey from the moment I first heard about the tragic and senseless death of my son to my decision to forgive Tony and his family, I recognized three main steps in my process. I further developed these steps in my workshop, *Forgiveness: The Crown Jewel of Personal Freedom*:

1. Acknowledge you have been wronged.
2. Give up all resulting resentment
3. Reach out.

I call my workshop *Forgiveness: The Crown Jewel of Personal Freedom,* because I truly believe that forgiveness has the power to heal your grief. But, just as importantly, I believe that forgiveness has the power to create a world at peace. Each time we witness an act of forgiveness, we marvel at its power to heal, to break the seemingly unending cycle of pain. Forgiveness is something people aspire to do. And when we see it, we feel hopeful.

I present my forgiveness workshop in venues all over the world. It is also offered as a CD set with accompanying exercises. (For more information on this and my complimentary guided meditation, please refer to my Resource page.)

RELEASING VICTIMHOOD

The world has witnessed astonishing acts of forgiveness. Pope John Paul II made a comprehensive apology for the acts committed by the Roman Catholic Church against groups of people throughout history. Former Prime Minister Tony Blair of the United Kingdom sought forgiveness for England's role in the Irish Potato Famine. Following the September 11, 2001, attack on Americans, Palestinian and Israeli officials issued orders to pull back from aggression and violence.

The Truth and Reconciliation Committee led by Nelson Mandela and Bishop Desmond Tutu facilitated the forgiveness of countless atrocities committed by the apartheid movement in South Africa. More recently, the parents of the Amish children who were massacred in a Pennsylvania school shooting opened their hearts and forgave the murderer. Then, to the astonishment of most of the people who were watching this tragedy unfold, those same grieving mothers and fathers—along with many members of the Amish community—reached out in compassion by attending the shooter's funeral and creating a charitable fund for his family.

Choice is always present in forgiveness. You do not have to forgive, but there will most certainly be resulting consequences. Refusing to forgive by holding onto the anger, resentment, and sense of betrayal can make your own life miserable. It can cause disharmony in your relationships with others and with yourself. Without forgiveness, we remain stuck in our past, a place from which it's difficult to reach happiness and true abundance.

We often think that anger directed at another person hurts them, but at the end of the day it is really only hurting ourselves. Forgiveness is not condoning behavior. Forgiveness is simply seeing the divine essence in every human being. It is recognizing that when we forgive another, we are also releasing ourselves from the self-abuse that comes from holding onto hatred and resentment. There is nothing so bad that it cannot be forgiven. I mean nothing. Withholding forgiveness is the same as choosing to remain the suffering victim. In the victim mode, it is difficult—perhaps even impossible—to achieve success, fulfillment, and healing of your body, mind, and soul.

We sometimes forget that we are divine, spiritual beings. Forgiveness helps us to connect with that place in ourselves that is a never-ending and limitless source of inspiration. When you choose to forgive in an authentic manner, you will experience a transformational shift; you will manifest a miracle.

Over the next three chapters, I will describe to you the three main steps of forgiveness which helped me to reach fulfillment in my life. It is my sincere hope that these specially selected stories will inspire you to begin the process of forgiveness in your own life.

Before we begin with Step One, "Acknowledge you have been wronged," I would ask you to take a moment to consider . . .

Who is the Tony in your life?

True Love burns the brightest, but the brightest flames leave the deepest scars.

— Author unknown

Step One: Acknowledge You Have Been Wronged

Chapter Three

We have all experienced some form of divisiveness in our lives. For each of us, there is something or someone to forgive. This break in harmonious relationships with ourselves and others causes us deep emotional pain. I truly believe that the act of forgiveness has the power to heal your pain as well as to create a world of peace, one person at a time. But before you can forgive, you must first acknowledge you have been wronged. This is an important first step that you do for yourself, because the feeling that you have been wronged has created your inner suffering.

This wrongdoing may have been minor or extreme. It may have occurred yesterday or many years ago. It may have been an action by a loved one, an acquaintance, or a perfect stranger. But no matter what happened or when or by whom, because you believe you have been wronged, the result is that you have created negative emotions such as resentment, anger, and revenge which lie deep inside of you.

EMBRACING THE PAIN

You have a choice. You can remain frozen in your negative emotions or you can transform them into something positive, something that will help vitalize you and the world around you. We are all divine beings with a connection to our source; the

At a school event, this young one would not leave Azim's side. It had turned out that she too had lost a family member due to violence.

resources available to us are limitless. We all have the capacity for forgiveness, but it is not something that we often think about. In my case, forgiveness was not the first thing that came to mind when I found out my son had been murdered.

Imagine what it would be like if a bomb exploded in your heart, that you're broken into millions of small pieces that will never again be found. You know that even if you found them, the pieces would never come together like they were before. This is how I felt. Tariq's death was an event in my life that put me into a place where I had never been before. As parents, you never want to think that your children go before you. The grief is immeasurable and literally stops you in your tracks.

During Tariq's life, in my work as an international investment banker, I lived a fast-paced life. Most of my time was spent away from home traveling the world. I thought nothing of getting off a plane, changing clothes, and boarding another plane to go to yet another destination. My work week was typically eighty hours and often more.

After I lost my son, everything changed. It took all of my willpower just to climb out of bed. The person I used to be, who traveled the world without hesitation, was nowhere to be seen. All my energy was gone, literally sucked out of my body by the tragic news. I had lost all hope and could not even begin to imagine how I would ever find my way back to a normal life.

When Tariq died, I would say that the size of my wound was as large as Jupiter. Every time I talk about my son's death, it is like taking the scab off my wound. What I have learned over the years is that when the scab reforms, it's a little smaller than the one that came off. Today my wound is about the size of planet Earth (but it's still pretty large).

There's another side to this coin. Every one of us is a vessel of the divine spirit. When Tariq was alive, the capacity of my vessel was like the size of a wine barrel. If you liquefied me, that's probably all you would fill. Today, almost twelve years later, the capacity of my vessel is like the state of California. I'm able to contain so much more love and compassion in my heart, so much more divine spirit and peace.

So what is this process that increased my capacity for love and goodness? It is the gift of forgiveness. Having survived the deepest crisis in my life, I am now able to see the immense value of this wonderful elixir, and I hope that I will be able to show you that it will also be valuable to you. You see, there is no quality of life being a victim. And yet, paradoxically, when we take that first step of forgiveness and acknowledge that we have been wronged, we automatically engage the "victim mindset."

Though we don't want to stay in victimhood too long, this first step of forgiveness is necessary. Whether someone else is truly responsible for our suffering or not, if we believe that it is so, it is important that we also acknowledge that belief. This first step of forgiveness allows us to fully embrace all the negative emotion that is attached to victimhood—to feel it, to honor it, and then to finally be able to take the next step of letting it go.

It is vitally important that we accept and bring to the surface all the painful emotions we hold onto. Without our embrace of these shadow parts of ourselves, the feelings will gain strength and end up controlling the decisions we make as we go throughout our days. When Tariq was murdered, I could easily have ended my own life. That was the depth of my pain and despair. At that stage, my mind was not able to deal with the crisis. Sometimes in life you are given problems that your mind cannot solve. You are given problems that your heart cannot heal. You need this third dimension, which I have named the *soul-ular* level. There are many words for it—human spirit, higher power, source—but we all have the natural ability to connect with this amazing reservoir of compassion. I truly believe there is no problem in life that we cannot solve when we are in alignment with that soul, that divinity, that power.

Today, when I look back at the way I responded to the tragedy of my only son in those first few days, I don't know where I found the will. I could not see or feel any strength in me at all. I had no clue that I had this inner power within me that would be able to transcend all the negative that could so easily have come from this tragic incident. I was unable to envision that through the power of forgiveness, I would ultimately create something so loving, so compassionate, and so beautiful. The Tariq Khamisa Foundation (TKF), the organization that I created in my son's memory, has helped millions of children and youth to live lives of nonviolence and peace.

MEDITATION AND RITUAL

It is incredible for me to wonder how I was able to move from a sense of utter desolation to inspired grace. I believe two important elements were involved. One was the spiritual preparedness which came from my twenty years of practicing meditation. There are no problems that cannot be solved at the soulular level, and meditation is a way that we are able to connect with our source and the limitless resources within.

Ritual is the other element that was so critically important in helping me move from devastation to inspiration. It gave me a safe and structured outlet for the overwhelming grief that I felt. Tariq's death was a defining moment in my life. Depending on the choices I would make over the next few months following the tragedy, my life would either cave in upon me in despair and negativity or I would expand the capacity of my vessel to new and transformative possibilities. At that time, I was not conscious of which way I would go. This was not a matter for my mind to solve or for my heart to heal. This was a matter for my soul to transform.

Spiritual preparedness through my regular meditation practice all the years before prepared me for the moment of

Tariq's death. After being held in God's healing embrace, I was sent back into my body with the wisdom that there are victims at both ends of the gun. I was on my way to forgiveness.

But it was ritual, specifically, which gave me the strength to deal with my grief from this tragedy. When Tariq died, I knew that I wanted his burial to be within the rites of my Ismaili faith, which is rich in traditions and rituals. We believe that when a young soul dies we are all diminished, and fourteen hundred people congregated at the central mosque in Vancouver, Canada—my parents' home and Tariq's birthplace—to share in our grief. According to our tradition, Tariq's body was shrouded in an unstitched white cloth, with only his face showing. For two hours in a single line, our friends and neighbors walked around his body chanting in unison an Ismaili prayer for the salvation of his soul.

To hear this chanting was electrifying. I could feel the energy in the room shift. As we lifted Tariq and began to move him through the hall, one by one everyone came up and touched the corner of the litter supporting him. It was as if each and every one of them was giving me a hand and helping me to carry my load. I cannot emphasize enough how important these rituals were for me. The gathering of our friends and neighbors, the chanting as they viewed Tariq's body, the sharing of our family's loss as we moved his body to the gravesite—all of these ceremonies and rituals gave me the strength to bury my son dust to dust.

At the site, I had to step into the grave to receive my son's body. Every cell of my being wanted to stay with him. I could not bear to leave him there by himself. My best friend, Dan Pearson, offered me his hand and pulled me out of the grave to reluctantly start the rest of my life without my son.

After I returned home, I had people coming from my mosque every day bringing breakfast, lunch, and dinner. I live by myself, and there was so much food I didn't know what to do with it all. Every person who came asked me to repeat the story, and I remember feeling that I couldn't tell it one more time. I would say, "Tariq . . ." but then couldn't say the word "died," because it sent a 20,000 volt shock through me. But with each person who came with food and love, I told the story once more. I didn't recognize the value at the time, but now I see that the ritual of repeating the story over and over again was a very important part of my healing.

The Cure is in the Pain

At forty-six years of age, I had to relearn how to live. It would be difficult to begin anew, but I also knew somewhere deep inside that I did not want to live the life of a victim. I did not want people to feel sorry for me. I had to find a way to climb out of my grief just as I had climbed out of my son's grave. But it was not easy, and I remained confused in the darkness of my sorrow.

During this time I continued to meditate; I journaled and took long walks by myself. All of these spiritual practices helped me to stay connected with my soul. Rumi says, "The cure for the pain is in the pain." And so I allowed myself to feel my pain—deeply. Grief and sorrow are natural parts of life, and allowing ourselves to feel these emotions is an integral part of being able to fully develop into the radiant beings that we are meant to be.

In his essay "On Pain" in *The Prophet*, Kahlil Gibran writes, "And the cup he brings, though it burn your lips, has been fashioned of the clay which the Potter has moistened with His own sacred tears." We all know that once the moistened clay has been formed into a pot, it is placed in a high-temperature kiln for several hours. It is through this firing process that the pot gains its strength and beauty. I know what it feels like to go through this kind of heat and intensity. Exposing myself to the seemingly unbearable pain of my grief was truly the only way for me to be able to reveal my radiance as a divine being. It was the only way for me to expand my faculty for forgiveness and love. I'm a better person now than I was before my son's death. That is not an easy thing to admit, but it is true. Before the tragedy, I was focused mostly on myself and my investment banking. Now I am committed to serving humanity. I am more at peace. But this did not happen overnight. After my son's burial I struggled with my grief and remained confused in the pain of my sorrow.

TRANSFORMING GRIEF

When my mind and heart could not give me any solace, any direction, or any solution to my despair, I turned to the spiritual teachers of my Ismaili Muslim faith (in the Sufi interpretation) for wisdom and for strength. According to the ritual of my faith, we say prayers for our departed at the funeral, ten days after, thirty days, forty days, three months, six months, nine months, one year, and every year thereafter. My teacher reminded me that it is important to grieve, but it is also important to have a sunset on your grieving.

"For the first forty days after the soul dies," he said, "it stays in close proximity of its family and loved ones. But the forty-day prayers end that grieving process, and the soul then travels to its new consciousness in preparation for its future journey. Continuous grieving by family and loved ones impedes the soul's journey. I know there are going to be moments where you are still going to grieve, and my recommendation to you is to do good deeds, because good, compassionate deeds are spiritual currency. They transfer to the departed soul and help fuel the soul's journey."

I lost Tariq six weeks before his twenty-first birthday. We had some wonderful plans to celebrate this occasion, but how could I plan a celebration for my son who was no longer here? I recalled the advice I'd received from my teacher and thought that here was a way I could do something for Tariq. This burning desire to transform my grief into good deeds became my inspiration for creating the foundation in my son's name, which by its very nature as a charitable organization would do good, compassionate deeds.

When we experience a loss such as I did, or a loss of any kind, it is important to acknowledge that we are hurting and allow ourselves to fully experience the resulting emotions. Grief, sorrow, and pain are all natural parts of life. In his essay "On Joy and Sorrow" Kahlil Gibran says that those two emotions are inseparable. "Together they come, and when one sits alone with you at your board, remember that the other is asleep upon your bed," he writes in *The Prophet*.

THERESA

My writing partner, Karen, faced a tragic loss of her own in 1993. Her third child, Theresa, was born with Down syndrome and congenital heart defects. At the age of two, she was diagnosed with leukemia and died four months later. After attending one of my forgiveness workshops, Karen told me that her ten years of Reiki practice and her ritual of daily self-treatment prepared her to be able to walk that fine line between life and death.

"In those last weeks, I was living in the 'opposites,'" Karen says. "I sat on my little girl's bed as she slept, and I kept at the task of knitting the blanket I wanted her to be wrapped in for her burial. The knitting itself was like a ritual where I was embracing all the joy and sorrow of her life, one stitch at a time. I sat with Theresa for hours, not wanting to leave her side, knowing that these might be her last days. Episodes of our life together for the past two years flew across my mind like scenes in a movie. My heart was overflowing with love for my daughter, and I knew with every cell of my being that she was going to live.

"I also knew that she was going to die. It wasn't either/or. It was that both possibilities seemed entirely real to me, and they existed simultaneously with each breath I took. I did daily self-treatment and shared Reiki with my daughter as she slept. These practices allowed me to move into that place of stillness and love where there is no tension or resistance. It is my most sincere belief that the Reiki provided healing for Theresa in her final days. I also believe that through the ritual of Reiki self-treatment which I had incorporated into my life several years before, I was being emotionally and mentally supported in preparation for her death.

"When Theresa died in November of 1993, the pain was excruciating and I wailed as only a mother can. Like Azim I lost all my energy, and it was only through the grace of having two other children that I was able to get out of bed every morning. I have no doubt that my love for my older daughter, Colby, and my son, Thomas, kept me alive in those days. But the pain of losing Theresa was almost paralyzing.

"Contrary to others' expectations of how I might grieve, though, I never once had a moment of anger when I felt that Theresa's life had been cut short or that she had been taken away from me. Although I was in mourning for a long time, I've always understood that Theresa's life was whole and complete. Why did I never go to anger? I believe that my daily ritual of Reiki self treatment prepared me for that day and provided the support and healing I needed to be able to accept my daughter's death instead of feeling the need to resist or fight it. The grief of knowing I would never hold Theresa again, or smell her hair, or hear her sweet voice was overwhelming, and the sadness never entirely goes away because a child is a part of you forever. It's been thirteen years since her passing, and the sorrow still washes over me from time to time, but knowing that Theresa's life was beautiful and perfect just the way it was makes my heart smile."

Forgiveness is Possible

Karen went deep into her pain as did I, but that is not something our Western culture supports. On the contrary, it pushes us toward masking our suffering with pharmaceuticals. These are temporary fixes, though. It is only by first going into our deepest hearts that we are able to become the radiant beings that we are meant to be. As we all know, there is a time for all seasons. There is a time to grieve, and there is a time to rejoin the world. By creating spiritual currency for my son through the creation of the Tariq Khamisa Foundation, I brought purpose back into my life. But even though I knew with all my heart that there were victims at both ends of the gun, the reality was that Tony had shot and killed Tariq. My son was his victim. And my family and I were also his victims. Before I could move more fully into compassion, I had to acknowledge I had been wronged. This was step one on my journey of forgiveness. And Tony was the person I needed to forgive.

Acknowledging that you have been wronged creates a certain amount of completion, because now you are able to speak about the wrong that you felt was done to you. In the case of self-forgiveness, acknowledging that you are responsible for a wrong allows you to begin the process of healing yourself. We are in the human condition, and none of us is perfect. None of us is beyond mistakes.

I think the greatest historical example of forgiveness is Jesus the Christ who said, "Father, forgive them for they know not what they do." At the same time, forgiveness is not something reserved for the saints or for enlightened people. Sometimes we believe that forgiving is such a hard thing to do, which sometimes it is. But I want you to know that forgiveness is possible for all of us. It is not reserved for people who have a higher consciousness. I am an ordinary person. I am a person who makes a living as an investment banker and who only came to realize the process of forgiveness through the tragedy of my son.

With the practice of forgiveness, you reduce a lot of the stress in your life. A teacher once came up to me at a school and said, "Mr. Khamisa, I've been watching you for the last nine years, and I thank you for bringing your message of peace, compassion, and forgiveness to our students. Our students love it when you are here. They are all so moved. But Azim," he asked, "are you always this peaceful?"

"You know, I really wasn't always," I said, "but I am now, because through forgiveness I am almost always connected to this very peaceful core of my being."

You can find this place of peace within yourself, too. Take some of these pieces in your life—the little things that cause you distress and pain—and begin to forgive the small stuff; begin to develop your own forgiveness muscle. Then you'll find that forgiveness will become very much a practice and a habit. It will be like getting up in the morning and brushing your teeth. It will be a process you will live with on a daily basis, and the more you practice, the more you will find that the stress in your life lessens.

You can see that acknowledging you have been wronged is an important step in your healing, because it allows you to honor the depth of your emotions. However, as I said at the beginning of this chapter, by the very nature of your acknowledgment you also take on the victim role. When you choose to hold onto the negative emotions that grow out of your sense of victimization, the capacity of your vessel is limited and there is not much room for love and joy to flow into your life.

Through forgiveness, those negative emotions can be diffused and transformed. Through forgiveness, you will stop living your story of victimization. You will find a purpose. You will take the negative energy that lies deep inside you and move it through the prism of your inner spirit, your higher self. And as you take this energy through the light, it will be transformed into something positive, into a laser of compassion, of empathy, and of peace. Step Two will show you how.

Put love first. Entertain thoughts that give life. And when a thought or resentment, or hurt, or fear comes your way, have another thought that is more powerful—a thought that is love.

— Mary Manin Morrissey

Step Two: Give Up All Resulting Resentment

Chapter Four

In the last chapter I talked about how my many years of meditation prepared me for that moment when I first heard Tariq had been killed. Leaving my body and going into the arms of my God was not a conscious choice I made. Rather, it was an immediate, spontaneous spiritual experience which propelled me upward into the higher level of understanding that there were victims at both ends of the gun.

It is one thing to understand this concept on the mental, intellectual level. Even on the emotional heart level, an idea like this can be warmly embraced. But it is something else to gather the bits and pieces of inspiration and wisdom we gain in our lives and put them into practice. Even as I suffered in my grief and despair, I knew that I did not want to remain a victim of this tragedy. Through the rituals of my Ismaili faith, I was able to move through the fire of my pain and discover that hope was waiting on the other side.

DEVELOPING COMPASSION

Acknowledging I had been wronged was an important first step toward forgiveness and fulfillment, because it allowed me to bring forth and honor the strength of the reality of my experience. I have a beautiful daughter, Tasreen, but I had lost my one and only beloved son. Tariq was gone, and my family and I were

To help heal hearts of the young, Azim and Ples support school children to plant a tree in the "Garden of Life" in memory of anyone that they may have lost.

devastated. And someone—Tony Hicks—was responsible for firing the bullet that killed Tariq and taking him away from us.

We are structured by our society and culture that when something bad happens to us, we immediately go toward the attitudes of resentment and revenge. "So and so did this. He hurt me. She angered me. They were unfair to me. I am the victim. He, she, they are the offenders. They did me wrong and have to pay." Our society and culture also reinforce the notion that we ought to feel guilty for those things we've done or said where others have been hurt.

We have all had these types of experiences. We have all been there with feelings of abuse or self-abuse. But when you have axes to grind with others or with yourself, you can never be present to this moment. When you replay the experience of suffering in your mind and determine who is playing the part of victim and who the perpetrator, you remain always in the past. It is inevitable. But happiness is a present concept. We can never experience true joy if we remain in our past and in our suffering.

Our sense of victimhood lies solely in our thoughts, and we carry this immense burden of negativity around with us moment by moment, day after day. We're often not even aware that the negative attitude is present or of how much effect it has on the life choices we make. The resentment and anger and guilt build up, and over time they become a reservoir of pessimism, cynicism, and invalidation of the fact that we are all divine human beings. The idea that we are separate from one another is an illusion. We truly are all connected by divinity, source, God. When we make the choice to give up the resentment within ourselves, we not only create peace in our own hearts, but we also create peace beyond ourselves to others, to our communities, and to the world.

Once you are ready to give up the resulting resentment, it's helpful to look beyond the problem so that you can develop compassion for the perpetrator or for yourself. This is done through empathy. You learn to reframe the difficult or painful experiences so that you can see them in a totally new light. Remember that it is important to first go through the process of acknowledging you've been wronged and to feel the depth of your suffering so that you can honor the fullness of your experience. But just as there is a time to grieve and a time to end the grieving period, so too there is a time to feel you have been wronged and then a time to put a stop to the belief that you are a victim.

It is important to develop empathy for the person we are angry with or hurt by so that we can give up our negative feelings and move on with our own lives. Through empathy we create a shift in ourselves. This shift replaces the reservoir of negativity with creative energy and allows us to reframe our thinking about the difficult and painful experiences in our lives which have been the root cause of our suffering.

In my workshop, Crown Jewel of Personal Freedom, there is a beautiful empathy exercise called "Just Like Me." In this exercise you make a series of statements that help to create a bridge of empathy and compassion between you and the other person. For example, I would say, I forgive Tony for murdering my son.

Just like me, Tony is seeking happiness in his life.

Just like me, Tony is trying to avoid suffering in his life.

Just like me, Tony has had behavior that was motivated by fear.

Just like me, Tony has known sorrow, loss, loneliness, and hopelessness in his life.

Just like me, Tony is seeking fulfillment in his life.

Just like me, Tony is learning about life.

Just like me, Tony acted in ways in which if offered an opportunity, he would make a different decision.

Just like me, Tony is not perfect.

For the exercise, you would choose someone appropriate to your situation. This is a wonderful and safe way to explore the experiences of joy, pain, and suffering that all of humanity has in common.

When we are faced with situations that our mind can't fix and our heart can't heal, we can reframe and transform the experience by connecting with our soul, our source, our higher self. Meditation, Reiki (a Japanese hands-on healing technique), and Ho'oponopono (an ancient Hawaiian healing art) are but a few of the many spiritual practices people use to reframe their experiences and connect with their core, that place in themselves which is a source of inspiration and love. The more time we spend in that higher plane connected to our higher self, the more likely we are to act from a place of empathy, compassion, and forgiveness.

Self-Identity through Ho'oponopono, developed by Kahuna Morrnah N. Simeona, is an updated version of an ancient Hawaiian healing system. In her wonderful book, The Easiest Way, radio and TV host and author Mabel Katz talks about how Ho'oponopono helps us to solve problems by "lifting the fog, erasing our unconscious memory tapes, and eliminating that which no longer works in our lives. Ho'oponopono is a process of forgiveness, repentance, and transformation," Ms. Katz says. "Every time we use any of its tools, we are taking one hundred percent responsibility and asking for forgiveness (from ourselves). We choose if we are going to react and engage when a problem comes up, or let it go and let it be resolved by the part of us that knows better."

In her book, Ms. Katz quotes her teacher Dr. Ihaleakala Hew Len (one of Mornnah Simeona's students) on how a problem can be looked at differently. "A problem is only a problem if we say it is, and a problem is not the problem," Dr. Len says. "How we react to the problem is the problem."

"The conscious is the part of us that decides whether to assume one hundred percent responsibility by saying, 'I'm sorry, please forgive me for whatever is going on in me that has created this' (Ho'oponopono), or to point fingers and blame someone else," Ms. Katz says. "The intellect was not created to know. It doesn't need to know anything. The intellect is a gift. The gift that we have to choose. We learn that everything that appears in our lives is only a projection of our 'programs.' We can choose to let them go and observe them, or to react and get caught up in them. We all have an eraser incorporated within us, a delete key, but we forget how to use it," she says. "Ho'oponopono helps us to remember the power that we have to choose between erasing (letting go) or reacting, between being happy or suffering. It is only a matter of choice in every moment in our lives."

Reiki is another means of reframing difficult life experiences. Usui Shiki Ryoho Reiki Master Upasana Grugan has a public practice in Eugene, Oregon. She says, "Reiki self-treatment for me has always been a touchstone. It's a touchstone to who I really am, to what I can do in life, and to what I can be. At the same time it's a way for me to connect with my heart and to connect with what really is. When I put my hands on myself in the protocol of self-treatment, it connects me with something that is so much bigger and so much greater. And it soothes me. At the same time it takes me away a little bit, takes me up, enables me to be able to see whatever it is from a different perspective. And then it looks differently to me, and it's easier to act rather than react.

"There were difficulties with the birth of my youngest granddaughter," Upasana says. "It was a life and death situation. I had to travel from the U.S. to Chile to get there, which is a big trip. And that whole time I held my Reiki hands on myself. It was a way of containing myself and my emotions. In Chile there was so much strife and so much pain on the outside. I was there to support my daughter, especially, as she was going through this. It was so difficult to look at my granddaughter in the hospital, this little creature so defenseless and so full of tubes, that I would always come back to my room and give myself self-treatment. That practice would always bring me back to a place of knowing that everything, no matter what the pain and no matter what the result, that everything was okay."

We all want to be happy, and we all want to be free from suffering. In fact, this is one of the messages of the Dalai Lama, with whom I had the good fortune to spend time. I have studied everything the Dalai Lama wrote, and one of the things he talks about is the commitment to ending the suffering of humanity. He says, "I have committed my life to making sure that every human being is happy and is not suffering, because when that happens I will also be happy and not suffering."

We can get very comfortable in our own personal suffering, especially if we've held onto negative emotions over a long period of time. There is a sense of deservedness that at first glance seems to make us feel better. But when we look harder, we see that it truly does not bring ease. So long as we suffer in our negativity, no matter to what degree, we keep a part of ourselves closed off from the fullness of peace and contentment which is our true nature.

CALLING FORTH EMPATHY

Empathy—the ability to look beyond the incident toward compassion for the other person—will move you toward forgiveness and the personal choice to give up all the resulting resentment. When I realized there were victims at both ends of the gun, this was an expression of empathy. If you just look at the incident, what you see is a perpetrator and a victim. But if you look beyond the system, what you see is a deeper problem. It is a societal problem. For instance, if you take Tony and hang him, or if you give him the electric chair, how do you improve society?

I would ask you to consider what it would take to choose forgiveness and to give up all the resentment you hold. Remember, forgiveness is a process. It takes practice, and it requires a choice. When you choose to live the life of a victim, you continue to bear the scars of the original event. The emotional negativity prohibits your ability to find positive meaning in your life. This element of meaning is important and was primary in my own process of giving up the resulting resentment.

Through taking the first step and acknowledging I'd been wronged, I began to understand the need to heal my wounds. I did not want to live my life with a victim mentality, but I didn't know how to untangle myself from that despair of the suffering soul. By initially reaching out to Ples and asking him to help me with my work at TKF, I slowly began to understand that this was a way to bring meaning back into my life. With each passing day, as I saw the beautiful outcomes of our nonviolence programs, my heart grew more receptive and willing to open. And because I had already made the choice to give up all the resulting resentment, those negative feelings I was holding slowly began to melt away. It took time. As I say, forgiveness is a process, not an event. It requires patience and commitment. But the results are well worth it.

Empathy and compassion have helped me in another way to give up all resulting resentment. I sometimes think this tragedy is harder on Ples than it is on me. Tariq died. There is this big, empty hole which will never, ever be full again. I cannot bring my son back. But there is a completion there. Now think about Ples for a minute. He has to get up every day and worry whether or not his grandson is safe in his prison home. For both Tony and Ples, this has been an ongoing battle since the day Tony entered an adult prison at the age of sixteen.

So when I look at that with empathy and compassion, I can give up all the resulting resentment, because I can see that Tony and his family are also suffering. This second step of forgiveness comes from the ability to have perspective. It comes from the ability to look not only at the incident where you can easily see a perpetrator or offender and a victim, but also to look beyond that. You see how the system or society or family contributes to the process. You realize that perpetrators were at one time victims of something or somebody themselves. I've never met an offender who was not a victim at one time. When we understand this, then we can call forth empathy.

I ask you to look at each "offense" in your life as an opportunity. You do this through empathy and compassion. Whether it's a conflict with a member of your family, your business partner, your ex, or anyone or anything else, try to look and see that this is an opportunity to create brotherhood, sisterhood, and unity.

Nelson Mandela made famous the saying, "Resentment is like drinking poison and waiting for your enemy to die." (The original quote is by Cindy Clabough.) Archbishop Desmond Tutu talks about how it's important that your enemy become a friend, and then a partner. South Africa was able to heal the atrocities of the apartheid movement by creating a Truth and Reconciliation Committee, where all the sins of the apartheid were forgiven after the truth was sought. The South Africans made the choice not to stay in the resulting resentment, but to instead create a unification of their country. Tutu said, "Without forgiveness, we have no future." This is a beautiful example of how it was possible to give up all the resentment that had built up over many decades of apartheid rule.

A lot of people want to forgive, but they don't know how. Acknowledging you have been wronged is relatively easy. Giving up all the resulting resentment is harder. First you must decide that you want to give up your sense of victimhood. And then from that place, you can begin the process of developing empathy for the other person or for yourself. This is the way to reach compassion, and it's through compassion that you will find peace. But once you decide you want to unburden yourself from all the negative emotions, what exactly is the process to reach empathy, compassion, and forgiveness? It is called intention.

My good friend, Brian Klemmer, teaches that intentions equal results. Intentions are powerful, but they must be clear to be effective. Confusing messages do not bring results. However if the intention is clear, the Universe will conspire to help make the manifestation real.

The intention of Ho'oponopono is to clean and clear the memories within us which cause suffering. James Piver of Beaufort, North Carolina, talks about how, through his commitment to the practice of this healing form and his forty-year intention to surrender his life totally to God, he one day experienced the manifestation of a physical healing. "The greatest miracle of Ho'oponopono to me is that whatever problem I may be experiencing or perceiving in another, I have the choice to take one hundred percent responsibility for it and to clean and erase the erroneous thoughts in me that have created the problem.

"I had been diagnosed legally deaf for twenty-one years, and I learned of Ho'oponopono about a year ago. I soon began practicing in earnest, and my hearing began to improve little by little. A few weeks ago I turned on my iPod, put on the headphones, got in the recliner, and began listening to a score from the opera Tosca. Oh my God, I could hear it so clearly. The voice sounded so natural, the orchestra so clear and full. 'What is going on here?' I thought. I was back in that heavenly place, and the music soared while tears of gratitude and joy began streaming down my cheeks, my body almost electrified. Words can't even begin to describe this experience."

As Jimmy's story so beautifully demonstrates, intentions are powerful things. Whether your intention is to forgive yourself or another person, it is important to sincerely consider the Buddhist concept of nonattachment. The "how" and "when" of the outcome is not important. It is the clarity of your intention that will connect with that place of divinity in yourself, and it is from letting go and surrendering to that place of divine inspiration within yourself that miracles happen.

THE POWER OF MEDITATION

What bailed me out of my deepest crisis was my ability to meditate. It is because of my preparedness from years of meditation that I had the spiritual awakening which showed me there were victims at both ends of the gun. From this point of empathy, I was able to move toward compassion, forgiveness, and peace. Meditation is a spiritual practice that helps us connect with our higher self, our source, the Universe, God. But we are thinking beings, and our thoughts distract us from our own holiness. How then do we turn off our thoughts so that we can feel this connection to divinity?

The practice of meditation gives us a way to dip into the gap between our thoughts and enter that space wherein peace lies. In this gap there is no thought, no mantra. It is pure emptiness. Through my years of meditation practice, I have experienced an increase in the size of that gap, and I blissfully exist in that state of safety, security, and inspiration for longer and longer periods of time. When I come out of my meditations, I feel like I've taken a dip in the river of wisdom, compassion, and love.

It is in this river that your intention will take hold, unfold, and blossom into the manifestation of the forgiveness you seek. Some of you are familiar with meditation techniques; some of you are not. Over the years I have practiced a variety of forms of meditation and finally developed a technique of my own. In one of my meditations, I was asked by the Universe to create a guided meditation and to share it with all who are interested. A Preamble, which explains my technique, and the Guided Meditation itself are available as a free download on my website, which you can find listed in the Resource section of this book. I am happy to share this forgiveness meditation with you, and I will be pleased if you will pass it on to your friends, family, and acquaintances. The more people who find forgiveness in their own lives, the closer we will be to world peace.

Before you begin your meditation, set your intention to give up all the resulting resentment so that you can forgive whomever you have held ill will toward, whether it is someone else or yourself. Make sure your intention is clear and precise, not confused. Remember that the energy of the Universe is there for your calling. Also remember to remain compassionately nonattached to the outcome. Release your thoughts about how it will look or when it will happen, and surrender to inspiration. In your meditation period, you will relax and expand as you dip into the gap between your thoughts. When your intention to give up all the resulting resentment is clear and strong, you will be supported and inspired toward the compassion that will lead you to inner peace and forgiveness.

RECLAIMING YOUR POSITIVE ENERGY

Ho'oponopono is another method of finding peace within oneself. Joanie Chappel, founder of the Ho'oponopono forum at powerfulintentions.com says, "The Ho'oponopono practice of cleaning is surrendering a problem (memory) to Divinity to transmute. By using the process, we can get ourselves into a place of appreciation and love, of others and ourselves—a feeling of ONEness. In this place, Divine Guidance can then download into us, and it's a gift. In each moment, no matter what else is going on in our lives, we have choice. We have free will. We can blame someone else for a problem we're having, or we can take one hundred percent responsibility and love that person—love ourselves. In the end, all forgiveness is self-forgiveness."

Yes, forgiveness is a gift to ourselves. Giving up all the resulting resentment is the stage in the forgiveness process when you decide to look at who you are, how you want to be, and how you will choose to experience the rest of your life. This step comes after you decide you have experienced enough pain from your memories of the past, and you choose to put the past to rest. You know that you do not want to remain the victim any longer; instead, you choose to reclaim the positive energy of your life.

You realize that your willingness to forgive is an attitude and behavior which will serve you the rest of your life. There is immense personal healing just from deciding which attitudes and behaviors you want to let go of so that you can begin to envision and experience your life free from the resentment, anger, or even hatred you have carried for so long. This defining moment is a pivotal decision that happens at the soulular level. It is the soul's cry for a deeper experience of love, peace, joy, and fulfillment.

True forgiveness can only occur once you've allowed yourself to feel the depth of feelings associated with the experience you have been through. Once you have worked through the pain and grief with the use of ritual and other healing practices, the road to restoring your lost sense of self will begin to emerge. Forgiveness allows you to get back onto the road of living a fulfilled life. Without giving up all the resulting resentment, you will be held hostage to your past and will never be able to release those binding memories and grow beyond them.

The biggest gift my son gave to me is that through his death I was kicked onto my path of teaching forgiveness, the path of my foundation, the path of stopping children from killing children. When you're on path, it is amazing how the Universe supports you. So many times I see people going through life who have no clue what their purpose is. Because of the negative emotions they cling to in their victim mentality, they cannot open their hearts to their full potential. When you choose to give up the resulting resentment, you will find that all your relationships begin to improve for the better. You will feel more peace and harmony in your day. And your heart will begin to open to all the creative possibilities of your life. We all have a reason for being. We all have a path. Are you on yours?

There is perhaps no greater personal tool for healing than forgiveness. When you allow yourself to forgive, you are truly demonstrating an important element of self-love and the recognition that you are ready for a lighter and brighter future. I teach that this process of forgiveness begins with first acknowledging you have been wronged and then giving up all the resulting resentment. This is done by viewing your life circumstances with the broader perspective of empathy and compassion. The third and final step is reaching out. In some cases this will involve face-to-face contact with the offending person. In other cases, completion will come through different avenues. In the following chapter, I will show you the way.

The holiest of all spots on earth is where an ancient hatred has become a present love.

— A Course in Miracles

Step Three: Reach Out

There is no timetable for forgiveness. Depending on your specific situation, steps one and two might take a day, a month, a year, or longer. In the first step, you acknowledge you have been wronged. Through ritual and spiritual practice, you give attention to your deepest and most heartfelt emotions so that those parts of yourself can be validated and honored. In the second step, you develop empathy for the person who hurt you, and you set a clear intention to give up all the resulting resentment.

In the third step you reach out, but this is not simply reaching out in a systematic way. This step involves reaching out with love and compassion. It may seem that this would be very hard to do. How can you find the courage to reach out to someone who has hurt you, to somebody who by his or her action has created all this grief and anguish for you? And why would you want to? Wouldn't it be better to keep your distance from this person so you could avoid the danger of being hurt again?

COMPLETING THE PROCESS

Once again, this is a choice for you to make. If you have been successful with the first two steps, this process will come more naturally for you, because the decision to forgive will be rooted in empathy, love, and compassion. If you choose to reach out, you will

Ever since the tragedy, Azim and Ples have worked side by side like brothers in teaching, as an example, the principles of peace and forgiveness.

complete the process of forgiveness by totally freeing yourself from this individual. By reaching out you can begin to heal that place in yourself that still feels vulnerable, afraid, and broken. And, depending on your situation, through this third step you may find a way to recreate harmony in your relationship.

This doesn't mean that you will become lifelong friends, although that may, in fact, be the result. But when you reach out in forgiveness to the person who wronged you, when you connect in some way with sincere respect and compassion, you will open yourself to the beautiful journey of transcending the pain of separation to a place of unity, peace, and harmony. When the reaching out process is an act of forgiveness toward yourself, you will see that the old wounds will heal, and you will once again have a free heart.

The most important aspect for practicing the third step of forgiveness is to make sure that your own personal safety is the first priority. For some, completion will not involve face-to-face or physical contact with the perpetrator or offender. However, if it does, and since you are doing this of your own volition, it is very important that you keep your own safety in mind. If there is any risk at all, do not feel that you need to do this step in person. There are other ways to reach out and still maintain your personal safety.

Be aware that the person you are ready to meet may not be ready to meet you. Have respect for this possibility, because forcing this third step to look a certain way will not serve you well and will not give you the desired result. At some point I realized that I would not feel complete with the healing process until I came eyeball to eyeball with my son's murderer. But when I finally made the outreach to Tony, he wasn't ready. He prepared for six months before agreeing to see me, even though he knew I had already forgiven him. When we finally did meet, it felt totally right to me. My intuition had been very strong that I had to take this final step, but it took a while for me to reach that point. The clouds of sorrow really didn't begin to part until three and a half years after Tariq died. I remember my family thought I was crazy to want to reach out to Tony, but I was very strongly driven.

Although it seemed like it would be a very hard thing to do, in the aftermath of the meeting I was quite surprised to realize that it had not been so difficult after all. I think that is because I, like Tony, had taken time to prepare. I remember that it took a thousand hours of meditation to heal from my divorce, and it took several

Over the years, TKF and Azim's speaking engagements have reached out to over 8 million children, either in person or via media broadcasts into the classroom.

thousand hours of meditation to get to a place where I was ready to meet the person who had taken my son's life. You'll want to take time to reach this third step of forgiveness. There is no set timeline. Some of you will get to this point of healing quickly. For others, the entire forgiveness process will take more time. There is no one right way to go through this. It all depends on the gravity of the situation and the person you are dealing with. Remember that forgiveness is never the same for everybody.

The separation, the divisiveness which needs to be corrected by this third step could be at your workplace, where perhaps someone was promoted over you or your boss fired your friend. It could be at home, where there has been difficulty with one of your family members. It could be a result of divorce, where there have been alimony or child-support issues. Or it could be with an acquaintance or a stranger who committed an act of negativity toward you. Your situation, like mine, may have involved a violent act. There are a variety of circumstances that beg forgiveness. This third step of reaching out can help to heal the fractured relationships you have with others and with yourself.

A professor of sociology at the Oahu campus of Brigham Young University heard me speak at a conference in San Diego. When he learned that I was scheduled to give a talk to social workers in Honolulu, he invited me to his campus to address his students, who were all doing their masters in social work. After I'd told my story, I watched one young lady during the Q&A portion of the talk. She was probably in her mid to late twenties, and I could see the emotion welling up and her eyes becoming teary. I watched her entire demeanor change as I was speaking, and I knew that she was experiencing a soulular transformation.

At the end of my presentation, this young woman, still full of emotion, came from the back of the room, handed me a letter, and offered me a thank you that came from a very deep place of gratitude. I gave her a hug, and then she left. Later that night, after I'd had dinner with the professor and had gone back to my room, I found her letter as I emptied my pockets. I had given two presentations that day, and my heart was wide open. Reading her words brought all the emotion that was in me up to the surface, and I cried like I hadn't for a long while.

"Dear Brother Khamisa," she wrote. "I know that you've spoken these words many times before, but I wonder if you know their power. Five years ago after my vicious rape, I had built a wall of hatred, of anger, of irreverence, of revenge, and of resentment. And your words pummeled that wall with a wrecking ball. The wall now is gone. I feel honored. I feel privileged to build something more reverent in its place. I shall seek the path of forgiveness and help wayward youth make positive choices."

I was deeply moved. By choosing the path of forgiveness she would begin to heal herself, and as a gift to me she would commit to helping wayward youth. For five years she had carried this burden of anger. Because of the viciousness of the crime against her, she was naturally fearful of entering into an intimate relationship. The possibility of having a family seemed out of the realm of possibility to her. But after hearing my story, she was immediately able to get to that place of forgiveness and see the possibility of reaching out and saying, "I forgive you." Through her forgiveness, she could transform her wall of hatred with healing. And through the creation of something more reverent in its place, she could fill her soul with love and compassion and offer that sense of peace and harmony to her future loved ones.

OPENING TO THE LIGHT

I realize that this process of reaching out takes a lot of effort and may seem very hard to do. Let me reassure you that it does take courage, but it is not as hard as you think it might be. It was actually easier than I ever imagined, and the healing that has come to my family as a result of Tony and I now having a loving relationship is profound.

You might feel insecure or tentative about reaching out to this person in your life. You might have trepidations, but I hope you will take the step, because this is where the real fruits are. I have traveled the country telling my story and teaching about forgiveness. I know that for many people the situation requiring forgiveness is nothing as dire as my case, where I reached out to the family of my son's killer. I find that most often the person you want to reach out to is somebody you were at one time close to, and that there is now a rift that needs to be healed. What I'm offering by this third step of reaching out is a way to recreate a closeness in that relationship you once enjoyed. Once you complete the process of forgiveness, there will be an instant behavioral shift, a change in yourself at the soulular level, and you'll find the quality of the relationship not only coming back, but also coming back at a more profound level.

I once gave a talk at a church in San Diego. A father came up to me afterward and told me that he had not talked to his son in ten years. He said he was so inspired by my talk that he was going to call his son the next day.

"If you are so inspired by my talk, why are you going to wait until tomorrow? Here's my cell phone," I said, "Call him now!" I put him on the spot, but he took my phone and dialed the number. I thought it was amazing that after ten years of not talking to his son, he still remembered the number. They connected, and I was amazed again. How many times do we dial someone and get their voice mail? But when divine inspiration is working through you, miracles happen all the time.

He took my cell phone and walked to the other side of the room, while I continued a conversation with a small group of people. Just a minute or two later, he came back and fell into my arms. So filled with emotion, he didn't care that there were other people around. This grown man sobbed so deeply, I literally had to hold him so that he wouldn't fall to the ground. After a short time he recovered from his emotion, and between tears he thanked me for the gift of reuniting him with his son.

I tell you this work is profound. It can literally take hearts that have turned dark and cold over years of resentment, and in a moment open them to light and love again.

When we contemplate the need for forgiveness in our own lives, we often think of situations with friends and family. But forgiveness can also be taken into the workplace. Mr. Morii, the chairman of a large, Japanese multinational company, had a young executive working for him. This young man, Masauki, worked under Mr. Morii for many years until one day he was caught stealing money. I think that in most corporations (especially in the United States), Masauki would have been fired. The chairman, who was a wise, enlightened human being, decided to do some research into his employee and learned that Masauki, who was a very good worker and showed a lot of promise, also had a very bad gambling habit.

Instead of seeking revenge and retaliation, Mr. Morii decided to reach out to his young executive. He forgave Masauki for stealing from the company, and he went the extra step in getting the young man help to deal with his gambling habit. Masauki apologized to everybody in the company, and over the next few years he paid back the money he'd stolen . . . with interest. He went through treatment and was able to kick the gambling habit completely. Later he became a significant vice president of Mr. Morii's company.

I had met Masauki in my work as an international investment banker when we were on a joint venture project. This involved a large real estate development in a major U.S. city and included office buildings, retail, and a hotel. It was a one hundred million dollar plus project, and I was dealing with Masauki, whose company wanted to provide the capital for my clients. Halfway through the negotiations, Masauki died of a heart attack! I thought, "My God, this project is now doomed because I don't know who else is going to pick up on this. We're going to lose all the work we've done up to this point."

We didn't lose it, though. The project was kicked back to Mr. Morii, so I started to deal with him. He told me that he really wanted to see the project through in memory of Masauki, because this was the man's favorite project. We continued working on it and, fortunately, through Mr. Morii's commitment in his colleague's memory, the project came to fruition. This is now a wonderful landmark project which is lighting the skies of one of our cities.

It was during my negotiations with Mr. Morii that I learned the story about Masauki having stolen the money. Mr. Morii said, "I want you to know that Masauki became a very wealthy person. He was one of our top vice presidents, and when he died we were inspired to find that he had left two thirds of his estate to the company. This was much more money than we had originally invested in his project."

Because the company forgave him for stealing and gave him a second chance, Masauki left the bulk of his estate to them in his will! So even in the workplace, even when it's very easy to fire someone, there is a place for compassion and forgiveness.

FREEDOM FROM THE PAST

Most often we know whom we need to forgive. But sometimes, especially in circumstances involving violence, you won't know the offender. Juan, one of our panelists in the TKF nonviolence programs, told me about his brother's murder. He said that he and his friends had heard that a certain person had committed the murder, and they drove over to a liquor store to kill him.

"I took a stand that day," Juan said. I told them, 'Turn the car around, we're not going to go do this.'"

He said, "My cousin called me all kinds of names. I'm a sissy and all of that. But that day I stood for something, because like TKF says, 'If you don't stand for something, you'll fall for anything.' We later found out that the person we were going to kill was in jail when my brother was killed, so he was not the person who committed the murder anyway."

To this day Juan doesn't know who killed his brother. "But whoever it is that did it," he said, "I have forgiven them, because I met Mr. Khamisa and I see how he has dealt with the loss of his son, and I'm finally at peace."

Even if you don't know the offender, it's still important to take this last step of forgiveness and reach out. This gesture will move you forward, so that you can begin to live free of the past. You can reach out on an energetic or symbolic level by writing a letter, or by having a friend take the offender's physical place. Forgiveness frees the forgiver. You do this for yourself even if you don't know who committed the crime. Through your compassion for the unknown offender, you will feel even more compassion and love for yourself.

If you are ready to take this step of reaching out, and the situation involves a crime, please remember that your safety is of the greatest importance. There are ways to have safe communication with an offender through facilitated letter writing and dialogue opportunities, and there is never a reason to put yourself at risk. "Victims of crimes can always rely on third-party facilitators for the preparation and communication bridgework, so they never have to go it alone," says Ted Lewis, restorative justice program manager at Community Mediation Services in Eugene, Oregon.

Options for victim/offender meetings vary depending on where you live, but a good place to start is with an inquiry to the VORP Information and Resource Center (Victim-Offender Reconciliation Program at www.vorp.com). Your state's Department of Justice may have an office of restorative justice, or you can contact your local victim's services department, which is usually in the District Attorney's office.

If the person you need to forgive is someone you know, you can reach out by going to see him or her. If for some reason you don't feel that you'd be safe in his or her presence—emotionally or physically—you can reach out through writing a letter or sending a recording. And even if you sense that the person will not be receptive to your outreach, you can still continue the process of forgiveness by writing a letter and burning it in the fireplace. This symbolic act of reaching out can be equally inspiring.

FROM SCAR TO STAR

Through this sharing of my three steps of forgiveness, I have given you what I call milestones in the journey. For some of you the healing process between each of the three steps could take a long time. Or, if it's a minor matter, you could complete the process in a single day. The important thing to remember is to continue on the path; let it become a new habit. Once you have journeyed through these three steps of forgiveness, you will find that your life energy is restored. The capacity of your divine vessel will have increased, and you will be free to live your life from a place of inspiration and love. You will see that by living with an open heart, the ripple effect of forgiveness will extend to your loved ones, your community, and eventually the world. Forgiveness is a process, not an event. There is no timeline. Simply listen to your own loving heart, and I know you will find your way. You may wonder, "How will I know I've forgiven?" When the person who has wronged you has a safe passage through your mind, that is true forgiveness.

I see today that through forgiveness my life experience has become so much more. My heart is wide open so that I am able to contain enormous amounts of compassion and empathy for humanity. This has enriched my own life, as it has enriched my family's life. You forgive for yourself so that you can create that space in your heart, in your spirit, to bring back joy. Forgiveness is for giving. And if, through your giving, the other person is moved to open his or her heart to healing, that is icing on the cake.

There are many ways for you to share your compassionate heart and energy. If you are so inspired, we would be happy to have you become part of the TKF family, helping us with our work of stopping kids from killing kids. You could also offer your heart and energy to the Peace Alliance Foundation. This is a nonpartisan citizen action organization founded by Marianne Williamson, which is responsible for the national campaign to establish a U. S. Department of Peace. I'm sure you can think of many people and organizations that could benefit from your energy, your compassion, your creativity, and your love. The ripple effect of forgiveness can extend to all of humanity, one open heart at a time.

Dark cannot destroy dark. Only light can destroy dark. Because of this I remember to live from the higher vibratory levels of compassion, peace, and love. It is possible to take something where there is a horrible scar—something even so dark as a murder—and create a truly magnificent star. This is our job as people who care about our planet. When we see darkness, we look around the room and find a power outlet. We plug ourselves in and cast light on the dark. As Gandhi said, "An eye for an eye, and soon the whole world is blind." We have tried that approach since the beginning of time, and what has it gotten us? Now it's time to try forgiveness. I think it is a much better strategy, not only for our country, but for ourselves.

I truly do believe that forgiveness is a blessing and a gift. And I believe that a blessing is when preparation meets grace. You begin with an intention. Whoever the person is, or whatever the thing is in your life—or even if it's yourself—start with the premise that you have the intention of forgiving. Intentions are powerful. But your intention must be authentic. It has to be sincere and in integrity. You cannot expect the Universe to support something that is otherwise.

From an authentic intention you can create an aphorism such as, "I want to forgive this person, I want to get beyond the suffering." From there you go to a meditation, and from a meditation you go to a prayer. This is that place where you are connected with your source. I believe that all prayers which are authentic, which are in integrity, and which are sincere and for the highest good are answered. It is my appreciation and my guarantee that if your intention is authentic and sincere, if you will do this on a daily basis—it may take a week, a month, a year, or even a lifetime—you'll wake up one day with a wonderful sense of freedom where this huge load, this albatross around your neck, has been lifted. You'll feel light and free and spacious for the love, compassion, and joy to flow back into your life. With a commitment to this process, you will be able to heal this thing in your life that has kept you from feeling complete happiness and freedom. Even if you've been suffering for years, you will now be released from it.

When we go through life, we hold onto so much of our past and suffer from all the anger, grief, and resentment that has built up over the years. It interferes with our ability to live a peaceful, joyous life of freedom and compassion, because all of these resentments are like an anchor preventing us from moving forward. Through forgiveness I've let go of a lot of the suffering from my past. I get along with my family and my siblings. My ex-wife, Almas, and I are very good friends. I get along with the killer of my son and his family. Ples and I are like brothers, and I have a good relationship with Tony. I'm never in the past anymore. But what about the future? So long as my thoughts remain there, I cannot be present. I once asked the Dalai Lama about this problem. "I've read that enlightened people are always present," I said to him. "How do you give up the future?"

He answered, "You are very fortunate that you've been able to heal your past. A lot of people can't do that, and they're stymied in the present from living a full life, because there is something in their past that is always coming in the way. That's a big step, and forgiveness is a good way to do that. As far as the future's concerned, it's important to put out the effort but not to be married to the outcome."

The Buddhists have tremendous richness in their teachings about nonattachment. This doesn't mean you don't put out the effort, but rather it's the realization that sometimes the unexpected results are the ones that are best for you and best for the Universe. When I sat with him, what I saw in the face of the Dalai Lama was the embodiment of peace and compassion through the practice of nonattachment. He lights up an entire room without making a sound.

When you practice forgiveness and release your attachment to outcome, you are able to transcend that which is negative. Gandhi said, "Become the message you want to create." This is an exercise that we do one human being at a time. The purpose of the forgiveness process is to first create that peacefulness in you. The more people who are at peace, the more people there will be who are living in trust. One person at a time, we will eventually create a world of peace practitioners who are committed to practicing a life of forgiveness, goodwill, and compassion toward all.

If we are to have real peace in the world, we shall have to begin with the children.

— Mahatma Gandhi

The Tariq Khamisa Foundation (TKF)

Chapter Six

The Tariq Khamisa Foundation was built upon one beautiful moment of inspiration which dutifully rose from the tragic death of my son. In the arms of God, I was embraced with Love, and in the midst of that peace and safety I understood that there were victims at both ends of the gun. My son was a victim of the shooter, Tony Hicks. And Tony himself was a victim of society.

SOCIETY'S CHILDREN

Who is society? Is it something outside of ourselves? Or is each and every one of us responsible for our culture and our norms? We have 75 kids in our country getting shot every day (kids aged twelve to eighteen), 13 who die, and another 237 who are arrested for violent crimes with a weapon involved — every single day. We, all of us, have a real problem. Who is this society that should be caring for our children? It is nothing less than the combined hearts of every one of us.

Before Tariq's death, I did not take much time to consider the overall welfare of society's children. I took care of my own children in the best way I knew how. (Those of you who are parents will agree that parenting is not an exact science.) But like so many also believe, I thought that other children were the responsibility of their own parents. Little did I know how many children in our country live with and are influenced by parents

73

The trusted TKF Board of Trustees. From Left: Derek Myron, Mark Fackler (Board President), Martin Shapiro, Dianne McKay, DeAnna LoCoco, Azim Khamisa (Founder, Chairman of the Board), Ples Felix (Vice Chairman of the Board), Johan Oeyen. Not shown: Richard Taylor, Peter Deddeh, Cheryl Rhodes (Treasurer), Harriet Carter (Secretary), Lou Adamo.

The Tariq Khamisa Foundation staff. From Left: Front Row Jenifer Finkelstein (Program Coordinator), Betsy Frank (Finance Director) Middle Row - Mayra Nunez (Program Coordinator) Back Row - Robin Hart (Program Director), Donna Pinto (Strategic Alliances), Lisa Grogan (Executive Director), Niki Kosteck (Development Coordinator), Suzanne Bacon (Development and Program Associate) Not shown: Katie Bowles (Development Director), Maslah Farah (Program Coordinator).

and guardians who are living lives of violence. How then are these children supposed to live differently when violence, and not nonviolence, is promoted as a way of life?

Tariq was killed by a boy who came from a loving home with his grandfather. Still, because of many problems throughout his young life, he was angry enough that when he was told by the gang leader to shoot a pizza delivery man for two lousy pizzas, he did. Tony knew he'd done the worst thing he'd ever done in his life, and he also knew that it could not be reversed. When he was holding the gun, he was an angry fourteen-year-old who had come from an extended family of gang members and violence. He was a victim of childhood abuse and neglect. In that moment he simply didn't value the life of another any more than he valued his own.

When I became aware of the violent youth statistics in our country, I began to ask some fundamental questions. First and foremost I asked, "Why do our kids join gangs?" The answers I found horrified me.

Joining gangs is a macho thing to do. Kids join to get a sense of respect. Or they join for protection because they live in an area where if they don't join *this* gang, then they're targeted by that gang over there. Kids also join gangs to get a sense of belonging. But the fact that kids join gangs represents a gross lack in what our families and our communities offer the children in our country. If the lack did not exist, there would be no need for a youth to join a gang to gain respect, to feel safe, or to have a sense of belonging.

Statistics reveal the likelihood that if a kid joins a gang, he or she will either be in prison or in the ground by the age of twenty-five. This is a tragic fact. It's a tremendous loss of youthful energy that could have been focused toward more positive rewards. This is our nation's loss, and it will take our national will to save these children.

STARTING MY FOUNDATION

After I learned the truth about gangs and youth violence, I knew in my heart that I had to do something to save these children from becoming victims of society like Tariq and Tony. I also knew that I couldn't do it alone. During the time these thoughts were running through my mind, I was reminded by my spiritual teachers that there is a time to grieve and a time to stop grieving. After our forty-day ritual, it was time to let Tariq's soul fly to freedom. And my teachers reminded me that it was by doing good deeds that I could accumulate spiritual currency to help my son's soul on its way.

The Tariq Khamisa Foundation (TKF) was born of this dual inspiration: to do good deeds to advance Tariq's journey and to give my life's attention to helping children learn to make nonviolent and peaceful choices. If I could save one child, I would feel that I had done something that made a difference. The burning desire that I had to do something to stop kids from killing kids burst forth and took root. Today it has blossomed into a fully-staffed nonprofit organization which successfully implements several youth and parent programs.

For the past twelve years, as I have devoted my life to ending the epidemic of violence within our society, the work of the foundation has touched millions of children through in-school assemblies, video presentations, and broadcasts into the classroom. We have touched at least as many adults through extensive national and international print and electronic media coverage, as well as television and radio exposure. These students, teachers, and parents—as well as many others I reach through my forgiveness workshops and speaking engagements at conferences and other venues—are coming to the self-empowering realization that they always have choice. They learn that even though they've been exposed to one way of living, that does not mean they have to pattern their lives after it. Violence begets violence. It is never a good choice.

Through its violence prevention educational programs and services, TKF offers inspiration to students. I'm happy to say that many of these kids are being sidetracked from a destiny of violence. In partnership with community and educational partners, we're cultivating new attitudes and behaviors by role modeling integrity, kindness, empathy, understanding, peace, forgiveness, compassion, and respect. TKF empowers future leaders by inspiring young people to choose nonviolence. Through our programs, we are nurturing a generation of peacemakers who will create a world free from youth violence.

THE TKF MISSION STATEMENT

Stopping kids from killing kids and breaking the cycle of youth violence by inspiring nonviolent choices and planting seeds of hope for our children's future.

TKF Executive Director Lisa Grogan says, "As our violent and aggressive world goes on, the Tariq Khamisa Foundation will peacefully evolve to continue its mission of 'Stopping Kids From Killing Kids.' Today's children are sponges of knowledge who absorb enormous amounts of energy—both positive and negative—from the environments in which they are surrounded. At a very early age, children become programmed with the mirrored morals and values of the ones who are in their daily lives, such as parents, grandparents, older siblings, other relatives, and neighbors.

"Unfortunately, in our society these morals and values are not always of a peaceful nature," Lisa continues. "Just as powerful as these people are in the molding of our nation's children is the media through television, the Internet, magazines, and video games. These messages of violence and aggression are conveyed into their lives on a daily or even hourly basis. In many instances the messages are of extreme violence, and the aggressive behaviors are portrayed as being powerful, cool, hot, or whatever the hip word is for the day. Children witness these negative accounts constantly and without the awareness of the consequences which would naturally follow these malicious behaviors. This is how the cycle of violence persists in our society today with no end in sight."

TKF's programs are an antidote for the rampant youth violence in our society. Since gang members begin pressuring kids at the fifth-grade level to join gangs, our prevention strategy focuses on youths in the fourth to eighth grades. Our messages of nonviolence and forgiveness instill in the kids the desire to be peacemakers, not gang members. And the strength of our belief that TKF's programs make a difference is backed up by measurable results.

It is obvious that we have a powerful story to share here at TKF. But I never wanted us to be a traveling circus. My desire has always been to make a measurable difference in stopping kids from killing kids. As a businessman I know how to measure widgets, and I've often been referred to as a statistical junkie. But from the earliest inception of the foundation I wondered, "How do you measure whether TKF's programs are really transforming the kids?"

DEVELOPING A MODEL

Soon after starting TKF I reached out to Dick Madsen, professor of sociology at the University of California San Diego (UCSD), to help me develop a quantitative and qualitative statistical model that shows beyond doubt that TKF's programs are exemplary in terms of outcomes and results. I told him that I could see the kids transforming before my eyes, but I didn't know how to measure social change. He told me that they have methods to do so and asked if he could come to one of our assemblies to see for himself. We usually do back-to-back assemblies in the schools, because they have such large student bodies. The day Dick showed up, we had three assemblies in a row. They are all basically the same except for the kids in the audience, and I was quite surprised to notice that Dick stayed for all three programs.

He came up to me afterward. "I've been a sociologist for thirty-six years, and I've never seen anything so powerful," he said in tears. "I want to help you." Dick went to his department at the university and put together a meeting of a dozen of his peers, all Ph.D.s and people who'd been working with youth for a long time. I presented the TKF video to them, and from that initial four-hour meeting the statistical model we use today to measure outcomes was drafted.

My good friend, Kit Goldman, who was instrumental in the creation of our very first *Violence Impact Forum Assembly*, spent an extensive amount of time and effort in developing our initial quantitative and qualitative statistical model. With the help of Kit, San Diego State University, the Institute of Public Health, and other consultants, we have substantially and consistently improved upon that model.

THE CORE VALUES OF TKF

INTEGRITY: We behave with integrity.

COMPASSIONATE CONFRONTATION: We believe in compassionate confrontation in a context of peace and respect.

FORGIVENESS: We forgive others and seek forgiveness.

Integrity is defined as "soundness, incorruptibility, and a firm adherence to a code of ethics." Our integrity demonstrates the strengths and weaknesses in our character. People of integrity are honest and genuine in their dealings with others. People of integrity hold fast to their commitments rather than their desires. We make many commitments to TKF, to ourselves, and to our community. At TKF we understand that at times these commitments are in conflict. At these times of conflict, we must work to remain steadfast to our true and deep commitments. We must bring these conflicts to the light and work with each other to resolve them. We strive to live a life of integrity.

Confrontation is defined as "to bring face-to-face, to cause to meet, a clashing of ideas." In the context of TKF, we believe in confrontation that occurs with compassion in order to achieve a higher understanding with mutually beneficial results. Compassionate confrontation requires compassionate listening. We understand that compassionate confrontation is a healthy ingredient to human interactions. Confrontation is honest. Confrontation creates opportunities for change. We embrace compassionate confrontation. We confront each other with a loving and compassionate intent.

Forgiveness is defined as "the act of giving up of resentment." At TKF we see forgiveness as a process, starting with the acknowledgment that we have been harmed. Through this pain, we tap into the power of forgiveness, the release of resentment. Ultimately, we reach out with love and compassion to the offender. We forgive others when they have wronged us. We forgive others who have wronged someone else. We ask for our own forgiveness when we have wronged others. We will not harbor feelings of resentment after forgiveness. We acknowledge that we are all human and at times will fail in forgiveness. We help each other to forgive, to accept forgiveness, and to accept each other through the process. We strive to forgive.

As an organization we are committed to helping kids make better and safer choices in their lives. We are also committed to a set of Core Values which provide a living foundation on which we continue to build TKF. These core values are a guiding light we use to illuminate our path. In difficult times and in difficult situations our core values provide us with direction, and they are often tough to adhere to. But at TKF, we help each other live by the core value standards in all that we do.

Of the core values, TKF board member Dianne McKay says, "There have been times when they really did guide me in deciding how to resolve a difficult situation. Something came up recently with one of my bosses, and I kept thinking about the core values. I thought to myself, 'What would Integrity have me do?' Before approaching her, I thought everything through and waited a few days until my anger had subsided. Then we had a very productive conversation. We talked for about half an hour, and our relationship improved. It was because I used the core values. I'm grateful to our president, Mark Fackler, and to TKF for putting the core values in writing, saying this is who we are and this is how we want you to strive to be, whether you're with TKF or not. The core values are magnificent and have really affected my life for the better."

TKF Program Director Suzanne Bacon sees them as providing a nice framework for dealing with problems. "Sometimes it's not easy to talk about something that you don't agree with or that is difficult in some way," she says. "The core values give me a nice way to open the conversation. I'll say to someone, 'I'm going to compassionately confront you,' and then they know that whatever's coming is probably going to be a little bit difficult. However, the framework of the core values provides some preparation for the difficult conversation."

The core values are an important part of our foundation, because they ensure that we are doing everything we can do to walk our talk. When we go into the schools to teach peace, nonviolence, and forgiveness to the students, they know whether or not we are speaking the truth. Kids are very much in tune with "vibes," or energy vibrations, and if they sense that we are not speaking from a place of integrity, they'll stop listening.

TKF Program and Marketing Communications Coordinator Megan Thomas Wescott says that it's all about what you take away from TKF — what you learn about forgiving, letting go, and about not reacting with anger. "That's what we try to teach the kids, so I really feel like when I talk to them I'm living exactly what I'm saying. I'm being truthful with them, and I think that's why they're so receptive of it. The kids really grasp the core messages of TKF."

BREAKING THE CYCLE OF VIOLENCE

Our foundation is dedicated to breaking the cycle of violence by inspiring youth to say "no" to gangs, guns, drugs, alcohol, and violence. It is clear that prevention is the ultimate solution. We must keep our vulnerable youth from joining gangs and engaging in other risky behaviors that can destroy their own futures and cause serious harm to others.

Lisa speaks to the problem with these heartfelt words. "How does one break this dreadful cycle of violence, which is often promoted in our society? As the executive director at TKF, my vision for the future of this powerful organization is to make these children, especially the ones who have been predisposed to vengeful and aggressive behaviors, aware that there are consequences for their actions. The consequences run much deeper than simply 'doin' some time' in juvenile hall. I want them to be aware of how one mindless violent decision, such as the one Tony made, can affect many lives for generations to come. I want them to be aware that there are other decisions which can be made. I want them to know the power of a peaceful decision and a forgiving heart. I want the children to know that Tony had a choice that night to pull the trigger on that gun or not to pull the trigger.

"When Tony made that one violent choice in that one moment, not only did Tariq and Tony's lives change, but also so did other lives of infinite proportions," Lisa continues. "Maybe Tony, who wanted to become a doctor, would have saved people's lives which in turn would have affected so many other people. Perhaps Tariq and his fiancée would have had children, who then would have had more children, who all would have done wonderful things. The world will never know. That is the power of one poor, thoughtless, violent choice."

TKF's mission is to teach kids they have a choice and to lead them toward living lives of peace and nonviolence. To this end, we have developed several programs within the framework of our comprehensive strategy. Two of these programs are the *Violence Impact Forum Assembly (VIF)* and *Ending the Cycle of Violence*. Both are held during school hours and are facilitated by TKF and/or school staff. All of our programs are designed to inspire the kids to learn and essentially live by TKF's six key messages:

1. Violence is real and hurts us all.
2. Your actions have consequences.
3. You can make good and nonviolent choices.
4. You can work toward forgiveness as opposed to seeking revenge.

5. Everyone, including you, deserves to be loved and treated well.
6. From conflict, love and unity are possible.

The reinforcement of these key messages through our programs and curriculum really turns these kids around and away from some of the bad choices they've been in the habit of making. We at TKF understand the temptations these kids face. "It's very frustrating," Ples says, "because we as parents and grandparents understand that there is a drumbeat out there in the community that goes 24/7. That drumbeat goes, 'Come on and be with me, come on and be with us. We'll protect you, we'll defend you, we'll take care of you. We're your new family now, and all you have to do is do what we say.'"

With TKF's continuing success, our programs and curriculum will one day be established in schools all across our nation and, with grace, possibly even the world. If we can teach these key messages to all of our kids—to the future leaders of our country and the world—if they can truly learn how to live lives of nonviolence and then passionately desire to create love, unity, brotherhood, and sisterhood from conflict, then the only possible outcome will be world peace. What is more important than that?

Our programs are designed to transform kids by offering them education beyond the basics of reading, writing, and mathematics. Many of the principals, teachers, and counselors at the schools where Ples and I speak tell us that our messages are exceedingly important, because no matter what other future life choices these kids make, most of them are going to become parents one day. And as parents the skills that they will most certainly need are those that we teach: nonviolence, compassion, and forgiveness. We at TKF are committed to helping these kids create new patterns of thinking.

"All children growing up experience certain kinds of emotional things that they need assistance, help, and support with," Ples says. "And to the extent that they get that support in a setting that's safe, secure, and nonjudgmental, then that certainly helps the kid understand, 'I'm not by myself in this instance, I'm not alone, I'm not the only one experiencing some of these emotional kinds of spikes and valleys based on loss.' They understand that their experience is a common one.

"And they also understand," Ples says, "'I'm in this setting learning practical, usable tools to help me not only address the trauma from my loss experience, but to also help me navigate the course of my life in a way that will be of value to other people.' They understand that they will express that value in dealing with issues not only of loss, but also of loss prevention by virtue of minimizing or otherwise alleviating anger. And they learn to look at alternative approaches to resolving conflict with the intention of a win-win outcome.

"Through our programs," Ples says, "we help the students develop tools that allow them to walk a mile in someone else's shoes. It's about exercising empathy and compassion. And those are tools that we want to be able to help instill so that not only do they learn them and practice them, but also the very people that they're receiving the instructions from are models of how to practice compassion, empathy, and forgiveness."

Stopping kids from killing kids and breaking the cycle of youth violence by inspiring nonviolent choices and planting seeds of hope for our children's future. This is the Mission Statement of the Tariq Khamisa Foundation. In the next chapter, I will introduce you to the programs that help us achieve that goal.

*If human beings can be trained for cruelty and greed and
a belief in power which comes through hate and fear and
force, certainly we can train equally well for greatness
and mercy and the power of love which comes because
of the strength of the good qualities to be found in the
soul of every individual human being.*

— Eleanor Roosevelt

Violence Impact Forum Assembly (VIF)

Chapter Seven

The first and oldest of our programs is the *Violence Impact Forum Assembly (VIF)*. This is a powerful, interactive in-school assembly that shares the real-life TKF story of Tariq and Tony, which clearly and powerfully demonstrates to the students the devastation and consequences of violence. We open the assembly with a video presentation—a reenactment of the shooting and its aftermath—which impresses upon the students those consequences, as well as the truth about gangs and the reality of prison life. The goal of the *VIF* is to create resilient youth who are empowered to make positive choices. Through our focus on forgiveness and choices, students come to fully understand the lifelong consequences of the one deadly choice made by Tony and the critical importance of choosing pathways to nonviolence.

NEED FOR THE PROGRAM

Because kids in the fifth grade are often pressured to join gangs, we take the *VIF* into elementary and middle schools, beginning with the fourth grade. If we can get to the kids first, and if we can impress upon them that they have the personal power and free will to make nonviolent and peaceful choices, then we have the potential to save them from the lives of violence that they may otherwise have chosen.

"I am a peacemaker." Towards the end of each Violence Impact Forum, children make a pledge to practice the teachings of nonviolence, forgiveness and peace.

"There is such need for our programs," TKF Development Director Katie Bowles says. "Youth violence is very real. We have had teachers say our assembly was more needed than almost any other curriculum. 'Every child can benefit from this assembly,' a middle school teacher told me. 'Our students were so engaged.'

"In one survey, seventy-five percent of the students questioned said they are afraid of violence from other kids," Katie continues. "Forty percent say they are afraid of violence in their schools. Our programs empower kids to forgive; they save lives and teach nonviolent choices. Azim and Ples know what it is like to forgive; they know the consequences of bad choices and the ripple effect of violence, something most people do not even think about."

At the time of this writing, most of our *VIF*s are held in at-risk schools. Even so, we know that not every child is going to join a gang or be pressured to join. However, violence comes in many forms: bullying, starting a rumor, name calling, segregation. Every child at least once has experienced some form of violence, so we teach the kids what violence looks like, and we impress upon them that it has many forms.

THE ASSEMBLY

Before the day of the *VIF*, an information sheet is sent out to the students' parents. An opt-out letter is also included in case of the possibility that a parent does not want his or her child to attend. Many of these kids come from families where gang activity is the norm. We include the opt-out letter, but it is rarely returned.

We also provide a teacher's guide for the *VIF*. Each school that participates agrees to do a follow-up session with their students. Our teacher's guide facilitates that follow-up with the TKF Vision Statement, an abbreviated version of the TKF Story, a description of the *VIF*, objectives, the teacher's role, and a Student Debriefing Agenda. "Tariq's Philosophy of Life" essay and Tony's sentencing speech are also included in the teacher's resource packet.

The *VIF* is an immersive, intensive, and transformative experience for the kids. After they take their seats, we turn down the auditorium lights and begin the video reenactment of the shooting. The kids are immediately drawn in by the rap music. Those who are still talking to their friends quiet down as the dramatic scene unfolds before them of street-smart youths hanging out in the shadows while the pizza delivery man becomes more and more frustrated by his inability to find the right address.

When "Tony" points the gun at "Tariq," any remaining noise from the students' normal energetic distractions dissolves, and the school auditorium is perfectly still. The hush is palpable, the students' breaths drawn in. And then, with the sound of the shot, it's as if the students exhale in one united breath. What they have just witnessed is something they may never have witnessed before. Or, if some of them have, the dramatic video likely may have triggered memories of events from their own lives.

With the video over and the lights becoming brighter, Sal Giacalone, Tariq's boss from the Italian restaurant where he was working the night of the shooting, comes on stage and welcomes the students. He thanks them for having TKF come to their school, for their respect, and for paying close attention to the video and to the speakers who will be coming on stage. He tells the kids that members of TKF have come to talk to them about making choices, and he instills in them the idea that each of them has the power to make different choices than Tony. He impresses upon them the notion that they can make positive choices to stop the cycle of violence.

"Today you are going to be meeting people who have been deeply affected by violence and how it hurts," he tells them. "Each of you is important. We care deeply about each and every one of you, and we don't want to lose any of you to violence."

Sal then talks about his relationship with Tariq and how they were more than boss and employee, about how they had grown to be good friends. "I was at home on my day off the night I got the call saying Tariq had been shot. I thought it must be a mistake and told my employee to find out what happened and call me back. The next call was from my store manager. He said it was true. Tariq was lying in the street . . . dead."

As Sal continues with his personal story of the events of that tragic night, some of the students are antsy. Some of them are captivated. All of them are listening. He describes how he went to the restaurant and told the police officers every detail he could remember about Tariq's last day at work. Not yet knowing who had shot him, the officers were trying to accumulate as much information as possible.

"The restaurant phone rang," Sal says. "It was Jennifer, Tariq's fiancée, wondering where he was. I told her I didn't know and that she should call back in a little bit. A little while later, the phone rang again, and one of the police officers grabbed me by the shirt and said, 'Don't answer that. We have people trained to make those phone calls.' The phone kept ringing and ringing and ringing, but I didn't answer it.

"Still to this day," Sal tells the kids, "when I hear a phone with that tone, it brings me right back to that night that my friend was murdered. And I don't care where I am. I don't care if I'm at a show, at a store, at work, in somebody's office, I relive his death every time."

By the time Sal finishes his story and introduces me and Ples, the kids are curious. "What exactly does all of this have to do with me?" some of them might be wondering. "I'm not in a gang. I'm not robbing pizza delivery men."

Ples and I walk out on stage and take two seats next to each other. Sal walks behind us and lifts his hand over Ples's shoulder and then mine saying, "This man's grandson murdered this

91

man's son." He repeats it. "This man's grandson . . . murdered this man's son. And today they sit in front of you in the spirit of compassion and forgiveness."

Sal introduces me and I stand up to speak. The kids are intent on finding out more about this story about Tariq and Tony, me and Ples. I share with them the pain I felt when I heard my son had been shot and killed. I talk about how he was my only son and had been shot for no good reason.

"Violence is extremely painful," I say. "It hurts very deep. It scars the soul, and sometimes it scars it forever." I talk to them about how we see a lot of violence in our culture through movies, television, and video games. "But you don't see the pain that violence causes," I tell them. "I really believe that if we knew this excruciating pain that violence causes, as human beings we would never, ever be violent."

The kids listen as I speak to them about the different forms violence takes, whether it's bullying someone, spreading rumors, starting fights, or harassing others in some other way. Some of the kids shuffle in their seats. Maybe they've been the bully. Maybe they've been the one on the receiving end. They all know what I'm talking about.

Then I ask the hard question, the one that will really open some of their hearts to our assembly. Without their knowing it, they've been prepared for the question by watching the video reenactment and by listening to the stories Sal and I shared about our pain and our loss. Because of the groundwork we so carefully laid, they are willing to answer my question.

"How many of you have lost family members as a result of violence?" I ask. Often, two-thirds of the students raise their hands. Two-thirds! On many occasions TKF staff are approached post-assembly by teachers, counselors, or vice principals with shock and sadness on their faces. "We didn't know," they'll say. "We had no idea so many of our children had been exposed firsthand to this kind of violence."

I tell the students who've raised their hands (and I know that I'm also speaking to some of those who didn't), "I understand the pain of losing someone you love. When Tariq died I felt like a nuclear bomb went off in my heart. How many of you have brothers and sisters?" Many hands go up.

"Tariq had an older sister, Tasreen. Maybe you lost a brother or a sister. A mother or a father. An aunt, an uncle, or a cousin. Perhaps this violence has happened in your family. If not, imagine that your brother or sister was killed in an act of violence. How many of you would seek revenge? Raise your hand if you would seek revenge." Almost all of the hands in the auditorium fly up in unison.

"I completely understand that you would feel like you wanted to have revenge," I tell them. "But what would revenge do? Would it bring Tariq back? Would it stop the pain in my heart?" The kids shake their heads no. "What would it do?" I ask them.

"Make it worse," they say. "Cause more violence." They understand in their hearts that violence doesn't make things better. Deep inside of them, they know that revenge and violence are never the answer.

"I understand that it can be difficult," I say. "In some of your homes you are encouraged to not be violent and at the same time you're told to get revenge if anyone is bullying you or harassing you. These mixed messages can be difficult to understand. But I'm here to tell you," I say emphatically, "never to choose revenge. I'm here to tell you that violence is never a solution. The consequences of violence are always going to be negative. When Tariq was killed, instead of revenge I chose forgiveness, and I reached out to Tony's grandfather, who is now like a brother to me and is one of my best friends. I point to Ples sitting in his chair on stage. He is looking at me. "I would do anything for Ples, and he would do anything for me," I say. "How many of you would like a friend like that?" All the hands go up. "Would we have this kind of friendship if I was seeking revenge?" They shake their heads back and forth in unison. "No," says the chorus of voices in the auditorium. I take a moment and then say, "This kind of friendship comes from forgiveness. And you find forgiveness in your heart."

The kids look at me standing in front of them wearing my pain on my sleeve and at Ples still sitting in his chair. They know that his grandson shot and killed my son. And they know that I have forgiven both Tony and his family for the tragedy. But they still don't know why.

I tell the kids that I know forgiveness is hard to do and that it is absolutely okay to be angry and to want revenge. I let them know it's okay to have the feelings, but that they don't need to act on them. I acknowledge the feelings they might have, and I offer an alternative to transform the negative emotions into something positive. "Forgiveness is letting go of your anger toward a person who has done something wrong to you. Every morning I wake up and I forgive Tony. Because I practice every day, my forgiveness muscle is very strong. It takes courage to let go of your anger, but I am healing from my pain because I forgive Tony every day."

MY BROTHER PLES

By the time I introduce Ples, and the kids see us hugging like loving brothers, they are very curious about nonviolence and forgiveness. Not all the pieces completely fit for them yet, but once Ples starts talking, it all begins to come together and make sense.

Ples is savvy and street smart and knows how to reach the kids at their "I wanna be tough" level. He tells it like it is and makes no secret of the fact that his grandson adversely affected many lives—including his own—by his one act of violence. Ples gets down to the nitty gritty and talks to the students about Tony and the bad choices he made—those bad choices which put him into the prison system. He talks about how he, too, lost a son, since Tony was as close to a son as he'd ever had.

He doesn't hold back any punches when he tells the kids that Tony's been serving a twenty-five-years-to-life sentence in an adult prison since the age of sixteen. "Tony's entire life has changed because of one bad choice he made after a day of hanging with his friends, drinking alcohol, and smoking pot. Tony woke up angry that day. And though he didn't know it when he woke up, this was going to be the last day of his life as he'd known it. Everything was about to change . . . for Tony and for all of us."

He tells the students that when we're angry, we're not thinking people. We're only reacting people. "And when we're reacting people," he says, "we're not aware people. We're not aware of what's going on around us. We're not aware of what's going on inside us. We're not aware of how on the edge we are to doing something that will put our lives off track. Because we're angry and reacting," he says, "we are not aware."

He tells them how Tony woke up angry that morning and decided to run away from home. He ran away because he was angry and didn't like the discipline at home where his grandfather required him to study, do well in school, and choose friends wisely so that he could have a successful life. Ples talks to the kids about what makes a good friend. "You might think someone's your friend, but if they bully you or tell you to do something that you don't really want to do, they're not a friend, so don't think they are. Tony thought these people were his friends. They weren't. One of them put a loaded gun in his hands. And after Tony pulled the trigger that night, these so-called friends told him to run, run, run and not drop the gun. They weren't concerned. They didn't care about Tony."

Ples tells the kids how Tony made his first bad choice when he decided to be angry that morning and that all day long he continued to make bad choices that finally resulted in his shooting and killing Tariq. "Azim and his family lost Tariq. I lost my grandson to the prison system. And as a result of one bad decision, Tony has lost his freedom. Even after he gets out, he will always have to report to the state of California. He will be living with the consequences of this one bad choice for the rest of his life."

Ples then asks the students how many of them have dreams. All the hands go up. "It's important that you keep your dreams close to you," he says. "Don't let anybody tell you you can't live your dreams. People will tell you that. They'll tell you you can't have your dreams. But you have to be strong enough to understand, this is *your* dream. It doesn't have anything to do with those folks. This is *your* dream. Accomplish your dreams. But you don't want to set obstacles up to prevent you from realizing your dreams by committing yourself to choices that are violent, that are not peaceful, that create consequences for you, your family, and the community."

Before Ples closes, he makes sure the kids understand who's responsible for the death of my son. He tells them that he knows some people think that if Tariq had given up the pizzas, he wouldn't have been shot. But with extreme emotion, Ples tells the kids, "That thinking puts the responsibility for his own death on Tariq. You can never blame the victim. There's no guarantee that if he had given up the pizzas, and done everything the teenagers told him to do, that the eighteen-year-old still wouldn't have told Tony to shoot him. No guarantee at all!"

Ples asks the students, "Let me hear it loud and clear. Who's responsible for the death of Tariq Khamisa?"

"Tony," the kids shout back.

Ples says, "Tony is responsible. You have to be able to take responsibility for your choices. Nobody makes you do something. When you do a violent act, you do it because you choose to do it. And you're responsible for it. So when you're out there making choices, understand that the choices you make are going to have consequences or benefits to you. So make the right choice. Be peacemakers."

PANELISTS

After Ples speaks, our panelists come on stage to talk to the kids. These speakers have been there, exactly where the students are now. They've been exposed to violence on the streets and in their homes. And they've been tempted to join the gang family for a sense of belonging and safety. They tell the kids that when they were their ages, they made the wrong choice.

Javier, a man in his fifties who looks much younger, begins talking to the kids with the language and slang of the streets. They listen. And they are curious about the dark shades that cover his eyes in their well-lit auditorium.

"My life of delinquency started when I was nine years old," he says. "My name is Javier Ortega, and I'm an ex-drug addict of thirty years. And I'm an ex-gang member of the same. I've been on both sides of the gun. I've shot people and people shot me in return. The last time I was shot, I was left for dead on the streets, and I thought I was going to die. But I didn't."

The kids listen intently. He is one of their own. They can tell. "All of the violence, all of the bad choices that I made in my lifetime caused me to take two shotgun blasts to my face," he says, raising his shades off his eyes, "nearly losing my life. But I'm here now to tell you that I feel sad, because I cannot see the beautiful human rainbow that's in front of me. But I say it could have been worse. I could have lost my life just like Tariq. I could have ended up in prison for the rest of my life just like Tony. Or I could have ended up paralyzed in a wheelchair, making it double hard for me to accomplish anything in life."

Javier talks to the students about his shattered dreams of being a great artist one day. He tells them he felt robbed and sad. He talks about how he can't see his children and grandchildren grow up. And he talks about the anger he had that instilled revenge in his heart. "But then I remembered that God had given me a second opportunity at life," he says, "and instead of continuing that cycle of violence in my life, I chose not to. Instead I reached out for help. I reached out to Mr. Azim

Khamisa and Mr. Ples Felix, and through the Tariq Khamisa Foundation I learned how to forgive myself first. Then I learned how to forgive others who have harmed me. Now I stand in front of you proud to say that I have finally accomplished that dream of becoming an artist. I'm an artist who uses the medium of wood and clay, and I'm also a writer. I'm not wasting my life as I was before. I'm doing things that make me feel good about myself and make me feel worthwhile.

"Hold onto that dream that's going to take you somewhere," he tells them. "Hold onto your education and most of all, be a good friend. Learn to be a peacemaker around your home, around your school, and all over the community. Be known as a peacemaker. Last but not least, love your parents with all your might, heart, and soul. If you have problems, you can call on us. We care for you. TKF, your counselors: you've got people who love you and want to see you do well. It's not weak to ask for help. It's strong."

Javier closes with these words. "In my life when I was able to see, I was blind. But now that I'm really blind, I'm able to see where I'm at, where I want to go, and how I'm going to get there. For that, I am grateful. My life is different now than it was when I was a drug addict and a gang member. My fulfillment is bringing my story and tying it in with this other tragic story of Tariq and Tony. All of us combine our common minds and give you the knowledge you need mind-wise to make a good choice, not a bad choice. Be a peacemaker in life. And be a friend to someone. You may save a person's life by being a friend. My life has changed for the good. Thank you."

The kids have been noticeably moved by Javier's talk— especially the boys. Our next presenter has a profound impact on the girls who attend our assemblies. Mayra Nunez is in her late twenties, the youngest of our panelists. She grew up in the neighborhood and started hanging out in a gang after her older brother was killed in a drive-by shooting.

"At that time, he was only eighteen and in a gang," she tells the kids. "I was twelve. I started hanging out with the homeboys not thinking, not knowing what a gang was. I knew about kickin' back at parties, and money, and cars, and about how the gang was supposed to 'back you up,' but I didn't really know anything about being in a gang. My brother was dead, and I thought by joining the gang now I was going to have thirty, forty, fifty brothers. They were going to love me and respect me the same way my brother did before he was killed. But that wasn't the way it was.

"A lot of kids go into the gang not knowing what it is," Mayra says. "They think the same as I did, that the gang will have your back. But in reality the homeboys never have your back. They're never there to support you. They're there to use you, and they especially take advantage of the younger ones. The older gang members bully the younger ones and tell them what to do, whether it's committing crimes or behaving in certain ways or doing certain things. As a younger member, you're never in control. You never get to make your own choices.

"As the youngest one and also because I was female, I had to deal with a lot of the consequences of being in a gang," she tells the kids. "Ending up in juvenile hall or ending up locked up or ending up dead. Those things are bad enough, but there are even harder consequences. Whether it's being blinded like Javier, becoming bound to a wheelchair, or being immobile for the rest of your life, these are consequences that a lot of kids who join gangs never think about."

Mayra tells the kids about how after the death of her brother, her parents couldn't bear the fact that she joined a gang and they soon divorced. She describes how she had to deal with that breakage of her family. "In the mentality that I was in, I continued to tell myself I didn't care. But the reality is that I did care. I just didn't know who to talk to or where to go."

It's wonderful to have Mayra as one of our panelists because she offers a unique, female viewpoint on what it's like being in a gang. A lot of the questions she gets are about how the females are treated. "It's harder for the females," she tells them. "The machismo mentality is always involved, regardless of ethnicity or gang or race. Females don't get the same respect that the guys do. They're always looked upon in a lower level. And most of the females in the gang are used and abused, whether it's sexually, emotionally, or physically.

"The females are always the ones who are holding the weapons or drugs, planning the crimes and being drivers, or serving as alibis," she says. "So most of the time, the females are the ones who take the worst end of being involved in the gang. And what the females don't realize is that the consequences they take extend out a longer period of time than the consequences for most of the males. Involving pregnancy, emotional abuse or any other type of abuse, the consequences are long lasting."

Mayra speaks from personal experience. She dropped out of school at the age of twelve when she made the decision to hang out with the homeboys. And she continued to make negative choices after that. Those choices escalated from little things to big things, and she ended up in juvenile hall several times. It got to the point where she grew tired of never being able to go places safely, always having to watch her back, and never being able to make her own decisions.

"If you do the crime, you do the time," she tells the kids. "I knew I was harming my family and myself, and I told myself I didn't care, but I did. I felt sad, and my feelings were all bottled up inside of me. Basically, I just couldn't be free. It got to the point that I became pregnant when I was fifteen, I was on probation, on drugs, and I had a criminal record. I was reaching my breaking point and it was then that I made the decision to leave the gang.

"I didn't want my daughter to see the same things that I had seen," Mayra says. "I didn't want her around the same dangerous environment. I didn't want my child to have the same life as me. It was a tough choice. But neither of my parents could afford to move out of the neighborhood, so I had to stay and deal with my decision. I had to deal with the consequences of having the homeboys try to convince me back into the gang.

"How many of you think you can get out of a gang if you want to?" she asks the kids. Very few hands go up. Most of the kids believe the myth that if you leave the gang you're going to end up dead. But, in fact, that rarely happens. There are ways of getting out.

"The best advice I can give you is to never join a gang," she says. "But if you or someone you know is involved with a gang, you *can* leave. But it's a process. You can't say, 'I'm not gonna hang out with you no more,' or 'I'm not gonna do crimes with you guys anymore' and then still go to parties with them or kick back with them or still use drugs with them. You can't do all that. Once you say you're leaving, a whole transformation has to happen including change of attitude, change of dress, change of mentality. The time that was spent with the homeboys kicking back, which included criminal activity, that time now has to be invested, whether it's in school, in a job, volunteering, sports. That time has to be invested in something positive.

"If it's not," she says, "then you're going to fall back into hanging out with the homeboys and be involved in all the things you don't want to be involved in. And you're going to have to deal with all the consequences that come with that. If you want to get out of the gang, you have to invest your time in something positive.

"The gang will threaten you," she says. "But seeing it from the outside looking in, I can see that it's all scare tactics to try and get you back. It's really easier for them to get a fresh, brand new kid into the gang than it is to convince somebody back, because you already know what being in a gang is. The fresh, brand new kid—like I was when I was twelve—that kid doesn't know what it really is."

When she became pregnant at fifteen and decided to leave the gang, Mayra made the positive choice to go back to school. But because she'd dropped out when she was only twelve, she was so behind in credits that she had to attend a juvenile community school to complete her education. That one decision to graduate high school led to more positive choices in her life, including getting married and having children, and eventually brought her to TKF. After serving as a panelist for several years, I'm happy to say that Mayra was recently hired as TKF Programs Coordinator.

"I've been with TKF for almost five years now," she tells the kids. "Being a panelist with them has helped me find forgiveness as well. I used to have a lot of anger and a lot of hatred toward the person who killed my brother. I don't know who that is, but I do forgive that person not only because it's the right thing to do, but also because it frees me from carrying that hatred in my heart and in my spirit. I appreciate TKF for giving me the opportunity to work with them and to find healing of my own heart through forgiveness."

The assembly is winding down. We invite the students to ask questions. Sometimes they tell a story instead. For most of them, it's the first time they've met me or Ples or heard about Tariq and Tony, but they feel that we will understand their hearts. And they are right.

One kid tells us how his brother was killed in a drive-by shooting one year before the assembly. Another talks about how his father was shot by gang members when he was only two years old. A girl shares her sadness at losing her cousin. Another trembles as he talks about his uncle's death. The list goes on and on. These kids sit at their desks in their classrooms day after day burdened by their losses, and very few around them have any idea they are so heavy in heart.

At the end of the *VIF*, we tell the students that a lot of people care about them. "All of us at TKF want you to know that we love you and care for you very much," Sal says. "I care. Azim and Ples care. The entire TKF staff cares. We want you to know that you can call us at TKF and we will be there for you."

We remind them that at their school there are also people who care: counselors, teachers, principals, vice principals. These are people they can talk to. These are people who will listen and help them to make good choices, even as some of them are faced with people at home who are not making good choices in their own lives.

At the closing, we ask all the kids to stand and join us in a pledge of nonviolence.

THE TKF PEACEMAKER PLEDGE

I pledge on my honor to be a peacemaker;
In my home
In my school
And in my community.
I am a peacemaker.
I AM A PEACEMAKER.

GARDEN OF LIFE

Being able to express one's grief is a first step in healing, and so following the *VIF* elementary school assemblies we hold a special "Garden of Life" ceremony on campus. A tree is planted in memory of Tariq and any family members the students have lost, and the kids also plant flowers in memory of their loved ones. This garden becomes a place they can visit every day, a place they can go for healing or remembrance.

Ples has a beautiful perspective about the programs and especially about the Garden of Life. "I see and experience the programs as an opportunity to help children see the potential of divinity within themselves," he says. "I always project that when we finish one of the *VIFs*, I see these students walking around with this great, glowing light coming from their hearts. The light itself is symbolic of the inspiration having been turned on to make decisions that will change them for the rest of their lives. That's the kind of vision I walk away with from every *VIF*.

"But the Garden of Life accentuates that even more for me, because it ritualizes for the students and everyone else in attendance an opportunity through the planting of a flowering plant for the expression of grief. And for the expression of caring for someone lost. And it's done in such a loving, reverential, nonreligious kind of way that whenever that's done, I visualize those lights coming from these students being one thousand times brighter.

"Each of these students touched a living plant, dug a hole in God's Earth, and planted this flower with loving intention for its growth, blossoming, and beauty as a means of expression to memorialize or to say goodbye or to honor someone they've lost," Ples continues. "Some of these children are so reverent with respect to the application of the Garden of Life, even after they plant the flowers, they step back and just close their eyes briefly in silence. Then when the kids have completed that process, you can see that they have been unburdened. They have not only been unburdened, but they have also been freed to make choices that will prevent them from engaging in violence in a way that will really help their lives.

"I come away with this tremendous sense of well being and gratification. It's like the feeling a person would get knowing they'd provided nutrients and food for someone who was without. Providing warmth and comfort for someone who was in the cold. Providing a sense of hope for someone who up to that point felt hopeless. That's what I see and that's what I experience every time we come from a *VIF*."

As Ples so beautifully describes, the Garden of Life ceremony serves the kids in several ways. The planting of the tree and flowers allows them a beautiful expression for their grief. It also gives them a place of beauty to come back to again and again in memory of their loved ones. By participating in the Garden of Life, the kids become part of the TKF family, and there is a shared sense of unity and love. The Garden also serves as a visual reference for the *VIF* event in their school, and so everything we taught them is reinforced each time they pass by.

After all of our *Violence Impact Forum* assemblies—those held in both elementary and middle schools—the leaders use the provided teacher's guide and debriefing lesson plans to help encourage a discussion. This allows the students to process any thoughts and emotions brought up by the program. The students are also given a resource sheet with names and phone numbers of people who can help in time of need or crisis: police, various youth help and crisis lines, and TKF's contact information. The sheet also has key-point information on Taking a Stand Against Violence, Making Up Your Own Mind, and Getting Help. With these resources we are impressing upon the kids that they are not alone and that there is always someone they can reach out to.

During the debriefing session with their teacher, students can write a letter talking about their experience of the assembly. These letters can be written to any one of us who spoke at the *VIF*, to Tariq, or to Tony. Those who choose to write to Tariq are assured that their letters will most certainly be read, and when I read them, I am deeply and profoundly moved. I am proud to say that TKF has received over 60,000 letters from students who have attended our assemblies.

Most of the kids are not familiar with the TKF story beforehand. They come to the school auditorium knowing they're going to participate in a program about youth nonviolence, but they don't know much more than that. A lot of the kids leave the assembly feeling hopeful, inspired, and lighter of heart. But there are exceptions. "There are kids who come up to us who are very sad," Ples says. "They're very angry, and they don't feel as though anybody really cares about them. And you can see in their faces with the sadness and their shoulders slumped that they're just looking for someone who they can share some of this burden with.

"I think both Azim and I are very sensitive to these kids, but Azim is very good about this. He goes directly to the student, puts his hand on the student's shoulder whether it's a boy or a girl, and asks their name. He patiently listens while they tell him with tears in their eyes about the trauma or the loss they've experienced. And then he hugs them, and it's amazing. You know, in the presence of a hug you can observe a lot of things. And the first thing I observe is that the student is automatically put at ease. He's relaxed and seemingly no longer distressed.

"Just in that instant of a kind word and a warm, loving gesture like a hug, the student steps back and Azim says, 'You know, we need to make sure that you talk to someone like a counselor. Would you like to talk to a counselor?' You can see the student nod their head in affirmation. They'd love to talk with a counselor, they're just maybe a little too embarrassed to say anything about it. And they're not wanting the other students to know that they're at that level of distress or that level of need.

"Azim makes sure that the student is connected directly with a counselor. He tells the counselor in a sentence or two who the student is and what kinds of concerns they have and asks the counselor to take time to sit down and talk to the student. And at that point, when the student connects with the counselor through that introduction by Azim, you can see the student's hopeful glow, they just really light up, as if to say, 'I've really got a chance here to get some assistance and some help with what I'm feeling.'"

These are the goals of our *Violence Impact Forum Assembly.* We want these kids to know that someone cares, and we want them to know that they have a choice in this world. They don't have to keep their hearts closed off, and they don't have to harden their hearts with poor choices, bad decisions, or violent actions. Through the telling of our story—Tariq and Tony, me and Ples, Sal and the panelists—we instill in the kids the knowledge that they are responsible for the consequences of their actions.

In the words of my friend, Joan Adamo, "Since the norm in our society is to seek revenge for an act of violence, I'm delighted that you are trying to turn the world on its head. Not only children tempted by gangs need to hear your story and other heroic stories of forgiveness that are transforming lives— everyone does."

By the end of the VIF, the students know that bad choices, violent choices, can only lead to more violence. The only way to a peaceful life is by living peacefully. We come to the schools with hope, and we leave with the knowledge that a lot of the kids we've spoken to that day have been transformed. They've become true peacemakers. It is with their efforts and their wisdom as they grow older that our world will eventually be transformed into one of peace and nonviolence, one peacemaker at a time.

*Let us put our minds together and see what kind of
life we can make for our children.*

— Sitting Bull, Lakota Chief

More TKF Programs

Chapter Eight

Peace Ambassadors

An important part of the *VIF*, which is evolving into a stand-alone program, is our *Peace Ambassadors* program. Before TKF arrives for the *Violence Impact Forum Assembly*, the school chooses several students to represent the student body. These students are chosen on the basis of their leadership skills. Some are involved with student council or participate in the school's peer mediation group. A letter is sent home to the parents letting them know their children have been chosen for this honor and special opportunity. The students receive training on how to be a peace ambassador, and they represent their school all throughout the program day.

Peace ambassador activities include attending the pre-assembly VIP reception, where they meet the panelists and other specially invited guests. They help to pass out wristbands at the assembly, and in the elementary schools they assist with the Garden of Life tree planting ceremony. Being chosen as a peace ambassador is a huge recognition for kids of an age where they are naturally seeking to be acknowledged. By being given the role, trained, and then recognized during the assembly, the students are empowered to become positive decision-makers, peacemakers, and role models for their peers.

This role of peace ambassador extends beyond the day of the assembly, which is why it seems to be evolving into a

111

Through TKF programs, children have an opportunity to see a choice that is different than the one offered by gangs and a violent society. Here children plant flowers in thier "Garden of Life."

program unto itself. Throughout the year, some of our peace ambassadors are given various opportunities to express themselves and to promote nonviolence. In 2006, we invited a few of the ambassadors from one of our middle schools to participate in our *Seeds of Hope Society* fundraising event. The kids were so excited to come to San Diego, California, to a town called La Jolla, where many of them had never been before. We treated them to a nice hotel breakfast, and the kids felt really special. At the fundraising event, they spoke about being peace ambassadors, mediating peer conflicts, and being peacemakers. As a thank you to them for coming and presenting at our event, we took them to see the film *Freedom Writers.*

Sometimes our peace ambassadors take the initiative to start a peer mediation group or to get our after school leadership club, *Circle of Peace*, going at their schools. We invite all of our peace ambassadors to submit an essay for our *Gandhi Nonviolence Awards Ceremony* youth scholarships. Each year one male and one female youth receive a $500 scholarship. We also encourage them to go to myspace.com and participate in our forums, where they can continue to support each other and encourage other young people toward peace.

We're very proud of our *Peace Ambassador* program, because the kids who are involved truly are being empowered to make a difference. The recognition they receive on program day and after serves to reinforce their commitment to being peacemakers and to role model that behavior for their peers. These kids have already shown leadership skills in their schools, and through their roles as peace ambassadors they're taking yet another step in the direction of peace for their communities and ultimately for our nation.

ENDING THE CYCLE OF VIOLENCE

In partnership with Discovery Education and Victress Hitchcock, founder and president of Chariot Productions, we developed *Ending the Cycle of Violence,* an educational video series based on the TKF story. "Azim was looking for a way to replicate the *VIF,*" Victress says, "which could then be distributed to schools in other areas besides those in southern California which the TKF programs were already reaching.

"I was contacted by Beth Ida Stern," she continues, "an educational producer I had worked with before. Beth had recently met Azim, and she told me about his story. I remember that I started to cry on the phone, so I knew there was some connection happening there for me. All I heard was the bare bones of the story, but that was enough.

"A meeting was set up between me and Azim," Victress says. "We agreed to work with each other, and then Discovery Education got involved and decided to fund the project. We went through a rocky period with different people having different ideas about how this should all look. Azim went to bat for the project. He really championed the whole thing.

"Once contracts were signed, the program director and I used the key messages TKF had already developed as the road map for the video series. In the first video we wanted to try to look at all the different angles of the basic story. For the rest of the series, we took each of the TKF messages and explored them more fully with the Tariq and Tony story and also with other people. One of the things we did in this series, which is an expansion of the *VIF* program, was give Tony a voice."

We developed *Ending the Cycle of Violence* to be used primarily in middle schools. Geared toward grades six to nine, it is a youth violence prevention series of six videos with accompanying curriculum that addresses the realities of violence. Through narration, interviews, re-enactment, animation, and documentary segments, the series explores the causes of violence and its ripple effects; the consequences of choices; the healing power of empathy, compassion, and forgiveness; and the power each of us has to stop the cycle of violence. The accompanying teacher's guide and student workbook amplify each of the TKF messages presented in the videos.

The goals of the program are the same as those of the *Violence Impact Forum Assembly*: to identify different forms of violence and its ripple effects; to raise awareness of youth violence and to teach and encourage nonviolent choices; to communicate the message of forgiveness; to stop kids from killing kids; and to offer hope to every child for the opportunity to live a peaceful and successful life.

In the *Ending the Cycle of Violence* program, the students watch one video at a time and then participate in activities designed to emphasize the themes and key messages in the video. For example, after seeing the first video of the series, "From Murder to Forgiveness," the kids are asked to answer questions such as, "How did Tariq's family react to this death? Why did the Khamisa family choose forgiveness? Do you think Mr. Khamisa's response was unusual? Why? Have you ever forgiven anyone? Is forgiving someone easy or hard?" and "Does it depend on the circumstances?" These questions help the kids as they wrestle with their emotional responses to the video which they've just seen.

Students are then given a copy of Tony's sentencing speech. After they read it they're asked to answer more questions: "Why do you think Tony chose to plead guilty? How do you think the guilty plea affected Tony's family? The Khamisa family? Do you think Tony tried to make excuses for his actions?" and "Do you think the Khamisa family should have had a say in Tony's sentencing?"

In another activity, students are instructed to write a first-person short story from the point of view of one of the people in the video: myself, Tariq's mother or sister, or someone from Tony's family. Their stories may take place anywhere during the timeline of the TKF story itself: before, during, or after the shooting, and up to the present day. The students are encouraged to think about what it would be like to be in that person's shoes and then write from that perspective. Through this writing exercise, students can learn important concepts such as empathy. All of the activities outlined in the *Ending the Cycle of Violence* student workbook are meant to help the kids integrate the six key TKF messages into their lives.

By utilizing the many elements of the TKF story, the video series and accompanying curriculum provide a comprehensive, in-depth understanding of the realities of youth violence and the principles of forgiveness. The first video, "From Murder to Forgiveness," focuses on the story of Tariq's death, Tony's incarceration, and my response of forgiveness, first extended to Ples and then to Tony. The video explores the psychological and emotional factors impacting Tony and the choices he made that led up to the shooting. Tony was interviewed for this project at the age of twenty-six while incarcerated at Pelican Bay State Prison.

Branching out from the first video are five more, each one expanding upon one of TKF's key messages. The second video in the series, "Violence is Real and Hurts Everyone," explores the devastating impact of violence on all those involved. It illustrates various forms violence may take, its ripple effects, and the emotional pain created by even a single violent act.

The third video, "Everyone Deserves to Be Loved and Treated Well," introduces the principles of respect and empathy as tools to facilitate understanding between people and as necessary steps toward forgiving. The video takes a look at Tony's younger years, the abuse he suffered, and his exposure to violence and neglect. The video also emphasizes the importance of and strength in asking for help in times of need.

"Actions Have Consequences," the fourth video in the series, explores in detail the series of choices Tony made leading up to the tragedy and raises awareness of the power we have to control our own choices. It looks at actions with both positive and negative consequences and encourages youth to be the "authors of their own scripts."

The fifth video, "Choosing Forgiveness Instead of Revenge," illuminates the process of forgiveness, for others and for oneself. It acknowledges the difficulty of forgiveness, and emphasizes the difference between wanting revenge and acting on that impulse. Forgiveness is offered as a viable solution to release anger and facilitate personal healing.

The last video in the series, "Making the Nonviolent Choice," uses examples of youth who are working together to promote peace as an inspiration for other young people to "make the nonviolent choice" and create love and unity from conflict. It explores the concept of nonviolence as a proactive choice and shows that young people can have a powerful voice as peacemakers. It also provides real-life examples of youth programs dedicated to positive activities and community service.

Through cartoon illustrations, the second through sixth videos also walk students through the process of what happens when a person takes a moment to think before they react. Through this demonstration, students are taught that it is possible to consciously change their thinking and, subsequently, change their lives.

The comprehensive curriculum developed by TKF involves six modules or sections, which can be incorporated into the students' class work over several weeks or months, depending on the individual class's needs. The classroom workbook has over seventy activities, which help the students incorporate what they've seen on the videos with what's going on in their own world.

From answering questions on how they'd react to violence to learning about brain activity to practicing forgiveness, the hands-on activities promote understanding and compassion for the students themselves and for others. Combined with the videos, they make a strong statement about how each student is responsible for and has the power to make his or her own choices, which will then determine the course of their lives.

School counselor Fred Laskowski, MFT, shared his thoughts about the *Ending the Cycle of Violence* (ECV) program with TKF:

"I am the fifth grade counselor at Dana Middle School in San Diego," he says. "I have been implementing the ECV program in all of my fifth-grade classrooms . . . [The program] is very friendly to use. It is well organized with lots of choices of activities to implement. In my very busy days, I am always thrilled to find a program that is classroom ready. And even better, this one is of *excellent* quality. It is amazing how the foundation has been able to put together a series of lessons on such a topic as violence and murder and do it in such a tasteful manner that is appropriate for students at this age level.

"They do not focus heavily on the gore of murder," he continues, "but rather on the issues in people and society that lead to such crimes. They focus more on the character liabilities and the interventions that can be put into place to make a positive difference in the students' everyday lives when it comes to different forms of violence that we all face.

"What I am most thrilled about is the deep and thoughtful response of the students to the material. The videos are tastefully done and hold the students' attention. The discussions that are generated afterwards are phenomenal. I have been a school counselor for over twenty-two years and have led hundreds of classroom guidance lessons, and I have never had such focused and deeply pensive discussions as this program has generated. . . .

"The depth of heartfelt sharing that is the prevalent feeling throughout the films is so impressive," he continues. "It is good to see this in our society. Hats off to the Tariq Khamisa Foundation for this program. From the bottom of my heart I thank you on behalf of myself and my students."

We are thrilled to receive this kind of response to our program. The *Ending the Cycle of Violence* series and curriculum, which is primarily for grades six to nine, is available for all schools in San Diego County and is also available for purchase by any interested party (see Resource page). It is our hope that other school districts across the country will soon utilize our program in their own schools to further the goal of ending youth violence in our great nation.

In addition to our *VIF* and *Ending the Cycle of Violence,* we have several other programs currently running or in development. Three of these programs are geared to the students, and one is for their parents.

CIRCLE OF PEACE

The elementary and middle-school students who participate in *Circle of Peace* are those who want to learn more after attending a *VIF* or are students who are required to attend because of their participation in the school's extended-day learning program. Sometimes the students chosen as peace ambassadors for our *Violence Impact Forum Assembly* will lead the way in setting up *Circle of Peace* with the help of teachers and counselors at the school. The program lessons and activities involve three main components:

Inner Peace Through question and answer discussions, games, and fun art activities, we teach the students how to go within and find their own core of peace and contentment.

Life Skills Through a wide variety of art activities and discussion, we teach the students life skills such as public speaking, expressing feelings, and team building. By extending their newfound sense of inner peace, the students also learn how to be at peace with each other.

Community Service Project Through the Inner Peace and Life Skills activities, the students have begun to develop a deeper appreciation for themselves and for others. Now they're ready and eager to take their new skills as peacemakers into the community.

Our Facilitator's Guide for *Circle of Peace* is made available to the teacher or counselor who heads up the program. The guide is organized into three modules which correspond with the three main components, and each module has several lessons and corresponding activities. The facilitator is encouraged to engage the students in a discussion involving the activity theme.

For the Inner Peace component, for example, our first lesson is "Welcome," designed to help the kids get to know each other better. The group gets in a circle, and the first person will say her or his name and add a body movement. The next person copies the first person and then says his or her name. The third student copies the first two, and on and on. It can be quite hilarious and is a real icebreaker.

Then the students watch the TKF video, and the program facilitator engages them in a discussion by asking questions such as, "What are your thoughts about this video?" or "Do you agree that there were two victims in this story?" Because the kids have already loosened up with the "Welcome" activity and are feeling comfortable with each other, they are forthcoming with their answers.

Each lesson and activity is designed to build continuing trust and to open the kids' hearts toward the notion of inner peace and living a peaceful and forgiving life. Time is allowed for them to make journal entries, but that activity is strictly voluntary. At different points in the program, the facilitator teaches a meditation technique or leads the kids in a guided meditation. These techniques are of real value and empower the kids with a tool they can use to relieve physical tension and emotional stress. Other lessons and activities in the Inner Peace module deal with judgment, nutrition, setting goals, anger, and trust.

"Some of these kids are dealing with difficult situations at home, and *Circle of Peace* is a place for them to celebrate who they are and talk about how they feel," says TKF Program Director Suzanne Bacon. "One day we did a relaxation technique where students listened to music, and I encouraged the kids to let go of their worries. Afterwards, I asked how they were feeling. A few students shared that they were feeling relaxed or tired or that they thought it was a weird experience. Then one student shared that she felt angry and another that he felt sad. Sometimes kids are so busy in their lives that they don't get the chance to sit and discover what they are really feeling. This program can bring up emotions, and it is my hope that the kids see the *Circle of Peace* as a safe place where it's okay to be yourself, it's okay to be real, and it's a place to challenge ideas you have about yourself and the world."

Module Two is about teaching the kids life skills. Lesson Two is called, "Working Together," designed to teach cooperation and how to work together as a team. In one activity, students split up into groups and are given ten pieces of paper. Each group is told to create a tower, as tall as they can. As they attempt to meet this challenge, the students take on different roles of leadership or of being followers or cheerleaders.

One student in a group that was feeling particularly frustrated said, "What does this have to do with peace? We're all fighting." It was an example for the students of how some conflict is natural when people work together to accomplish something. Through the team challenge, the students are given the opportunity to look at what their natural reactions to conflict are.

At the end of the activity, the teacher encourages a discussion by asking things like, "What role did you find yourself taking? What was easy or difficult about this task?" or "What worked or didn't work, and what could you do differently next time?" The kids have a lot of fun with the activities, and each one builds upon the next as far as developing a continuing trust with each other. Some of the other lessons in this module emphasize forgiveness, cross-cultural awareness, managing stress, building empathy, and expressing yourself.

Suzanne says, "'Sally' wrote about how she deals with anger by hitting the person she's angry at, screaming, and then running away when her mother calls. I asked her what happens when she reacts that way when she gets angry in class. 'I get in trouble,' she said in a low voice.

"I asked if she thought there was any way she could deal with her anger in a way that wouldn't get her in trouble, such as thinking of a nice place she likes to be. 'Sometimes I pretend that the whole world is made of candy,' she said softly.

"I encouraged her to write about that, and she wrote about the world being made of chocolate. A short time later, another student got Sally's paper wet. She jumped up and screamed, 'I'm going to kill you!'

"Instead of reprimanding her for her outburst, I said to the kids, 'Wow, it looks like Sally is very angry. What can Tom do?'

"A lot of the students said, 'Apologize.' Tom did, and Sally calmly returned to her seat. I wonder how often adults in her life recognize Sally's feelings instead of just her inappropriate behavior. In *Circle of Peace,* we provide a safe place for the kids to express their feelings, no matter what they are."

By the time the kids move on to the third module, they're eager to begin looking into a community service project. One that they like to do is called Peace Day. The kids brainstorm ideas for this day, and the facilitator makes sure the final plan is reasonable and doable. Some of the suggestions offered in the facilitator's guide for organizing a Peace Day are creating a mural; publicizing the event; recruiting someone for a musical performance; having a face painting booth, bake sale, or raffle; or putting on a talent show, and then sending out thank you cards to everyone involved with the service project. Other community service activities the kids engage in during the *Circle of Peace* program are food donation drives, beach clean-up days, mentoring, and tutoring.

Circle of Peace is a wonderful follow-up to our *Violence Impact Forum Assembly* and *Ending the Cycle of Violence* in-school programs. Through our lessons and activities, students first learn how to find peace on the inside. As the weeks go by, they build a continuing trust with each other, gain confidence in themselves and their abilities, and feel the desire to reach out to their communities as peacemakers.

"It sounds like a cliché," Suzanne says, "but peace does begin within. For peace to happen, people need to feel safe, loved, and comfortable with who they are. They need to believe that things will get better. Today a little girl asked why we call it *Circle of Peace.* I said, 'Well, a circle means that we come together, and in the circle we learn about and care about peace.'

"The wise little girl said, 'Peace will never happen if no one does anything about it!'"

These kids are our leaders of tomorrow, and they will be the ones who will lead the way toward global peace by embracing the concept of our sixth key message, "From conflict, love and unity are possible."

PARENT PEACE COALITION

Our *Violence Impact Forum* assemblies, *Ending the Cycle of Violence* video series, and *Circle of Peace* all provide education, support, encouragement, and inspiration for the kids. But what about their parents? We recognize that in order to fully support the kids in their efforts toward living nonviolent lives, their parents need education and support too. We created the *Parent Peace Coalition* to provide a safe place for parents to come together to discuss the different ways violence impacts their children, themselves, and their communities. Through printed materials developed by TKF, and with the assistance of a school staff person or parent coordinator, the parents discover that there are paths to prevention. They meet once a week for twelve weeks, and through their discussions they are inspired to go back into their families and communities to promote peace and nonviolence.

"They work toward understanding the cycle of violence," TKF Development Director Katie Bowles says. "A lot of times, the violence is not coming from school. It's starting somewhere else. Through the TKF materials the parents are taught how to work toward having a safe school, family, and neighborhood environment for their children. They're taught some of the same skills the kids are taught in their in-school programs. And they learn how to work with anger at home to break the cycle of violence."

SUBSTITUTE TEACHER CURRICULUM

As of this writing, our *Substitute Teacher Curriculum* is being further developed. The idea behind this beneficial program is to provide substitute teachers with life skills lesson plans to use during the regular teacher's absence. Oftentimes, the substitute teacher will come into a classroom and find incomplete lessons or no lessons at all pertaining to the subject at hand. When they find themselves in this situation, they have little choice but to act as babysitters for the students, which is not the best use of their abilities.

With our *Substitute Teacher Curriculum*, instead of having to resort to a quiet study period or something along those lines, the substitute teacher can pull out one of six lesson plans, each lesson being based on one of TKF's key messages about making nonviolent choices.

For each lesson, the curriculum describes fun activities the students can do including skits, art projects, games, and writing exercises. Through these activities the kids learn about the impact violence has on themselves, their families, their friends, and their communities. And through the understanding and incorporation of the key messages into their lives, the kids are inspired to break the cycle of violence and become peacemakers.

IN-SCHOOL SUSPENSION PROGRAM

Another program being developed as of this writing is the *In-School Suspension Program*. The concept and curriculum will be similar to that used in the *Substitute Teacher Curriculum*. Instead of leaving the suspended kids to sit at their desks (presumably studying), the attending teacher can use TKF materials to engage the students in activities and discussions that will inspire them toward making peaceful and nonviolent choices.

SEEDS OF HOPE SOCIETY

I started TKF nine months after Tariq was killed. Soon after, I asked Ples if he would help me with my work. We have now been working together side by side for twelve years, modeling forgiveness and brotherhood. As a nonprofit foundation, we rely on fundraising efforts to maintain, develop, and staff our programs.

"Youth violence is a national problem, and it needs the attention of *all* of us," Katie says. "TKF's programs are changing this situation, and there are so many more schools in need. How do we do this work? Who funds our programs? People like you and me! All the children in the world deserve to be loved and cared for. Our *Seeds of Hope Society* members are individuals who are committed to supporting our work. They are true leaders in the world, and they come from all walks of life. We have bus drivers, gardeners, housewives, school teachers, doctors, and lawyers: all types of individuals.

"We are more than ninety percent funded by *Seeds of Hope Society* members who have committed to being the change they want to see in the world," Katie continues. "With ten thousand members (or more), we could take our message of love and forgiveness into classrooms all over the nation."

Seeds of Hope Society offers a three-tier donation structure to our members. To support a classroom, the donation is $1,000 a year for five years, the price of a latte a day. To support a school, it's $5,000 a year for five years. And to support a community, the member gives $10,000 a year for five years. We are grateful to all of our individual donors who help us bring our prevention messages of peace and nonviolence to the students. And we also appreciate the organizations and corporations who have made the commitment to help us with our work.

Klemmer & Associates, Inc. is a leadership and character development company based in Petaluma, California. I met founder Brian Klemmer several years ago when I was asked to be a speaker at one of their trainings. We were each touched by the other's message, and I was honored to be asked to participate in Brian's leadership seminars.

"Our Heart of the Samurai training is the only level where we bring in outside speakers," Brian says. "Everything else is done by people I've trained. In this seminar, we do a whole experiential model around surrender, and then we have Azim come in and tell his story. He is a great example of surrender. By reducing his resistance to the tragic death of his son, he's made something incredibly good come out of it. Azim had a great impact on our students, and we've invited him back to speak at every Heart since.

"In Heart of the Samurai we do a lot of compassion work," Brian says, "and we work with people on their abundance and being able to fulfill their dreams. We do all kinds of money projects in this training, and I tell my students, 'I'm only going to ask you to use your own money for one thing, and that's Azim.' I ask them, 'Did you get value out of this seminar? Do you trust me? We have a war going on in this country, and Azim's doing good work. Fund him. Reach in your pocket. Put your money where your mouth is.' And a bunch of people do."

Our ambition and objective is to inspire students all over the world with our messages of nonviolence and forgiveness, and we are greatly appreciative of Klemmer & Associates in helping us to reach our tipping point toward the fulfillment of that goal. We are grateful to all of our individual and corporate donors, for without them the work of TKF could not go on. (Information on our *Seeds of Hope Society* can be found on the Resources page.)

GANDHI NONVIOLENCE AWARDS CEREMONY

We at TKF have a great passion for helping kids to understand that the choices they make today will create their lives of tomorrow. We have received international recognition for our programs, because we get results. If one student at a *VIF* makes a better choice because of the story we share, then we are a success. But the more students who have the opportunity to experience the *VIF* or view the *Ending the Cycle of Violence* series or participate in an after-school peace program, the better off they and our society as a whole are going to be.

There are many wonderful people working to improve society and making contributions to the youths in their communities. Since we are based in San Diego, California, we decided to recognize those individuals and organizations that promote, inspire, or help to build a culture of peacemakers and who make San Diego a more harmonious and peaceful community for all.

TKF Board Member Dianne McKay leads the team that puts on our annual *Gandhi Nonviolence Awards Ceremony.*

Each year we take nominations in eight categories. "There's a faith category," she says. "We have an education category—for example, a high school principal, teacher, counselor, or someone who does peace patrol. We honor one female and one male youth up to the age of eighteen, and each of the youth awards includes a $500 scholarship. We have a business (for profit) category, an individual community leader category, and a nonprofit community organization category. The eighth category is communications, which includes media and the arts—singing, dancing, painting, and poetry, for example."

All the work that these recipients do is related to nonviolence and enhancing the lives of our local youth. Nominations are submitted through the TKF website or to our office by fax or mail. The final winners, selected by a special TKF committee led by Dianne, are honored at our annual ceremony. We began this program in 1998 with Dr. Arun Gandhi and his beloved wife, the late Sunanda Gandhi (may her soul rest in eternal peace), as guests of the TKF "Island of Nonviolence" benefit event. Our *Gandhi Nonviolence Awards Ceremony* is named in honor of Arun's grandfather, India's greatest spiritual leader, Mahatma Gandhi, who died in 1948.

We hold this elegant evening event at the Joan B. Kroc Institute for Peace & Justice at the University of San Diego. "The Institute for Peace & Justice is the most stately theatre I've ever seen," Dianne says. "It is perfect for our program, which lasts for about ninety minutes. A youth singer opens and closes the ceremony. Our youth keynote speaker, selected by our committee, also introduces each award winner. Azim and Ples each say a few words, and beginning in 2008 Arun Gandhi will be a permanent guest speaker. We have a sunset reception beforehand, and a dessert reception afterwards. It is a beautiful gala that highlights the people in our area who are dedicated to improving the lives of San Diego County youth, is a gift to our community, and involves youth wherever possible."

I wish that Tariq were still with me. And I sometimes wish that TKF programs had existed before Tony decided to join a gang. I think that maybe if he had participated in a *VIF* or had gone through the *Ending the Cycle of Violence* curriculum, he would have been transformed from a life of violence to a life of peace. But these wishes are only impulses of the heart and have no substance in reality.

I know only too well that it is because of the death of my son at the hand of Tony Hicks that the Tariq Khamisa Foundation came into existence. This is what makes this story both a tragedy and a blessing. "He always wanted to leave this world a better place . . . and he has," Tasreen says about her brother. Yes, he has. Without the ultimate sacrifice of his death, TKF would not exist. And without the programs of TKF, many more children would remain lost in lives of violence, living without hope, living in the darkness of despair, revenge, and hatred.

I have great hopes for TKF. I believe that as we continue to accumulate data and results, more and more school districts will hear of our work and choose to make TKF a part of the mainline curriculum in all of their schools, bringing our message of hope and nonviolence to more and more kids. Just like going to a math, reading, history, or science class, kids will go into a TKF class and learn the core values we teach through our six key messages.

It is my dream that once we have achieved this goal in the U.S. school system, we'll go to places like Iraq, Israel, Palestine, and North Korea, where there is such dire conflict. I would like to see TKF go all over the world, because when we have been able to touch all the kids of the world and they have learned how to create brotherhood, sisterhood, love, and unity from conflict, then we will manifest a world at peace.

Lisa Grogan expresses my feelings very well when she says, "I look forward to the day when TKF will provide a violence prevention curriculum—kindergarten through twelfth grade—to our schools so that our messages of peace, love, and forgiveness will be practiced on a daily basis. I want our message to be branded in the minds of youths just as the messages of violence are branded on their minds today.

"I envision this curriculum to be nationally recognized," Lisa says, "with satellite TKF offices and staffing throughout our country and the world. The evolution of TKF will continue to take place in the hopes of inspiring a generation of peacemaking and nonviolence. If TKF can continue to play the 'good conscience' or the 'little angel on the shoulder' of youths in difficult situations for years to come, I believe the cycle of violence will be halted, allowing a new cycle of peaceful societal bliss to begin."

I've always maintained that no child is born violent. It follows that since violence is a learned behavior, nonviolence can also be learned. But who in our society teaches nonviolence? TKF does and does it successfully. In fact, San Diego State University has been so impressed with the results of our programs over the past twelve years, they have proposed creating a TKF endowed professorship on peace and nonviolence.

Since San Diego State is the highest teacher-producing university in the country, with the professorship in place, every graduating teacher will have been trained in our curriculum. The university also has twenty international centers, so through our partnership we will be able to take our programs into these other countries. Being involved with an institute that can support the research and development of our programs is a dream come true! Ples and I have committed the rest of our lives to the principles of peacemaking and teaching nonviolence, and, as Lisa points out, when the Tariq Khamisa Foundation meets its mandate, we will see the beginning of a new cycle of peaceful societal bliss.

Although attempting to bring about world peace through the internal transformation of individuals is difficult, it is the only way.

— Thich Nhat Hanh

CANEI, NYAP and Restorative Justice

Chapter Nine

In my first book, *From Murder to Forgiveness*, I devoted an entire chapter to Restorative Justice (RJ). This relatively new paradigm of justice invites active participation of all parties affected by a crime: the victim, the offender, families of both, and representatives of the victimized community. The focus is upon accountability and healing through repair of harm and dialogue whenever possible. Since the publication of my book in 1998, RJ programs have been incorporated into the criminal codes of many states and local jurisdictions. Professor Mark Umbreit, director of the Center for Restorative Justice and Peacemaking at the University of Minnesota, says it's now a major social movement developing all over the world. "It's not a household term, but contrary to when it began and I was involved with it in the 1970s, today there are thousands of programs," he says.

SHIFTING HEARTS AND MINDS

Restorative justice calls for a shift in one's mind and also in one's heart. It requires that all parties involved have a similar investment in the long-term restoration of the victim, community, and offender. As I've said so many times before, Tony shot and killed my son in a senseless act of violence. He is wholly responsible for his decision and his deed. But I believe there were victims at both ends of the gun. I believe the

135

Pictured left to right:
Mubarak E. Awad (Founder, NYAP, IYAF, and Nonviolence International); Marvena Twigg (President/CEO, NYAP); Azim Khamisa (National Director and Founder, CANEI Program).

same is true for any perpetrator of a crime. The victim is the obvious hurt party. But the perpetrator is often also a victim. It could be that they suffered abuse in their lives—either physical or psychological. Maybe they are simply victims of confused thoughts caused by misperceptions, lack of education, and/or poor role models along the way.

Whatever the reasons for someone's bad choices that end up hurting others, it is up to us as human beings to find compassion in our hearts for all people. It is up to us to promote the idea of having successful restorative justice programs flourish across our nation so that all parties involved in a crime have the opportunity to find healing and hope.

Ted Lewis, restorative justice program manager at Community Mediation Services in Eugene, Oregon, who was a panelist at a conference where I gave the keynote speech, says, "The availability and the spread of RJ are on the rise and are substantial. But the actual practice of RJ with respect to significant dialogue processes are not at that same level."

Professor Umbreit adds, "It's a little of both. Restorative justice has been endorsed by the European Union, it's supported by legislation in more than twenty states, and the United Nations has endorsed it. But to say all of that is not to say that there are *active* programs all over the place. Our surveys have found that there are RJ policies and practices in nearly every state in this country, in different communities within the state. Yet, we have also found more talking about restorative justice in many locations than actually implementing it."

Ted talks about crime being more than a breakage of laws. "If it's just a breakage of law," he says, "you're missing the breakage between people, between relationships. If that's not addressed, you're going to have all sorts of problems that'll continue."

In 1995, I created the Tariq Khamisa Foundation with the desire to stop kids from killing kids. Our programs were developed to target youth from fourth to eighth grade. We want to teach them tools of nonviolence before they make the bad choice to join a gang or get involved with violence in some other way. Our programs have been very successful, and we've won several awards over the years.

But even as we moved forward with TKF, adding new programs and strengthening the ones that were in place, I also recognized that we were leaving out a lot of kids. TKF was not touching those youths who already had turned down a dark path. These kids have either already

Azim is the National Director and Founder of CANEI (Constant and Never Ending Improvement). Shown from left: Nola Lawarre (Executive Assistant, NYAP); Azim Khamisa; Judy Strnad (Director of Program Development, CANEI); Scott Timmerman (Vice President of Planning and Organizational Excellence, NYAP); Mubarak E. Awad (Founder, NYAP)

committed crimes or their deeds have been of a lesser nature, but they are deemed "high risk" and have been referred to participate in some kind of social service program. Some of them still live with their parent(s), and others have been placed in foster-care homes. All of them are on a slippery slope in the choices they make and the consequences of those choices.

TKF cannot reach them through our programs, because our vision and our purpose is to reach kids before they get to this point of behavior. It saddened me to know that we had the motivation but not the way. It was around that time that I met Mubarak Awad, the founder of the National Youth Advocate Program (NYAP), and Marvena Twigg, the president and CEO of NYAP. It was from our heartfelt conversations with each other that the seeds of CANEI were sown.

NYAP AND CANEI

Mubarak, Marvena, and others from NYAP had heard about the TKF story in 1998 and invited me to be one of the keynote speakers for the twentieth anniversary celebration of the National Youth Advocate Program, headquartered in Ohio. I was in good company, as Nobel Laureate Archbishop Desmond Tutu also spoke at that five-day conference. I gave the keynote on the fourth day, telling the story of Tariq and Tony, me and Ples, and how the act of forgiveness can transform lives. Tutu, a phenomenal and brilliant speaker, gave his keynote on the last day of the conference and spoke about apartheid in South Africa.

A few days after I'd returned home, I received a call from the conference program person who had tallied the results of the attendee feedback forms. I was shocked to learn that I had received the highest rating of all the keynote speakers. I don't believe this is because I'm a better speaker than any of the others. I do believe that my talk touched the heart of the audience, because they understood that there is a Tariq and a Tony in every American family. Our story touched the hearts and souls of the people at the conference, because they understood that ours is a familiar story, relevant and important to every one of us.

"I've been to hundreds of professional gatherings and conferences," Marvena says. "When Azim spoke, you could have heard a pin drop in a room of five hundred to six hundred people. This was a very seasoned, experienced group of professionals.

To move such a group is quite extraordinary. Azim's amazing keynote speech really touched people cognitively as well as emotionally."

In the TKF story, we see the bravado that's in Tariq, and we recognize that it's the same thing we see in many other kids. There is a Tony lurking inside every angry teenager, whether it's because of drugs and alcohol, family or social stressors, or emotional isolation—lurking with the potential to harm somebody. The conference attendees were savvy professionals who worked with youth day in and day out and who had been in this field for many years. They understood that our story represents two distinct societal issues: the bravado to stand up for what you believe at whatever risk and whatever cost, just as did Gandhi and Martin Luther King, Jr., and the potential for a person's mind to be ruled by emotions of anger and hatred leading to a dark path of violence.

A couple of years after the conference, Mubarak and Marvena approached me about working with them to develop a program for aggressive, defiant, and violent youth—a program which we named CANEI: Constant and Never Ending Improvement. The kids we'd be working with were the tough ones, the kids with attitude, hostility, and resistance. These were the kids who acted out their hurt, pain, and trauma, the ones who were headed for some serious trouble.

The very name of our new program spoke to the fact that these kids needed someone to make a heartfelt commitment to help them toward a better life . . . no matter what. The acronym CANEI is intentional. Our commitment to improving the lives of troubled youths is constant and never ending. We will not give up on them. So long as they are in our program—that is, so long as they are not referred out of our programs because of a court decision—we are there to support them, challenge them, teach them, and love them. Some of these kids have never before experienced this kind of affirmation and commitment from an adult. This is exactly why we promise it to them. The kids in our program learn about trust through our interactions with them. Through that trust they also learn about taking responsibility for their own actions.

I always had empathy for the at-risk youth population, and NYAP was well-established in this heavily regulated environment of youth social work. This made the work I wanted to do possible. Not only did they have all the licenses and accreditations required, but they also were very passionate about the work. This was a dream come true for me, because at TKF we are a prevention program. We are stopping kids from becoming gang members. But what about the kids who had already joined the gangs? This was my opportunity to work on the other side of the gun.

Mubarak founded NYAP in 1978, motivated by his passionate desire to help youth in danger and turmoil, especially those at risk of confinement in the juvenile justice system. Mubarak, ever the advocate for social justice causes, witnessed the violent death of his own father as a young boy. He and his siblings grew up in an orphanage, because his mother could not provide economically for him or his siblings. As he matured, a desire grew within Mubarak to do whatever he could to help children and families live free of violence. I have learned much from Mubarak, and he has significantly helped me in my work. He and I have much in common even though I am Muslim and he is Christian. Our Arabic names, our mutual loss of loved ones, our social activism, and our commitment to peace bring us together as brothers.

NYAP itself provides comprehensive services to at-risk youths and their families through a variety of state- and county-funded programs. Their administrative offices are in Ohio, with program offices in several Ohio cities. NYAP also has affiliate organizations in a number of states including Georgia, Illinois, Indiana, South Carolina, and West Virginia, as well as a sister program in California, which I helped establish. By the time of this book's publication, most of these subsidiary organizations will have been dissolved and incorporated into one national corporation, which will allow NYAP to more efficiently serve more kids and their communities.

My very good friend, Marvena, has been a great teacher for me in this work. She's been in the field of social work for most of her life and understands what disenfranchised children and families need. "The National Youth Advocate Program has always had a strong advocacy voice," she says, "believing that children belong with their families and in the communities they call home. And if children fail in their communities, it's because we as the adults and the service providers have not yet figured out how to reach them."

Through their comprehensive state- and county-funded programs, NYAP is able to reach many of these at-risk youths and their families. "We must find ways of continuing to reach adolescents using the natural supports of their community," Marvena says. "We must actively involve youth and families in defining their problems and developing solutions in the multiple and varied challenges they face. We must respectfully interact and engage with them in ways that we would want to be interacted and engaged with."

Through a variety of family- and community-based programs, NYAP helps youths and their families gain mastery over difficult life circumstances. NYAP was a pioneer in the concept of matching youth to caring and committed adults who would never abandon them. As an organization, NYAP works with a number of values and principles that guide its programming decision-making, concepts which each of us can nurture within ourselves. These are the principles of the National Youth Advocate Program: Children First, Advocacy on behalf of those who cannot yet champion their own cause, Advocacy for Systemic Change, Empowerment, Diversity, Community, Social Inclusion, Innovation, Peacemaking, and a belief in and a commitment to the Universal Rights of Children.

CANEI, as one of NYAP's funded programs, is committed to the same concepts and values. Constant and Never Ending Improvement. This is precisely what we offer and promise to our kids. We teach them that they have an internal navigation system. Tony was listening to an *external* navigation system when he shot Tariq. Antoine called out, "Bust him Bone," and Tony, listening to something outside of himself and apart from his own better judgment, pulled the trigger.

With CANEI we're trying to connect with the kids' souls so they don't have to rely on being controlled by what's external to them. When you are in contact with your soul, you know what is right and what is wrong. It's as if the decision of what to do is already made for you, inside yourself. When Mubarak, Marvena, and I were discussing the possibility of creating this program for at-risk youth, I was inspired by three main concepts, which became the Three Pillars of CANEI:

- ⚶ Spirituality
- ⚶ Restorative Justice
- ⚶ Literacy

EXPANSION

At its inception in 2001, CANEI was based on a concept shared by myself, Mubarak, and Marvena. Beginning in Columbus, Ohio, and then with our 2005 expansion into Atlanta, San Diego, and Chicago, we implemented the CANEI program using a few different modalities to see how and where we could be most effective with at-risk youth. In 2006 our wonderful administrative people from all the different sites came together. Under the competent guidance of NYAP Vice President Scott Timmerman and Director of Program Development Judy Strnad, we re-engineered CANEI into a fully integrated and comprehensive program. I reached out to Rudy Alexander, a professor of sociology at Ohio State University, for help in creating a statistical model for measuring results, just as I had done with TKF. With Scott's expertise and the commitment of the CANEI team, the assessment and evaluation model was taken to a new level.

Creating and implementing a program is one thing. But measuring its success is something else. I know the TKF story is powerful, but I never wanted to be a traveling circus. What has always been important to me is to have programs in place that are exemplary in terms of outcomes and results.

"We know that our outcomes have to be objective, measurable, and sustainable," Scott says. "So the current CANEI curriculum includes specific outcomes that we seek to achieve. What we are looking for is transformation in our youth. Those coming into the program are described as aggressive, defiant, and disruptive. They have an outlook on life that is very fatalistic, and they have a lot of despair. The mission of CANEI is 'To Provide Hope' that youth will find stability in their own lives and find meaning for themselves in relation to their community and to others."

I'm very good at measuring widgets. But finding evidence of transformation seems more elusive. At TKF we incorporated strategies to determine the effectiveness of our in-school and after-school prevention programs. At CANEI, Scott further developed and organized strategies to measure the success of these at-risk youths.

"The evidence of a transformation will be that youth are experiencing success in an academic or vocational environment probably for the first time in a long time or ever," Scott says. "Youth will demonstrate a positive involvement with the community through service learning projects and through engagement with other community processes, instead of running the streets or being truant from school and hanging out all day. What we're looking for is a marked shift in their orientation and focus because of what's now important to them.

"There will also be evidence in increased pro-social behavior. They'll experience a positive and stable home environment, whether it's their own family home, a kinship home, or a foster home. There will be a qualitative change in their stability in terms of incidents of disruptive behavior and episodes of truancy, running away, and being AWOL from placement.

"We do a pre- and post-program evaluation, and then following program completion we also do a three-, six-, and twelve-month longitudinal study," Scott continues. "We say that the behaviors that youth have coming into the program are learned behaviors. They're survival skills that the youth have learned in order to get through their day or to survive in their community. We want them to find alternatives to the gang or pre-gang type of activities they engage in, and to see an alternative to being in jail or dead by the time they're twenty-one.

"Our goal would be for youth to see many other kinds of possibilities for themselves other than that. Part of the approach of CANEI is to really be able to demonstrate that there is something different about this program. Part of the initial difference is contained in the Tony and Tariq story. The youth see that there's opportunity to be responsible for their own behavior and for forgiveness. That's what we seek to build on with our program and to allow youth time to explore. This is not the same program they've seen in the three or four other places they've been. There are concepts of the CANEI program—restorative justice, the importance of spirituality, the principles of the Circle of Courage—that resonate with the basic developmental building blocks that these kids have missed out on.

"To measure the success of our program," Scott says, "we collect information that reflects the youth's current and recent behavior at the time of discharge. We use two formal instruments: CAFAS (Child and Adolescent Functional Assessment Scale), and Albert Bandura's measure of Moral Disengagement. We're looking for objective and measurable behaviors that continue to reflect that a transformation did occur and has continued and is sustained."

Utilizing a 26-week curriculum that draws upon the "Circle of Courage," a youth development model rooted in Native American childrearing practices, CANEI staff help youth peel back the layers of their own aggression and hostility to uncover the core of brilliance within each of them. This program was

146

developed by three brilliant gentlemen, Reclaiming Youth International co-founders Steve Van Bockern, Larry Brendtro and Martin Brokenleg, and is detailed in their book, *Reclaiming Youth At-Risk: Our Hope for the Future.* Circle of Courage involves four aspects that every human being needs in order to survive:

- Belonging
- Mastery
- Independence
- Generosity

Our curriculum utilizes these components in the various lesson plans we've developed for our youth, and they fit in beautifully with the three pillars that ground CANEI.

THE FIRST PILLAR: SPIRITUALITY

With the first pillar of spirituality, we teach our kids to explore their own values, attitudes, and places in the world. Some of them have never felt like they belonged anywhere before.

"Most of our kids come from a history of broken attachments," Director of Program Development Judy Strnad, says. "They've either been ripped from their homes or ripped from their communities." Through the spirituality component of CANEI, we get our kids to take a look at who they are, where they belong, and how they can fit in and contribute to their families and their communities.

Week one of our curriculum is "The Nature of my Spirit." Spirituality is never confused with religion. We present a variety of wisdom traditions and activities to our kids to encourage and nurture their personal growth. Whether we have a Native American elder speak, teach meditation, or have an art or music activity, the kids gain invaluable life skills including decision making and conflict resolution.

The Second Pillar: Restorative Justice

The youths who participate in the CANEI program come from a background of personal victimization. They have all experienced suffering to some extent, whether it is adverse economic conditions, emotional or physical abuse, parental absenteeism, or some other traumatic condition of their childhood. The restorative justice component of CANEI helps these kids forgive others and accept themselves—both for their past circumstances and the consequences of their own behavior. For most of these kids, this is a radical paradigm shift in their thinking and in their understanding of relationships and responsibility.

The restorative justice model, whether it's being implemented for youth or adults, recognizes that multiple lives are impacted by a single incident of aggressive or violent behavior. As Ted Lewis, restorative justice program manager at Community Mediation Services, says, it's a breakage of relationships. Whenever a crime is committed, many lives are impacted. It was so when Tony killed Tariq, and it is so with every crime committed against another human being. In order for justice to be served, three things need to happen: the victim must be made whole again, the perpetrator must be integrated into society as a contributing member, and the community must be healed.

"I look at our program as having three legs to the stool to make it solid," Ted says. "That is the victim engagement, the offender engagement, and then the community engagement.

One of the reasons the community leg of the stool is as vital as the other is because the community has a role to communicate to offenders. We say, 'We want you to fit into our society or into our community in a good way. We want you to make things right.' The community takes the role of saying, 'This is what we expect of you.'"

CANEI has taken on that role of community that Ted describes. Our kids soon learn that we expect a great deal from them both in terms of their relationships with themselves and others and also in the ways we teach them how to generously give back to their families and communities. Right at the beginning of our program, the kids hear the TKF story and listen to the speech Tony made to the judge at his hearing.

"I shot and killed Tariq Khamisa, a person I did not know who was not doing anything wrong to me."

The kids hear that and they understand right away that Tony took responsibility for his actions. Then Tony says, "I pray to God every day that Mr. Khamisa will forgive me for the pain I've caused him."

Just like Tony did, we want our kids to take responsibility for the actions they've taken. Once they've admitted their wrongdoing to themselves, they can then reach out in the hopes that the victim will one day find it in his or her heart to forgive.

In his work with restorative justice, Ted Lewis feels strongly that forgiveness is a gift of the giver, rather than it being a request of the receiver. He believes that the victim of a crime or a wrong action shouldn't have the burden of forgiving someone when they're not ready or willing to take that step. Apology is also a gift of the giver. When these gifts of either forgiveness or apology are offered prior to a request for them, they are very powerful and healing.

In Step Three: Reach Out, I spoke about VORP, the Victim Offender Reconciliation Program. This program and others are available in many areas that have a restorative justice component. In these programs, a victim and an offender can come together in a mediated environment for the purpose of reconciliation. I worked with the district attorney to set up the meeting between me and Ples, and it was very healing for both of us to come together. When the time was right, after we had both taken time to prepare, Tony and I also came together in the spirit of reconciliation and healing. The same can also be true for other victims and offenders. Under the right circumstances, with both parties willing and prepared, reaching out and reconciliation are possible.

THE THIRD PILLAR: LITERACY

Most of our kids are greatly handicapped by a lack of education. "Many of the kids that we serve have tremendous gaps in their education," Judy says. "What we're trying to do in working with them is increase their desire to learn."

We cover the basics of reading, writing, and arithmetic and provide tutors when they are needed. We also teach other kinds of competency, critical thinking, and life skills that will help them long after they've left our program. Through the literacy component of CANEI, we help our kids become the masters of their own lives by the competent and intelligent choices they make, the positive attitudes they hold, and the manner in which they carry themselves and participate in their communities. Through our sustained and heartfelt commitment to our programs and our kids, they truly understand that we will not give up on them until they succeed.

Judy's been working with at-risk kids for close to thirty years. "I don't believe that these kids are bad," she says. "I believe that there have been environmental influences that have shaped them. Many of these kids have lived in states of poverty their whole life. They've had to scratch for everything that they've got. And they do it in ways that help them to survive. When you peel back the layers, these are incredible young people who have just not been directed in the right way in order to survive in a healthful way."

Our slogan at CANEI is "We won't give up until you succeed." We are sincere about this. Each youth in our 26-week CANEI program is assigned a full time treatment advocate and a full time treatment coordinator. For every ten kids in the program, we have a part time therapist on staff. The kids are involved in individual therapy, group therapy, and, if family therapy is needed, we also provide that.

The treatment advocate serves as a mentor who helps the kids learn to build healthy relationships with themselves, with others, and with their communities. They do two main things: (1) help the kids in a service learning project and (2) assist them with their independent living skills.

CANEI kids are already in the system and are connected with any number of human services organizations. These groups do wonderful work—I honor them for what they do—but for the most part their budgets and their programs do not include care for the kids once they reach a certain age. We fill that gap by teaching our kids how to live independent, satisfying, and successful lives and instilling in them the desire to do so.

The CANEI treatment advocate is literally available for 26 weeks, 24/7. I asked Judy to share a story to illustrate the kind of commitment our staff has.

"We have an adolescent female who came into our care last year," Judy says. "The most fascinating thing about her was that she was incredibly angry, and she had been using violence as a means to get her needs met. She assaulted her last caregiver, because that person wouldn't give her what she wanted.

"When she came into our care, we immediately set up a safety plan for her of ways that she was able to verbalize, 'When I get upset, when I get angry, these are probably the things that would help me through that.' And we put it into the plan for her to follow.

"Her treatment advocate told me, 'You know, she still has a mouth.' I told her that I understood, and I said, 'We can't take all her tools for survival away from her until she learns that there are other ways that she feels comfortable with to replace the more aggressive ways. If she doesn't pick up anything and use it as a weapon, which is what she's been doing for the last seven years of her life, that's what we're trying to achieve.'

"Her treatment advocate had been working with her seven days a week for months, and she had chosen to do her service learning project with a recreation department in her city. Together they had gone to different parks in their area, in and around her home, and beautified the parks by painting benches and getting them ready for spring.

"So here she was now in the most stable environment she'd been in for years, and it was because the staff was so involved. Then one night, the treatment advocate called and said to me,

'I'm at her house for our appointment, and she won't come out of her bedroom. What should I do?'

"I said, 'You stay and you visit with the family for the duration of the time you would have spent with her. She has to see that she's not going to scare you away.' That went on for weeks! And the staff said, 'I'm getting discouraged.' 'Hang in there,' I said. 'The fact that you're not leaving, she's watching you. You don't want to disappoint her.'

"Eventually the adolescent came out of her bedroom, and when she saw my staff person pull up in the driveway, she was already out the door and in the van. It takes time with these kids. It's all about engaging. It's all about establishing relationships with them, because we know that when relationships are formed, kids improve."

IMPROVEMENT

Constant and never ending improvement. That's what we're offering to these kids and their families. With the three pillars of Spirituality, Restorative Justice, and Literacy grounding our program, and the Circle of Courage forming the basis of our 26-week curriculum, CANEI helps these at-risk youths turn their lives around. We help them gain a sense of belonging, perhaps for the first time in their lives. We help them realize that they are spiritual beings and have a spiritual connection to all living things. We guide them in mastering independent life skills and cultivating a genuine desire to generously give something back to their communities.

CANEI has come a long way since its inception. With the many resources available through NYAP and its contractual funding by state and county agencies, we are able to reach these kids, teach these kids, and lead them toward the satisfaction of self-responsibility they've been seeking. I am greatly honored to be connected with an organization as compassionate as NYAP. And the Circle of Courage social model frames CANEI's programs beautifully. Because of the synergy of the two, it is not surprising that I was recently invited to sit on the board of Reclaiming Youth International, and I have gratefully accepted.

For twelve years TKF has successfully guided kids toward lives of peace and nonviolence with our prevention programs. Now CANEI is an integral part of NYAP's overall vision and program goals. With its new and more rigorous structure in place, CANEI is ready to reach even more kids—the ones who are already slipping. As Scott says, "We don't want to be waiting at the bottom of the waterfall to scoop them up. Let's get them before they go over the waterfall."

Marvena adds, "We believe we do good work, and we want to grow and develop NYAP. We have a very aggressive plan for growth and development that is anchored around services to adolescents and their families. Part of our strategic vision is to continue to grow and deepen our work with socially and economically disenfranchised people. It is there that CANEI becomes a very important part of what we believe NYAP will be focused on for years to come."

At CANEI we show our kids how to survive using the brilliance of their own hearts. We lovingly impress upon them that we expect them to make the right choices and do the right thing. If they fail, if they lose their footing along the way and end up back on the slippery slope, we are there to pick them up, dust them off, and welcome them back with arms open wide. Constant and Never Ending Improvement. That is our commitment to youth in CANEI, and we won't give up until they succeed.

We are all cells in the body of humanity—all of us, all over the world. Each one of us has a contribution to make, and will know from within what that contribution is, but no one can find inner peace except by working, not in a self-centered way, but for the whole of humanity.

— Peace Pilgrim

The Ripple Effect: Finding Peace Through Forgiveness

Chapter Ten

There is a great paradox in life. Even as we go about our days feeling, thinking, and acting like self-contained, independent beings, we are all energetically connected to one another in ways most of us can't even perceive. Some people are sensitive and attuned to these energies; others are not. Regardless of one's experience, it is important to remember that the connections exist and that we are always influencing and affecting each other with our thoughts and actions.

Sometimes these influences and effects are obvious. When Tony chose to pull the trigger and fire a bullet in Tariq's direction, my son was fatally affected by that decision. Our immediate family members were not the only ones who felt the ripple effect of Tony's action. Tariq's friends, co-workers, and other people he knew in San Diego and elsewhere were also deeply affected.

Sometimes the influence is immediate. Other times weeks, months, or even years go by before the influence of a violent act upon another's life is apparent. Such was the case with Tariq's fiancée, Jennifer. After his death, she spent seven years trying to come out of her despair, but eventually she succumbed to her pain by taking her own life.

Azim's family is a perfect example of the ripple effect of love and compassion. Shown from left: Almas Khamisa (Tariq's mother), Tasreen Alaei (Tariq's sister), Khalil Mohamed Alaei, Azim Khamisa, and Shahin Tariq Alaei.

When something bad happens, the ripple effect is often negative. Similarly, when something good happens, that event can lead to more positive experiences in other people's lives. When I made the decision to forgive Tony, my heart reopened to the possibility of a fulfilled life, something I thought had been stripped away from me forever by Tariq's death. My very act of forgiveness propelled Tony toward a life of personal growth, contemplation, and forgiveness of others and himself.

In this chapter, I highlight family members, co-workers, friends, and students whose personal experiences are a testimony to the power of finding peace through forgiveness. It is my hope that through these heartfelt sharings you will be inspired to create a shift and transformation in your own life.

MY FAMILY
Almas Khamisa, Tariq's mother/TKF volunteer

As Azim was reaching out to Ples in forgiveness, forming the foundation, and getting national attention, I had withdrawn into my private world of anger and devastation over the loss of my son. My anger was not directed towards the fourteen-year-old who took his life, or the family who raised him, but towards my son who took such an early exit from this physical life. I believe we have free choice in this matter.

Since I raised him alone after the divorce, I blamed myself for many things. Most of his friends came from stable homes where fathers were involved, especially where father/son activities were occurring. I remember when he brought home projects that I could not help him with. He used to say, "Mom, you make a lousy dad." For not being able to give him everything he needed, I was plagued with guilt for many years.

I am no longer angry with my son or with myself. I have forgiven him, and the process of forgiving myself still continues. I believe that we create our lives with our thoughts. Resentment and all other negative emotions cause a lot of damage to our heart and our soul. Being aware of this, the best way I can continue to forgive myself is to change my thoughts to understand that I did my best with what I had in terms of emotional and material stability at that time.

Since Tariq's death, I am very aware that to change our society we will have to begin with the children. As a teacher, I am grateful that every day I can influence a child to deal with conflicts in a positive manner. There have been several occasions when I have stood in front of students at TKF *VIF* assemblies and talked about the pain of losing my son. I've said that my

The ripple effect continues. Azim's family includes his son-in-law Mehrdad Alaei, here shown with Shahin and Tasreen.

wish for them was to learn to treasure their lives and the lives of others. In working with children, especially the ones I see during the school year, I feel as if I have been given a second chance. This has been healing for me. If I felt that I had let my son down, this was an opportunity to make up for that, and that would help in the process of forgiving myself.

Tasreen Khamisa Alaei
Tariq's sister/former TKF Executive Director

I majored in sociology and emphasized in juvenile delinquency, spending two years in university studying why people like Tony commit murder. When I first found out that it was a fourteen-year-old who had killed my brother, I was really torn. I could empathize with Tony, but it was *my brother* who had been killed. Half of me was really angry, and that was something I was battling with internally. When my father decided to reach out and forgive Tony and start the foundation, it was a positive way for me to focus on the half that was empathizing with Tony and begin to let the anger go.

Living in Seattle, I was isolated from the tragedy and had gone into a depression. Eighteen months after my brother had been killed, my boyfriend committed suicide. I was on a really sad path. In 1998 I came to San Diego and embraced the foundation in my role as assistant executive director. Moving to San Diego and working with my father and Ples changed me as a person . . . for the rest of my life.

I fell in love with what I was doing, and after about a year I was promoted to full executive director. It didn't feel like a job to me. I was doing my life's work in the name of my brother, which made me work really hard. I also felt like I was doing Tariq's work, what he wasn't able to finish in the physical world, and it felt good not to have the tragedy be in vain. I felt very supported by my brother when I had my role at the foundation. Sometimes I would make decisions or something would come out of my mouth, and I'd think, "I sound just like my brother!" I really felt like I was working with him hand in hand, and I felt his presence very strongly.

You can run away from pain, and you can dive into pain. Working at the foundation made me dive into mine. Being immersed in an organization that is named for your brother, reliving the story of his tragic death every day, you're forced to look at it. Diving into the pain, I could first feel the hurt. The next step was to look at my anger and ask, "How is this going to serve me?" I knew that being angry wasn't going to help my brother. It wasn't going to bring him back. So for me to be angry, I was only hurting myself. And I didn't want to hurt myself anymore.

Through his death, my brother gave my family a wake-up call to really look at our lives. He put us on our journeys of our life's work and how we were going to contribute to the world. He connected me back to my soul again, and after my brother passed, I really got to start fulfilling what I thought my purpose in life was.

Tony's Family
Ples Felix, Tony's grandfather/TKF Vice Chairman

I maintained at the outset of understanding that Tony had murdered Tariq that I had a parallel purpose which developed out of the tragedy. My primary purpose was to be of support to my grandson and my daughter in terms of the impact of one of our family members having committed this senseless act of murder. At the same time, I prayed for strength to be able to be of support to Tariq's family, a family of people I did not know. It was one of my human responsibilities and obligations to seek an opportunity to extend to them directly, and face-to-face preferably, my heartfelt condolences and sympathy for the loss of their son at the hands of my grandson in this senseless act.

I committed to do anything I could to support them in their loss. That was a constant focus of my meditations and prayers immediately after finding out that Tony was responsible for murdering Tariq. Upon hearing from Tony's attorney about Azim's desire to meet with me, I realized that this opportunity I'd prayed for was beginning to form up. I was very appreciative of the fact that Azim approached this tragedy uniquely different from how tragedies like this are approached in our culture, and in cultures all over the world. When we first met, I was mindful to be sure and share with Azim that I was very much gratified by his compassion for my grandson and my family.

Upon expressing heartfelt sympathy and condolences, I shared with Azim that I was committed to make myself available in any way I could to assist him and his family with their loss. He said, "I'm determined to start a foundation to help prevent youth violence. Will you help me?" I recall distinctly the smile coming over my face and telling him that his request of me was really an answer to my prayer, that I would do all I could to help, and that I'd be delighted.

The only way I could see to even try to be of support in that loss was to be of support to the family in a real way, in a substantial, practical way. Not by just kind words and platitudes and cards and letters once a year, but by being and standing with Azim shoulder-to-shoulder, by serving in support of Azim and in support of TKF, serving as an example of how we as human beings can really work in earnest with sincerity to try and make something better.

I've always aspired to be a righteous person. I've just really never known exactly and clearly what that meant. My basic purpose to exist is to support Azim and his family. My vision of TKF is to support Azim's vision wherever that vision goes. If Azim wants to create an organization that will help children not make violent choices, I'm going to do that. If his vision is for us to have programs in every school in the country, then I'm going to support him in doing that. If asked about my own personal vision for TKF, my sincere answer is that I don't have a vision that's different from Azim's. What we can do together, what my support of Azim and his family can do to help our country and our world, that's my purpose.

Azim and I are water bearers for each other. I help him carry his load. He helps me carry mine. In our mutual assistance of each other in carrying this load, we're moving forward in a way to positively influence the lives of children and families in our communities, and each time we do that, the load gets a little lighter.

TKF FAMILY AND STUDENT LETTERS
Mark Fackler, TKF President

What draws me to TKF at this point is the magic of the organization. I get to save kids, and I get to learn about forgiveness. It brings tears to my eyes when I see a letter from a child who's been to one of our assemblies. TKF is dedicated to children, but it's my belief that the adults involved and associated with the organization learn just as much if not more. What I have learned about forgiveness is priceless.

When 9/11 happened, I felt terrible for the victims, their families, and their friends—the ripple effect that was caused by the tragedy. Just as quickly, I felt sorry for the terrorists. How these people who were born pure and perfect could live a life that could lead to something like this was so sad to me. At some point something went wrong, and this perpetual anger started.

That's why I love that we're working with children. To change an adult is hard. But if we can get the adults to raise the children properly, so they're not filled with this hatred and thoughts of revenge as opposed to forgiveness, then we won't have two buildings tumbling down and all the heartache that came from that. We won't have people willing to fly a plane into them either, and losing their lives just like Tariq's life was taken from him and Tony lost his life to the prison system.

That's a huge impact of this work on me. My heart aches for the criminals. I just had my Bluetooth earpiece stolen. I was angry, but I also felt bad for whoever took it. I believed the criminal should be punished, but I also wondered what experiences the person had in their own life which brought him or her to steal my headset. When I get angry at someone, it doesn't take long for me to forgive that individual. It's not that the anger goes away. Azim was once asked, "How long did it take you to forgive Tony?" His response was, "Well, it's not that I did, it's that I do. Every day."

It's a very powerful and universal message. Raised Lutheran I was taught, "Love thy neighbor as thyself." But at TKF I have this wonderful opportunity to see the message over and over and over again. When you're immersed in forgiveness, it helps.

VIF Assembly middle school student Q&A session, January 2007

It was like last year and I got a phone call saying that my, that one of my older brothers had died. And I didn't hear how it happened, but it just, it was kind of like part of me, inside of me, had died. And I just really wanted you to know that you made the pain go away just by this assembly. I really appreciate it. Thank you.—C.

Megan Thomas Wescott
TKF Programs and Marketing Communications Coordinator

My own life has been riddled with tragedies. Fortunately they weren't derived from violence, but I've lost a lot of people in my life. When I was eight months old, my mother tragically died in a car accident. My biological father had not expressed any interest in continuing to be in a relationship with my mother or in being a father to me, so my mother's parents—my grandparents—adopted and raised me. I have a great family. I never felt anger or resentment toward my biological father, but he never reached out to me, and I never felt the need to reach out to him.

A while back, Azim was a speaker for the KPBS "Love and Forgiveness Campaign." Decorated stationary was given out for people to use to reach out and write letters of love and forgiveness. I had saved some of this beautiful writing paper and matching envelopes for months, saving it for something special. That something special turned out to be reaching out to my biological father.

I found out he has pancreatic cancer, and hearing that he's in the hospital has definitely stirred up some emotions and thoughts. Even though I'm sure I would still have had the desire to make contact with him, if I hadn't been working with TKF, I think it would have been much harder to do. It's helped me to be aware of what Azim and Ples have done. If they could come together, then I really think it's true that everybody can do that. Working with the TKF core values, our six key messages, and everything Azim talks about in his forgiveness workshops, I'm reminded on a daily basis. That made reaching out to my biological father so much easier. And it definitely feels good, and I hope we can develop a relationship now.

VIF Assembly student letter

Dear TKF,

I want to thank you first off starting the foundation and take youngsters in consideration. You have great big hearts to actually take action and talk to schools about these things. Azim Khamisa you really are a great man for forgiving Tony and his family. It is really inspiring. Ples Felix it's really cool how you were there for Tony and how you and Azim have such a great friendship. Javier Ortega now I really see that when your in a gang bad stuff done really happen. Myra its a good think you got out of your gang for your daughter you're a great mom. I really liked Javier's and Myra's storys. I guess its because gangs really catch my attention I don't know why. In fact I started one but I realized that theres no need to bring trouble in my and the gangs life. I'm really sorry that you cant see Javier and sorry that Azim you cant see your son again. Thanks for coming to our school.

Sincerely,

M.

Katie Bowles
TKF Development Director

I love the heart behind this organization, and my experience working with TKF and Azim has been fabulous. I like having core values and striving to work out of integrity and compassionate confrontation daily. It is not always easy to do; however, it is what is the best for the organization and thus the people we serve.

It's really nice to work for a place that I know can make a difference, and TKF is an organization I am motivated to tell other people about. I heard Azim speak at a leadership seminar where I worked, and I was so moved. Honestly, I don't know if I could have done what he did if it had been one of my three sons. And yet I do see it's really the only thing that you can do to go on with your own life, to really have healing for all the people involved.

With issues that I have now and struggle with, I remember what Azim did and I think, "Okay, you know what? These things are not that important. I have my family. I can work through this." Everything to me seems so much smaller now in my own personal life. I love the first step of the forgiveness workshop, acknowledging that we've been wronged. I believe in my heart that the acknowledgment itself allows us to move to a place in our hearts where forgiveness can be sustained. But if we begin with forgiveness, without taking the first step, I think it's too easy to go back and feel like the victim again.

VIF Assembly student letter

Dear Javier,

I know you may not get to read this on your own. But hopefully someone gets to read it to you. You know what, I REALLY admire you. After you being a gang banger you became a serious man. You might get shot at but that doesn't stop you from being a nice person. Hopefully everything goes well with you.

Sincerely,

A.

P.S. Take care, Javier.

Suzanne Bacon
TKF Program Director

It took a while for me to understand forgiveness the way Azim talks about it. I had a lot of conversations with my fiancé about things like, can the Holocaust be forgiven? Are there certain people you just can't forgive? In our society, in some ways when you forgive somebody it's almost like saying, "Well, it's okay, never mind that you did that." But that doesn't have to be what forgiveness is. Forgiveness means not letting yourself be destroyed by anger.

When I finally understood that, I started to notice that I reacted differently to the little things that used to make me angry. It's a minor thing, but in terms of traffic, like road rage, I would sometimes get mad. But I began to notice that it was easier not to let it get to me. Instead of "hating" other people, even briefly, I began to try to connect to our common humanity.

At one of our board meetings, Mark asked us about forgiveness. His question made me realize that I'd been holding onto some anger which I'd been unaware of. I'd just had knee surgery from an injury in Mexico while playing soccer. After I kicked the ball, a girl on the other team pushed into me, and I could immediately feel something in my knee tear. Until Mark asked that question, I hadn't realized I was still holding a grudge against this fifteen-year-old girl whose name I didn't even know! Once I realized I was still holding the anger, I was able to begin the process of forgiveness.

VIF Assembly student letter

Dear TKF,

Thank you so much for coming to our school to share your touching and sorrowful experiences with us. Since we are in a neighborhood plagued with gangs and violence, I thought it was a wise choice to raise the awareness level of the fact that violence DOES affect us and others around us.

The speakers really opened my eyes to all the things that could happen if you pulled the trigger once. It made me realize how much violence would hurt people.

Again, thank you so much for coming.

Sincerely, T.

DeAnna LoCoco
Spiritual Advisor/former TKF Board Member

I've attended four of Azim's forgiveness workshops. In one of them a plan of action was revealed to me as he guided me through a meditation. It was a plan that was doable with some people in my life with whom I'd had a difficult estrangement. Just the fact that it resolved and softened in me was exciting; to know that I could make the shift by offering something different of myself was an epiphany. All we can do is work on ourselves, relinquishing any expectation that the other person may or may not get it.

That workshop was significant for me, and subsequently things began to unfold with these particular people. It's taking a while, but it was a shift in me. When you're dealing with people who know you, who've known you your whole life, say family members, the presumption is always their memory of how they remember you "when."

When I am more relaxed with myself and not constantly, frantically thinking about, "Well, how can I change this?" or "If it was different," or blaming or criticizing, then it all shifts, neutralizes, and dissipates. To continue to unfold and blossom and become unattached to some of these things, your energy literally can shift the situation. "Where your thoughts go, the energy flows."

Alex, VIF Assembly student

Alex was a fifth grader who had a lot of attitude. Even though he wasn't in a gang, he wore the color and insignia of a gang member. My daughter, Tasreen, was teaching a TKF course called Empathy, and its theme was, "You don't know

171

me until you've walked a mile in my shoes." The students' homework was to practice empathy all week and come back to share what they'd done. At week's end Alex put his hand up, and what he said was very powerful:

> *"I was walking in my hood last weekend, and I saw this kid give me a dirty look. Usually if a kid gives you a dirty look, you basically go and beat him up. But since you have taught me that you don't know me until you've walked a mile in my shoes, I walked up to this kid and asked him, 'Why are you giving me a dirty look?'*
>
> *The kid said to me, 'I'm not giving you a dirty look. I'm angry because my brother was shot and killed last night.'"*

Alex held the kid's hand and said, "I know how you feel." In that one moment, Alex became a healer for the rest of his life.

Dianne McKay
TKF Board Member

I've never had any personal experience with violence. When I watched the video showing Tony's mother sobbing in the courtroom, her pain always moved me to tears. But in the back of my mind I thought, "This could never happen to me." My son, Ian, was six years old when I started with TKF, and he's a wonderful kid—smart, well-adjusted, an artist and a thinker. But in sixth grade, he started hanging out with some guys and getting into a little bit of trouble. Real minor stuff, but his behavior was different than usual.

"What's with him? Why is he doing this?" I wondered. He knew about TKF, and he knew the core values we work with in the organization. So my husband and I intervened. We met with his teacher and principal, and we all talked with him. My son made his own decision to stop seeing those kids. That was the same year I was planning the first stand-alone Gandhi Awards event. Tasreen had suggested we have a youth keynote speaker, and my son wrote and submitted a speech. His subject was his "sixth grade adventures." It was ironic that my son became the keynote speaker at that event. He talked about why he started hanging out with these guys, to look cool and be accepted. Then he told the audience how he got himself out of it, how he brought in TKF and the core values. My son got a standing ovation. He was twelve years old at the time.

I thought to myself, "What happened to Tariq and Tony can happen in anybody's family." The reasons people hang out with the wrong crowd or join a gang are all the same. You want what you think will be acceptance, and you think people will care about you. You think you're cool. When I realized my own son had started to go down the wrong path, I thought, "Wow, TKF is really needed." The temptations are the same no matter what neighborhood you live in. This was my own family, and I'd been involved with TKF for years.

VIF Assembly student letter

Dear Tony,

What made you so angry to join a gang? What made you want to pull that trigger? If you had a chance to stop the shooting would you? I am a 13 year old girl . . . and after I heard the story of what happened between you and Tariq, I learned that violence isn't the answer. For me, I want

to kill the bullies at my school but now
I will try to forgive them. I have big
dreams of becoming an artist but I don't
want violence to get in the way.

Sincerely,

B.

Marcy Morrison
TKF volunteer/former Vice President of Marketing and Sales

I'd been struggling with a misunderstanding I had with my brother regarding money from a will. I was reading spiritual books and attempting to find resolution within myself, but I really didn't have the tools necessary to deal with the issue. Through my job at the time, I ended up corresponding with Mark Fackler who was the president of TKF. I kept noticing the tag line at the end of his e-mails: *To Stop Kids From Killing Kids.*

One day I clicked on the link, and it took me to the foundation's website. When I read Azim's story, I broke down in tears. It touched me and gave me so much hope. If somebody could forgive somebody for killing his son, then I could forgive my brother for something seemingly so trivial in comparison. One thing led to another. My business meetings with Mark ended up being at the TKF offices. While there one day I noticed a box that said, *Forgiveness: The Crown Jewel of Personal Freedom.* I asked Mark what it was, and he told me that it was Azim's CD forgiveness program.

At that point I'd known I needed to forgive my brother, but I didn't have any practical tools. Finding this CD series seemed like the Universe screaming at me, 'Here is your practical tool!' And so I ended up buying the CDs, and it was incredibly healing for me. The most powerful message I received is that we go through the process of forgiveness for ourselves.

VIF Assembly student letter

Dear Tony Hicks,

I'm going to start off how you said to the judge you messed up really bad and even more because you didn't even know Tariq. And the good thing about you later, you confessed that you killed Tariq, and that you didn't say, 'I didn't kill him!' You could have a chance to say to the guy that told you to shoot Tariq, 'I don't want to do it.' Maybe you were 'afraid' they were going to do something bad to you.

F.

Donna Pinto
TKF Director of Strategic Alliances

I went through Azim's forgiveness workshop in 2006 and chose to forgive my dad and stepmom in the exercise, because those were two people I'd had the most difficulty forgiving years earlier. They were the people I'd had the most anger toward. Going through the guided meditation and getting back to that deep place of surrender was important for me. In that place I recognized that I was not still harboring those resentments, and the recognition itself was healing. The process of letting go was most helpful too, because after holding onto anger for so long, it just eats away at you.

I want to make a difference in the world, to wake people up, and to help others to feel inspired that they too can make a difference. The opportunity I have to be a part of TKF is really allowing for that to happen. It's an honor and a blessing, and every time I work toward a "Cause Marketing" partnership with a company, I feel like I'm giving them the same honor and opportunity to be a part of the work Azim and TKF are doing.

OTHER FRIENDS IN FORGIVENESS
Jim Hart, CEO Senn-Delaney Leadership

In December of 2006, Azim came and spent several hours with our company sharing his message and personal story. We'd been through a lot of changes and were in need of letting go of the past, living in the present, and refreshing our understanding the role of thought has in our lives and how it tends to dominate. Our company and Azim teach that understanding, or awareness of the role thought plays, is fundamental in creating insights and shifts for people. Those shifts can lead to some profound changes in behavior and attitudes toward life purpose. Our message is that there's a sense of spirit, of goodness, in each and every individual, and the name we have for that is "innate health."

Azim's message creates a pathway for people to connect with that state of health. As our consultants are out there working in the world, there are opportunities for them to go up and down; we call it a mood elevator. The relationships that exist can be really good at times, and they can be frayed. In those times, it's easy for people to lose connection with their wisdom of their own innate health and form judgmental relationships with others in the organization.

As we are helping leaders to create healthy, high-performing cultures in their businesses, we're teaching them about getting connected to their own innate health and operating from that space, which is the same space forgiveness comes from. It is important for me to make sure that I and the other folks in our organization really understand what forgiveness is and what that space is really all about. If we aren't grounded in our own understanding of innate health and forgiveness, and if we don't live that as part of our lives, it's very difficult to go out and consult and teach others in that scenario.

Rev. Wendy Craig-Purcell
Founding Minister, The Unity Center, San Diego

Forgiveness is emphasized in all the world's major religions. As a minister, I certainly speak about it frequently. It's one thing for me to speak about the practice of forgiveness in the kinds of situations I've had to deal with; it's quite another thing to hear someone like Azim speak about the ultimate expression of forgiveness.

Hearing him speak at one of our programs about what he felt when he got the news, hearing him describe his inner and outer journey, was powerful and left a lasting impression. One can hardly imagine a more painful and devastating life experience than losing a child in such a senseless way. To have Azim standing there, vulnerable while at the same time strong, sharing about what all that was for him—what he did with his pain, how he could see that there were victims at both ends of the gun, how he eventually moved to a place of forgiveness and then created the foundation out of his great loss—was unbelievably inspiring to me.

Knowing Azim and hearing him speak so often inspires me to keep speaking about forgiveness and to help others learn how to forgive without exceptions and to begin right where we are with the people right in front of us. Forgiveness is for the forgiver much more than for the "forgiven." Forgiveness changes the one who forgives at depth, and when we're changed, our world—and everything in it—changes for the better.

THOUGHTS ON FINDING PEACE THROUGH FORGIVENESS

I had no idea when I reached out in forgiveness to Ples first and Tony later that the impact of this gesture would have such a profound impact on my family, my community, my country, and the world. Over the last twelve years, I have given over three hundred presentations around the world in various venues—schools, colleges, churches, conferences, rallies, corporations, and organizations—and invariably the impact is the same.

People young and old, rich and poor, and of all races, religions, and cultures are deeply transformed by this universal message of forgiveness. There is so much unquenched thirst for this knowledge and wisdom in our culture. There is so much grief that needs healing. There is so much pain that needs the soothing balm of forgiveness.

To be able to provide this depth of healing to so many was way beyond anything that I had ever dreamt. Through forgiveness, I went from a tough investment banker to a healer.

This has been a blessing and a miracle in my life and continues to provide me with solace, peace, and meaning on an ongoing basis.

Thank you, Tariq, for this profound gift! I love you, my son.

Am I not destroying my enemies when I make friends of them?

— Abraham Lincoln

9/11, Terrorism, Islam and Societies

Chapter Eleven

I travel the world teaching forgiveness, and I believe with all my heart that it is only through forgiveness that we will find peace—as individuals and as nations. I was faced with the horrible tragedy of the murder of my son and yet, by the grace of my upbringing and personal spiritual practice, I was able to move from anger into forgiveness, from despair into fulfillment.

This is evidenced by how my life changed when Tariq was so brutally taken away. He made the ultimate sacrifice. The gift he left was that his death put me on my spiritual path, which is to help our children and youth seek a life away from gangs, guns, and violence. It is now my life's work to show these kids that they can choose a life of nonviolence and peacemaking. Whereas the emphasis of my life used to be on my career as an international investment banker, my purpose now is to teach the process of forgiveness to people of all ages and from all walks of life.

It is one thing for me to practice forgiveness on a personal level and to teach individuals the benefits and joys of opening their hearts to empathy, compassion, and love. But what can I say when it is an entire nation of people who have been wronged? How can I impress the concept of forgiveness upon

In June 2004, Azim took part in the "Synthesis Dialogues" with His Holiness the Dalai Lama, held at the Pope's summer residence in Castelgandolfo, Italy. The Dalai Lama told a story that still inspires Azim to this day.

individuals who have risen up in unison with the mentality of an angry mob?

VIOLENCE BEGETS VIOLENCE

9/11 was a national tragedy of great proportion. I fully understand and have participated in the pain and suffering that has taken place in its aftermath, so please do not misunderstand what I am about to say. I am not condoning the actions of the terrorists, just as I do not condone Tony's action of pulling the trigger, an action which caused the death of my son. But when does an act of violence in reaction to an act of violence ever lead to nonviolence? In the history of mankind, war has always bred new wars. Violence never has and never will be the path to peace.

Our goal should be to make sure the children of our nation and, indeed, the children of all nations grow up in a safer world, in a world where they have ample opportunities to thrive, succeed, and live healthy and prosperous lives. The goal should not be revenge. The goal should not be retaliation. And the goal, most certainly, should never be to perpetuate violence.

How can we hope to encourage our children toward choosing nonviolence in such times as they are faced with personal conflict when we, the adults to whom they look for inspiration and guidance, choose otherwise? What is our role to be? Which path do we choose as individuals, and which path do we choose as a nation?

9/11 was a horrible tragedy. It is natural to feel anger and resentment and the desire to retaliate against the terrorists who committed this violent act. But is the world any safer as a result of our national outcry for war, or is it more dangerous? Are there more or less terrorists as a result of our violent response? By choosing war, what have we modeled to the rest of the world? Did we act like peace-seeking adults, or did we put up our fists and say, "Come on, let's see what you've got"?

I understand the outcry. Believe me, as a Muslim I have cried many tears over the fact that it was people from my own faith who committed this crime. But I would also ask you to understand that these people do not represent my beliefs. The Muslim faith, like all the major religions of the world, taught me the importance of forgiveness. The terrorists are as far outside of the Muslim faith as one could possibly be. We Muslims teach compassion to our children, not aggression. We promote good faith and sincerity, not attack against the vulnerable.

These fundamentalists claim that they speak for all Muslims, but it is not so. I, like you, have my own concerns about aspects of the world around me. I, like you, work to change those things — we stick out our necks to make our world a better place. As an American and as a Muslim I choose to do this, to make my stand in this the twenty-first century. I will not order my smart, beautiful daughter into a burqa and forbid her to leave the house. I will not abolish theater and music and the simple pleasures of being alive. I will never endorse the killing of people who follow a different faith or those who simply choose to live in this world, in this time. And I am a Muslim.

For whatever it is worth to you and to our country, as we continue to deal with our national outrage and pain, I offer my own experience of grief transformed into compassionate action. After 9/11, the public outcry against terrorists was undeniably strong. But labeling these people the "enemy" only served to create divisiveness among Americans, as well as a mood of combativeness among nations. Are we winning the fight against terrorism by acting violently against the terrorists? Indeed, can this so-called war against terrorism ever be won within the context of our national strategy?

I ask you to consider our responsibility to leave this world a safer place for our children and grandchildren. How do we as a superpower want to affect the rest of our world? If our actions have created and perpetuated a climate of aggression and violence, which I believe they have, what then should our role as a nation be? Who among us will be courageous enough to call for a change to the current paradigm of justice? We, each one of us, are the only ones who can end this cycle of violence.

When I teach the students in our schools and the adults in our communities that the way to peace, contentment, and fulfillment in their own lives is through forgiveness, mustn't I then also teach that the way to a nation's peace is by way of the same path? Is it not my obligation as one who has found salvation through my son's death and through the opening of my own heart to cry out for others to find empathy and compassion within their own?

I think it is. When I reached out to Ples and then to Tony, I recognized within myself a certain level of empathy. But I admit that I did not feel that same depth of empathy toward Antoine, the eighteen-year-old gang leader who gave Tony the gun and told him to shoot. Similarly, I have a certain level of empathy for the terrorists who have been raised in an environment of hatred and revenge since they were in the womb. But I do not have the same depth of empathy for the recruiters, the people who pay money to poor parents so that they will give up their children to join the cause and become suicide bombers.

I'm being honest with you about my struggle and my process. My heart tells me to have compassion for every living being. My mind, like yours, tries to divide people up into those who are more or less deserving of my compassion. But as a teacher of forgiveness I tell you, and I remind myself, that we need to look deeper into our hearts. We need to always look for that place of empathy for the circumstances of another person's life which would lead them to choose violence as a means to an end.

Tony is a good person, but at a young age he was exposed to sexual abuse, gang violence, and neglect. He grew up angry, and his anger festered until the moment he pulled the trigger and shot my son. At first I was angry—at a society that could create an environment where children kill each other. I asked myself who this society was that was responsible for the creation of these perpetrators and victims, and I realized that it was me. Societies do not just happenstance. Every one of us is reflected individually in the collective society which we have created together. I acknowledged my personal obligation to find a way to create peace for our children. I have taken my share of the responsibility for the bullet that took my son's life, and I truly believe so should every caring American.

ISLAM

Is it possible for us to look deep inside our hearts, past our pain, past our anger, and find a place of empathy for the terrorists? Can we find a spark of compassion inside us even for those who've caused us so much suffering and who continue to do so with each passing day? Perhaps it would help if we explored a sense of national responsibility for the scars and suffering of another nation. Have we ever asked the question, "Why do they hate us so?"

For years people have been asking me how I stay on the course of forgiveness and peacemaking instead of the expected avenue of rage and revenge. Since 9/11, non-Muslims are even more curious about the teachings of my faith. After all, our news is full of militant Islam, of Muslim terrorists killing innocents and quoting the Qur'an as their guide.

True Muslims, however, recognize the course I have taken. They understand that empathy, compassion, and forgiveness are the core teachings of our faith. Perhaps you can recognize in your own traditions the teachings that have guided me. All faiths teach forgiveness and compassion and taking care of each other. All faiths admonish us not to kill. Islam speaks respectfully of all people who follow the teachings

186

of Muhammad and the prophets who preceded him in bringing God's message to the world. The Qur'an tells us that all people worship the same God.

Our prophet, our messenger, brought us the teachings that all human beings were formed into nations and tribes so that we may know one another, not conquer, subjugate, revile, or slaughter. We are taught to reach out toward others with intelligence and understanding. The Qur'an tells us that whosoever kills one innocent human being, it shall be as if he has killed all humankind, and whosoever saves the life of one, it shall be as if he has saved the life of all humankind.

As an American Muslim, I want to impress upon you that these people who kill the innocent in the name of God are not practicing the tenets of our faith as they claim. I am aggrieved for these attacks on my country just as you are. I am also aggrieved for the violent highjacking of my faith by those who pervert Islam's teachings for their own political ends.

So, too, those of other faiths must be vigilant about not doing the same. All religions of the world have their own version of the "Ethic of Reciprocity" or, as it's commonly known in its New Testament interpretation, the Golden Rule: *Do unto others as you would have them do unto you.*

No matter the religious reference, the message is the same. (The following examples of the ethic of reciprocity were found at religioustolerance.org):

- From Judaism we have, *Thou shalt love thy neighbor as thyself.*
- From Islam we learn, *None of you [truly] believes until he wishes for his brother what he wishes for himself.*

- ❧ A Native American proverb teaches, *Do not wrong or hurt your neighbor, for it is not he who you wrong, but yourself.*
- ❧ Buddhism says, *Hurt not others in ways that you yourself would find hurtful.*
- ❧ Zoroastrianism teaches, *That nature alone is good which refrains from doing unto another whatsoever is not good for its self.*

No matter what religion or faith you practice, look deeply to make sure you are not highjacking its spiritual teachings for the sake of politics. When we label someone our enemy, what are we left with besides feelings of hatred, retaliation, and aggression? When will we choose to break the cycle of violence? Perhaps it is time to reevaluate our core values as individuals and as a nation so we can come from a place of compassion not hatred, empathy not revulsion, peace not violence. We all understand that there are difficult days ahead of us. There are threats to peace, and there is a world to be healed. I think all of us want to live in a peaceful, compassionate world. I assure you that Islam shares that vision.

His Holiness the Dalai Lama

I had the good fortune in June of 2004 to spend time with His Holiness the Dalai Lama at the third annual Synthesis Dialogues. He told a beautiful story about compassion that I would like to share with you. As many of you know, the Dalai Lama was exiled from Tibet by the Chinese in 1954 when he was a young man. He now lives in India in a town called Dharamsala.

At the June gathering, he spoke about a childhood friend who had been imprisoned by the Chinese during those turbulent times. Out of about six million Tibetans, 1.2 million were murdered. The Chinese also destroyed 6400 monasteries, and they imprisoned and killed many of the monks residing in them. This particular friend of the Dalai Lama's was a high profile monk and so instead of killing him, the Chinese officials imprisoned him for many years. He was finally released after thirty years of confinement, as there was a lot of political pressure on the Chinese to release some of these monks.

The Dalai Lama's friend made the journey from China to the Himalayas to pay pilgrimage to him, the spiritual and secular head of the people of Tibet. They embraced after such a long separation. After their warm reunion, the monk told the Dalai Lama that while he was in prison, he felt an impending danger on his life.

"Were you afraid that they were going to kill you?" His Holiness asked. "Were you afraid that they were going to take your life?"

"No, I was never afraid of dying," his friend said.

"Then what is it you were afraid of?"

"The impending danger in my life," the monk said, "was that I was afraid of losing compassion for the Chinese."

Think about that. The Chinese had destroyed 6400 monasteries in his land and killed 1.2 million of his people. They had imprisoned him for thirty years, and his fear was not that he would be murdered but that he would lose compassion for his captors. When I heard that story I wept, because I truly understood the essence of his message. If he had lost compassion, what would he have replaced it with? Anger? Resentment? Revenge? These are very corrosive emotions. What was our response after 9/11? Was it compassion, or was it something

189

else? Did we have in mind the Ethic of Reciprocity? When we decided to label the terrorists our enemy and attack them in the name of our dead, what did we accomplish?

TERRORISM

Outrage at terrorism is a reasonable reaction, but hatred in our hearts serves no one, especially ourselves. Rather, compassion and empathy can replace the anger and repulsion. I do feel compassion for the young who are manipulated by the extremists to engage in violence and to become suicide bombers. I grieve for them and for their families, and I hold them all in my prayers.

As I have said before, I also pray for Tony, and I do so every day. I saw him as a victim much like I see these terrorists who give up their lives for a cause, thinking they are trading their lives on Earth for a place in heaven. In my personal tragedy, the real culprit is not the fourteen-year-old who took my son's life, but societal forces that led a young African-American boy to become a gang member. It was that life which led him to hold a gun on a dark street and kill an unarmed, innocent pizza-delivery man to prove himself to the gang.

If you were to hang Tony from the highest pole because he killed my one and only son, how would that improve society? But if I forgive him and create room for him to redeem himself, and if I offer him a space to join the foundation and help make sure other kids do not make the same fatal choices that he made, do you not now improve society? I think you will agree that you do.

Concentrating on fixing the societal deficiencies leading to violence will eventually allow us to become a peaceful, compassionate, and nonviolent culture. Continually holding hatred in our hearts and seeking revenge will only lead to more violence. Are there fewer terrorists in the world today than there were on September 10, 2001? No, there are not. Can we create a peaceful world out of the resentment we hold as individuals and in the heart of our nation? I don't believe so. When will the overwhelming strength of our public outcry be for a path to peace?

When you look at the terrorist attacks, you have to look beyond the actual attack and ask yourself, "What are the societal forces that created the terrorist in the first place?" What part did we Americans play in the creation of these extremists? This notion may not appeal to you, but remember that Osama bin Laden was once an American ally whom we armed and taught to help fight the Russians in Afghanistan during the Cold War.

What foreign policies do we now have in place and what past policies have contributed to the current uprising of hatred against our country? How many times have our foreign policies backfired? What have we learned from these mistakes? Are we truly innocent? Or when we look deep into our hearts do we see that if we had made a different choice—even the more difficult one of nonviolence—we could have caused an entirely different set of circumstances to emerge?

I am not bashing America. There are too many wonderful things about our country, and I, myself, am a first-generation American. I came to the United States in 1974 fleeing the violence of Idi Amin's regime in Uganda, which was spilling over into my birthplace, Kenya. In leaving Africa, we lost everything material, but we gained something far more valuable—a safe and peaceful homeland.

When my children were growing up, I told them that my greatest gift to them was to live in this blessed, safe country. When I pledged allegiance to the United States of America as one of its newest citizens, I was filled with joy and pride. But the rage that followed Tariq's funeral burned away that pride. I felt I had made a fatal mistake bringing my family here. My American-born son had been killed on a street in the country I chose for my family, and I considered leaving. But where was there to go? My love for this country was stronger than my rage, and common sense told me that there was no place on Earth where I could escape the loss of my son. I had to stay, and I had to fight. I had to make some sense of the rest of my life.

People around me were expecting my anger to focus on Tariq's killer. But that made no sense to me. An eye for an eye? The wise Hindu Gandhi reminded us, "An eye for an eye and soon the whole world is blind." Tariq's life had been taken, but why would I want the life of his killer? He was a child himself who had lost what remained of his own childhood. He would surely lose much of his adulthood as well.

I somehow knew that the rest of my life depended totally on my reaction to Tariq's murder, and for a life to have quality, it must have spiritual purpose. So, too, does a nation need to have spiritual purpose in order to have quality. And if a nation's purpose is set in revenge, the heart of its people will continue to suffer.

FINDING EMPATHY

I do not like everything about the times we live in, and I am not in harmony with the aggression displayed toward us. But I do wonder what our national response would be if we contemplated our role as participants on the world stage of violence. We have often been the aggressors, taking the steps of violence toward our own political ends. We as individuals and as a nation have not always acted perfectly, and we seem to be caught in a spinning wheel of reactive violence to which there is no beginning and no end.

War begets war. This is a fact of history. And violence begets violence. War is a Band-Aid fix, a temporary or expedient remedy. As long as the scars of hatred, resentment, and revenge linger, the wounds of our nation will never be completely healed, and we will always remain vulnerable to the next violent act. True, there is a threat to be stopped and a world to be healed, but every faith and every great teacher of ethics and morality has taught us the same basic truth: Do unto others what you would have them do unto you.

What I'm proposing is empathy at all levels. It will take courage to shift the paradigm from violence to peacemaking. Surely there will be a price to be paid, but if we stay on this same path of retaliation and violence, there is a great price to be paid anyway. I sincerely acknowledge the men and women in our military who are putting their lives on the line in service to their country. When I say I am against war, I am not saying I am against our troops. I greatly admire their courage and patriotism, but it breaks my heart that we are losing so many of our young souls to war. I would much rather see our military train peacemakers, not soldiers, and have them be armed with compassion, not guns.

Waging war is an expensive enterprise. The war on Iraq has cost thousands of lives and hundreds of billions of dollars. Most people can't imagine that amount of money. I say, if you count one thousand one, one thousand two, it would take twenty-one years to count to a billion. Think of the transformations we could have made on behalf of our nation's youth and the youth of the world had we put that amount of money into efforts toward peace and compassion.

Choosing to live in a paradigm of forgiveness, we will at times be vulnerable to aggression, but the sacrifices made in the name of forgiveness will eventually create a peace dividend. The sacrifices being made every day in the name of violence and retaliation will never do the same.

I am very proud to say that we Americans have developed an incredible nation in two hundred short years. I feel fortunate to be accepted as a naturalized citizen of this great country, and, in turn, I pledge to always uphold America's values and commit myself to diligently serving my country and its people. Our free democratic, meritocratic, economic model is one of the best in the world, and we do share this with gusto. As one of the wealthiest and most successful nations on the planet, we enjoy freedom. I have always said that one of the things I love most about our country is that it epitomizes hope. Think about it— you can be a bodybuilder and become the governor of California! Another example is Oprah, born a poor, African-American girl in the South and abused as a child, only to become one of the most powerful icons in the world.

These kinds of opportunities are available to all Americans. They are something we should celebrate and in which we can take immense pride. However, when you compare our social model to our economic or technological model, it is pathetic. A myriad of social ills plague our country — homelessness, child slavery, teen prostitution, kids joining gangs, kids killing kids, children without health insurance, the plight of our inner cities, and domestic violence, to name only a few.

I often wonder why we can't build a social model that rivals our economic and technological platforms. Maybe that should be our main focus in this millennium. We desperately need to create an equal importance and focus for the social infrastructure of our society. I would love to see all of you who are successful business people and professionals to be inspired and to double and treble your efforts to help establish this model. Maybe we all need to become social entrepreneurs as exemplified by Bill and Melinda Gates and Warren Buffet. This would be the best gift we could give, because what happens in America eventually happens elsewhere in the world.

My life totally changed as a result of losing Tariq. Sometimes tragedies destroy you, and sometimes they make you a better person. In my case I thank the good Lord and my mother (who had a profound impact on my spiritual life) that I had the eyes to transcend the negative and arrive at a positive place by choosing forgiveness. I sometimes wonder what my life would have been if I had gone the other way.

UNPRECEDENTED OPPORTUNITIES

I am a passionate person, and had I chosen retribution and revenge, I could have done a lot of harm to myself, my son's spirit, and my family. To be sure, I would not have written my books and would have missed all the good that has come into my life. I would also have missed the good that the foundation has done for the kids in our country.

I have learned that hearts burning with hatred will not be changed overnight. But I will continue to reach out with my story and my compassion in the hope that I can help to transform other people's lives one heart at a time. I ask for your help in this great task. I am proposing to you a way of being consistent with the theme of forgiveness, which I acknowledge is sometimes very hard to do.

It is likely that the more hardened the criminal, the more victimization that person has endured. It is often those who act in the most terrible ways who have been treated the most horribly in their own lives. In the case of terrorists, they have been raised on hatred from the moment they take their first breath. As a nation, we must see that we are also responsible for teaching intolerance and hatred to our young. As soon as you label another individual or group as your enemy, an environment of revenge and aggression is created. It simply cannot be any other way.

There truly is no enemy. We are all children of the Universe. We are all connected to and by the same spirit. I believe that we as a human race must learn to create brotherhood, sisterhood, and unity from conflict. It is only when we begin to act like true family who would not want for others what they would not want for themselves that we will be on our way to peace. My heart reaches out to you to join me in my work.

As I previously mentioned, Ples and I would never have met had his grandson not murdered my son. Meeting under such dire circumstances, and further divided by race and religion, we were successful in forging a loving relationship as brothers and have now been together for over twelve years doing the work of TKF. This demonstrates that from conflict, love, unity, brotherhood, and sisterhood are possible. Both Ples and I are ordinary citizens. Neither one of us is trained in divinity or has any other special qualifications. We are working stiffs much like anyone else in our society. If I, an investment banker—which means that I have a Ph.D. in greed and avarice—and Ples, a two-tour Green Beret during the Vietnam War, who was part of the Special Forces and trained to kill, can come together as brothers in forgiveness, surely we can all do this.

Let's imagine for a moment that President Bush, Vice President Cheney, Ex-Secretary Rumsfeld, Osama bin Laden, the late Saddam Hussein, President Sharon, and the late PLO leader Yasser Arafat had all been TKF graduates and chosen to create unity and brotherhood out of conflict. What would the world look like today?

I acknowledge that conflict is part of life. There is conflict between spouses, ex-spouses, father-son, mother-daughter, peers, business partners, and in many other relationships in our lives. Conflict is not going to go away. What is important is that we shift our paradigm about conflict and view it as an opportunity to create brotherhood, sisterhood, love, and unity.

Unless we are able to do this, the human race will perish. When you look at 9/11 from this light as an opportunity to create unity, you can see that there are many other options we could have pursued besides those actions based in revenge and violence. Nonviolent options could have led to promoting peace, saving lives, escaping the grief of families who have lost sons and daughters to war, and saving many hundreds of billions of dollars better spent to strengthen and reform the social infrastructure of our society.

From this vantage point, 9/11 presented us with a singularly unprecedented opportunity for this generation to create a better world—a more peaceful world. If we only would have had the collective courage to choose forgiveness, we could have turned this conflict into a path to peace. I am not suggesting that I have all the answers to the complicated conflicts in the world. However, I do believe it is important that we engage in a serious national and global conversation to answer the questions I've posed in this chapter. I believe that the solutions which come from our collective conscious will provide answers to these questions. More importantly, the solutions will create love, unity, and a peaceful world that is safe for our children, one that gives them hope and opportunity to prosper and build a new and better world.

We Americans can cause all this to happen. It is our place in history to do so, but so far the national will is lacking. How will we find the courage and the determination to shift our consciousness to one of peace? We must begin small, in our own neighborhoods, in our own families. We must begin in our own hearts.

As a guide to this inner transformation, I would like to share with you my "Peace Formula," which came to me in an inspired moment soon after the 9/11 tragedy.

- *Sustained goodwill creates friendship.*
- *Sustained friendship creates trust.*
- *Sustained trust creates compassion.*
- *Sustained compassion creates peace.*

People ask me, "How do you extend goodwill to the person who killed your son?" I tell them it is through forgiveness.

As it is evident, it worked for me. As it is evident, it worked for my family. As it is evident, it worked for Tony. And as it is also evident, it worked for his family. It can work for you. It can work for your family. It can work for the United States of America. Indeed, it can work for the entire world!

Peace, my sisters and brothers, is possible. How do I know this is so? Because I am at peace.

*The forgiven world becomes the gate of Heaven, because
by its mercy we can at last forgive ourselves. Holding no
one prisoner to guilt, we become free. Acknowledging Christ
in all our brothers, we recognize His Presence in ourselves.
Forgetting all our misperceptions, and with nothing from
the past to hold us back, we can remember God.*

— A Course in Miracles

Fulfillment

Chapter Twelve

I have so often said that when I heard the news of Tariq's murder, I felt like a nuclear bomb had gone off in my heart. Shattered and crumbling, I spontaneously left my body and fell into the arms of my God. Here, in the peace and all-knowingness that is our true nature, I understood that there was not a perpetrator and a victim. I understood that both Tony and Tariq were victims of this tragedy. And I understood that I could no longer sit idly by and let the children of my beloved country continue killing each other.

With the love, support, and guidance of my loved ones and my spiritual teachers, my heart found a way to express my desire to help other children keep from making the violent choices that would put them in prison for the rest of their lives. I found a way to express my dream of helping kids learn to make peaceful and nonviolent choices so that other children wouldn't die the kind of senseless, violent death that Tariq did.

After the forty days of ritual mourning were over, I began to take steps toward this dream. With each step taken, I moved deeper into compassion. Nine months after my son's death, I held the first meeting of the Tariq Khamisa Foundation. At the second meeting, Ples met my family—Tariq's mother, sister, grandmother, and grandfather—and he joined me in my efforts to stop kids from killing kids.

Twelve years since the loss of his son, Azim has found fulfillment through the practice of forgiveness. "We know that we are here to do something wonderful" he says. "We know that we are meant to live fulfilling lives and to share our joy with others."

A Generation of Peacemakers

Now, twelve years later, I am privileged to be working with youth on both ends of the gun. I'm proud to say that TKF has grown into a fully independent nonprofit organization. Through our comprehensive prevention programs, we are teaching young students that they can choose self-respect and peace instead of gangs and violence. We are, indeed, creating a generation of peacemakers.

For at-risk kids who are already on the slippery slope and headed toward lives of continued violence, we have Constant and Never Ending Improvement. As one of NYAP's many programs serving youth and families, CANEI is flourishing and standing out as an innovative and successful approach to at-risk youth care and support. Our programs are continually evolving so we can serve even more youths in even more communities.

Today, I have good relationships with everyone in my family, with my staff and co-workers, and with my friends, old and new. Compassion has grown within me on a soulular level and I feel a warmth in my heart that I truly thought I would never know. It nurtures me like the warmth of the sun nurtures all living things. I feel truly blessed to be living a genuine, authentic, and purposeful life, and I am grateful to my son for the sacrifice he made which put me on my spiritual path. His death was a part of his own destiny, and it was also a part of mine.

Tragedy can sometimes destroy a person. It almost destroyed me. I spent weeks barely able to get out of bed. But with purpose in mind, and with the knowledge that I could help Tariq on his soul's journey by the spiritual currency of good deeds, I was able to begin to heal. Slowly at first. One day at a time. But eventually, I grew stronger both in body and in mind. As I began to work with kids, sitting with Ples, telling our story over and over again, my heart also began to heal. Every time I spoke about Tariq's death, the pain came back and the scab came off. I began to notice over time that the wound grew smaller. We have now reached millions of kids with our messages of peace and nonviolence through TKF's *Violence Impact Forum* assemblies and direct broadcasts into the classrooms.

If we choose to let tragedy destroy us, there can be no light to share with others. Dark cannot destroy dark. It is only light can transform the darkness. I found light through my compassion for the boy who shot and killed my only son. I found light through my brotherhood with his grandfather, who committed himself to helping my family in the work we are doing at TKF. Ples has truly become a brother to me, and my relationship with Tony is deepening. I look forward to the day when he joins TKF and works alongside his grandfather and me.

Through the healing of my relationships with others, I also found more light. And in that light, I found forgiveness for myself. Though at one time I was spiraling down into the depths of despair and darkness, the continual opening of my heart through compassion and forgiveness eventually brought me to fulfillment. I did not know it was there waiting for me, and perhaps you do not know it is also there waiting for you. But I can tell you that it is. When you get on the path, when you find your direction and purpose, you will find that fulfillment awaits you just as it did me.

Quantum science tells us what sages have been telling us for eons. Every living thing is vibrating energy. Negative emotions keep us vibrating at a low frequency. And from a low-frequency life, you can never reach fulfillment. If you think about this, you will know in your heart that it is true. Feeling anger, hatred, resentment, bitterness, self-pity, or guilt prevents you from feeling the more positive emotions of empathy, love, compassion, joy, self-love, and fulfillment.

When you choose to release the negativity and allow your heart to open to forgiveness and love, you will begin to vibrate at a higher frequency. This in turn will allow you to attract more love into your life. This is one of the spiritual laws of the Universe called the law of attraction. Like attracts like. So when you come from a place of positive emotion, you will attract more of the same into your life. Likewise, if you continue to choose anger and resentment, this will be your fate.

I found fulfillment through my work with TKF and CANEI and through my healed relationships. But it is not a stagnant thing. The more time I spend helping others find fulfillment on their own paths, the more fulfilled I am. It is circular. It is truly a circle of love moving out, coming back, and moving out again. My heart is full, and my soul is climbing to new heights with my son's spirit by my side. He is ever present. And I know that he is pleased with all that has transpired since the day of his passing.

Tariq often said that he wanted to leave a mark on this world. His sister, Tasreen, said, "When I think about Tariq now, I see him beaming. That's the image I get when I close my eyes, and I see a lot of joy in him and around him. I know that's how he is right now in life, smiling down at everything that's being done in his name."

From Forgiveness to Fulfillment

In the twelve years since Tariq's death, I have transformed my forgiveness into fulfillment. It is not something I strived for or wrote out as a life goal. Fulfillment is not something you can plan. It is a seed that grows within your heart and soul through living a life of spiritual purpose. The way to your own fulfillment is by choosing a path of peace, by letting go of negative, hurtful emotions, and by sowing your own seeds of transformation through empathy, compassion, goodwill, and forgiveness. It is by living a life of love—self-love and love for others—that you will find your own spiritual purpose, for it cannot be found in the darkness. It can only be found in the light.

Nobody is perfect. I still have moments where anger begins to rise, but I choose to pre-empt it before the anger has a chance to take hold. I live with integrity toward the principles I teach, and I have made the choice to live a peaceful and nonviolent life. Through my work of helping others to heal their pain and suffering, I live in an open-heart environment where I vibrate at the higher frequencies of love and forgiveness. The more I love, the more love I attract. The more love I attract, the more fulfilled I am.

When you live in an open-heart environment, you wear your heart on your sleeve. With all the teaching I do—by spending so much time with people who are being transformed by my message of forgiveness—I find that my tears often flow. I cry easily because I have a very open heart. And in this heart space, natural shifts continue to occur in my life. I move deeper and deeper into compassion, and I move higher and higher into love.

Many people struggle with understanding their purpose in life. We can easily get sidetracked by choosing paths that do not satisfy our souls. But deep inside, we know that we are here to do something wonderful. We know that we are meant to live fulfilling lives and to share our joy with others. Each of us is a spiritual being in physical form, and each of us has a unique soulprint. While I am not able to tell anyone else what his or her own life path is, I can tell you that when you are on path, when you are living your spiritual purpose, you will also be serving humanity.

When you find yourself on your spiritual path, the Universe will work in partnership with you. Through my story, day after day kids and adults are being transformed. Their hearts empathize with my loss and with the choice I made to forgive Tony, and through their empathy they open to compassion. Through their compassion, their desire increases to reach out to others in forgiveness. And through their forgiveness, their own hearts are healed.

As other people heal, I heal further. My story shows that something meaningful can come from something meaningless. As I wrote about in the Forgiveness chapters, when Tariq died my wound was the size of Jupiter. Today, my wound has diminished and has shrunk to the size of planet Earth. When I lost my son, the capacity of my vessel to hold the divine spirit was the size of a wine barrel. Today, I feel like the capacity of my vessel is the size of the state of California.

I know I am now a better person. By connecting with the higher power in me, I am now able to serve humanity in a much bigger and better way. As I contemplate the completion of this book I meditate, and all I see are beautiful skies ahead. My fulfillment will continue to deepen, and my capacity to hold the divine spirit will continue to increase.

It is my most sincere wish that you will find fulfillment in your own lives. Choose forgiveness and allow the light to flow back into your hearts. Allow the sadness to dissipate and realize that when you shine brightly, others will be inspired by your example. The more people who shine—the more people who are inspired toward love, compassion, and forgiveness—the more healed souls will walk this Earth in harmony and unity.

We often feel alone, but we truly are not. In spirit, in truth, we are all connected and we are all the same. There is no enemy; there is no victim. There is no past, there is no future. There is only Now and the choices we make in each moment to hate or to love. When we choose forgiveness, our suffering is transformed. And through this transformation and fulfillment of our spiritual purpose, our hearts reach out to embrace our brothers and sisters in spiritual unity. I ask you to please join with me on this path. When you choose forgiveness, you are helping me to heal our world one loving heart at a time.

Afterword

Azim Khamisa's contribution to a world without violence is perhaps more vital today than at any other time. As I sit writing this afterword, our nation is informed by the media that gang violence is at an all time high. On television we see graphic depictions of young men killing other young men, women and children in meaningless wars, as well as other forms of violence such as nationalism, corporate greed, genocide, the plunging of our planet's natural resources, to name a few. Azim shines a bright light of hope for all of us at the point where all change begins: within our own individual hearts.

Azim's life and his life's work are one and the same: examples of the courage of a mind and heart ablaze with the utmost faith in the inherent capacity of human beings to forgive one another, which results in a world infused with love, peace, and a level of respect that honors the dignity of all beings. His home-grown yet revolutionary programs for youth are not motivated by the sociological statistics created by academia, but from his personal experience of tremendous loss, grief, and anger over the murder of his beloved son, Tariq. And, like others who have contributed to the upliftment of our world, he first worked in the laboratory of his own heart to bring about a transformation from anguish and anger to forgiveness and love.

It has been my privilege to attend several of Azim's seminars. They always brought to my mind the words of Jesus the Christ when he said to "forgive seventy times seven," a statement which also acknowledges the challenges inherent in the act of forgiveness. Azim walked triumphant through those challenges, and now he is teaching countless youth and adults how to do the same.

From Forgiveness to Fulfillment underscores the teaching of Dr. Martin Luther King Jr., who tells us that the act of forgiving "must always be initiated by the person who has been wronged, the victim of some great hurt, the recipient of some torturous injustice, the absorber of some terrible act of oppression. Without this, no man can love his enemies. The degree to which we are able to forgive determines the degree to which we are able to love our enemies." This echoes the teachings of Gandhi and Jesus about separating the doer from the deed: "Forgive them for they know not what they do," which is exactly the premise of Azim's work that victims are "at both ends of the gun."

The question is: Will we practice the principles in Azim's programs to transform our individual lives and therefore our world? I personally ask all of you who have read this book to recommend his programs and books to schools, organizations — anywhere you believe that the methods for achieving peace and harmony are needed.

As the Hindu *Mahabharata* reminds us: "Forgiveness is the might of the mighty. Forgiveness is holiness; by forgiveness the universe is held together." Let us all — each and every one of us—apply the heart-centered practices taught by Azim Khamisa for holding together our world by the might of forgiveness and love.

Michael Bernard Beckwith
author of *A Manifesto of Peace*
July 2007

Epilogue

From murder to forgiveness. From forgiveness to fulfillment. This has been my journey for the past twelve years. Today, I am no longer a victim, and I have committed my life to peace, nonviolence, and forgiveness. Because most of my time is spent in the higher vibrations of love and compassion, the energy I lost when Tariq died has returned to me and multiplied. I use this strength to serve humanity, and it is through the service of teaching forgiveness to children, youth, and adults that I have attained true fulfillment in my life.

There is one more book on my heart, which is titled, *From Fulfillment to Enlightenment.* This will be my next frontier. Just as I lived and breathed forgiveness when I wrote my first book, and fulfillment as I wrote this one, my next book will rise from that place in my heart that is completely at peace . . . Enlightenment.

I will meet you there, Inshallah, God willing. Namaste.

Resources

The Tariq Khamisa Foundation (TKF)
7490 Opportunity Rd., Suite 202
San Diego CA 92111
(858) 565-0800
www.tkf.org

- ✍ *Ending the Cycle of Violence* video series
- ✍ *Violence Impact Forum Assembly*
- ✍ *Seeds of Hope Society*

Azim Khamisa - ANK Enterprises, Inc.
www.AzimKhamisa.com
(858) 452-2541

- ✍ *Azim's Bardo: From Murder to Forgiveness, A Father's Journey*
- ✍ *Forgiveness: The Crown Jewel of Personal Freedom* CD set
- ✍ *Complimentary Guided Meditation*

CANEI, IYAF, AND NYAP

CANEI (Constant and Never Ending Improvement)
> 4305 University Ave., Suite 520
> San Diego CA 92105
> (619) 819-5503
> www.canei.org

NYAP (National Youth Advocate Program)
> 3780 Mill Ridge Dr
> Hilliard OH 43026
> (888) 688-9964
> www.nyap.org

IYAF (International Youth Advocate Foundation)
Mubarak Awad (mawad@iyaf.org)
> 4545 42nd St NW, Suite 209
> Washington DC 20016
> (202) 244-6410
> www.iyaf.org

RESTORATIVE JUSTICE

Center for Restorative Justice and Peacemaking at the School of Social Work, University of Minnesota

  1404 Gortner Ave, 105 Peters Hall

  St. Paul MN 55108-6160

  (612) 624-4923

  www.rjp.umn.edu/index.html

VORP (Victim-Offender Reconciliation Program) Information and Resource Center

  PO Box 306

  Asheville NC 28802

  (828) 301-6211

  www.vorp.com

Peace, Forgiveness and Violence Prevention

The Peace Alliance (Campaign to establish a U.S. Department of Peace)
www.thepeacealliance.org

Marianne Williamson's website:
www.marianne.com

Dr. Michael Beckwith
Agape International Spiritual Center
5700 Buckingham Parkway
Culver City CA 90230
(310) 348-1250
www.agapelive.com

Children's Defense Fund
25 E Street NW
Washington DC 20001
(800) 233-1200
www.childrensdefense.org

M.K. Gandhi Institute for Nonviolence
c/o University of Rochester
510 Wilson Commons
Rochester NY 14627-0423
(585) 276-3787
www.gandhiinstitute.org

Chariot Videos: Victress Hitchcock
PO Box 7509
Boulder Co 80306
(303) 449-4528
www.chariotvideos.com

PERSONAL DEVELOPMENT

Klemmer & Associates, Inc., Leadership and Character Development
  1340 Commerce St, Suite G
  Petaluma CA 94954
  (800) 577-5447
  www.klemmer.com

Senn-Delaney Leadership
  3780 Kilroy Airport Way, Suite 800
  Long Beach CA 90806
  (562) 426-5400
  www.senndelaney.com

Mabel Katz (Ho'oponopono: *The Easiest Way*)
  www.mabelkatz.com
  www.businessbyyou.com
  (877) 262-7470

Stranded!

They were about a mile from Janie's house when Ross's blue Civic sputtered and died.

"What's the matter?" Janie asked shrilly. She glanced out the passenger window. She could see only dark woods. No house, no store, no streetlights.

"Out of gas," Ross moaned.

He turned to her, his dark eyes glowing.

She shrank back against the car door.

Faith, Paul, and Ian warned me. They warned me not to go with Ross.

Cold panic rolled down her body.

They were out in the middle of nowhere, she realized.

There was no one to help her.

No one.

Books by R. L. Stine

Available from ARCHWAY Paperbacks

FEAR STREET®
R·L·STINE

The New Boy

A Parachute Press Book

AN ARCHWAY PAPERBACK
Published by POCKET BOOKS
New York   London   Toronto   Sydney   Tokyo   Singapore

AN ARCHWAY PAPERBACK *Original*

An Archway Paperback published by
POCKET BOOKS, a division of Simon & Schuster Inc.
1230 Avenue of the Americas, New York, NY 10020

Copyright © 1994 by Parachute Press, Inc.

All rights reserved, including the right to reproduce
this book or portions thereof in any form whatsoever.
For information address Pocket Books, 1230 Avenue
of the Americas, New York, NY 10020

ISBN: 0-671-73869-0

First Archway Paperback printing January 1994

10 9 8 7 6 5 4 3 2 1

FEAR STREET is a registered trademark of
Parachute Press, Inc.

AN ARCHWAY PAPERBACK and colophon are
registered trademarks of Simon & Schuster Inc.

Cover art by Bill Schmidt

Printed in the U.S.A.

IL 7+

chapter

1

Two weeks before the murder, Janie Simpson saw the new boy at Shadyside High for the first time.

The boy was good-looking. He had the smooth, graceful stride of a natural athlete. He was tall and lean. His slender face, topped by curly brown hair, had a solemn expression. Janie wondered if he ever smiled.

Studying him, Janie couldn't stop staring at his eyes. Dark, brooding eyes.

Troubled eyes, she thought.

Sad eyes.

She had to blink to interrupt her gaze. She could feel her face growing hot.

Big deal. So the guy has great eyes, Janie thought,

turning her head into her gray locker as he passed her. Why am I being so melodramatic?

Two Tigers cheerleaders passed by in their short-skirted maroon and white outfits. Janie recognized Corky Corcoran and her friend Kimmy Bass. They were giggling and shoving each other playfully.

Janie turned back and watched the new boy disappear around a corner. Had he noticed her? She didn't think so.

"Janie, you've *got* to get a life," she scolded herself, muttering in a low voice.

The bell above the lockers rang loudly, startling Janie. She tossed her books to the floor of her locker. The hall was nearly empty now. Most kids had headed home or to their after-school jobs.

Janie wanted to get home to work on her social studies term paper. But she had a job to do first.

She started to slam the locker shut but changed her mind. Pulling the door open all the way, she glanced impatiently at herself in the small mirror attached to the door.

She smoothed her straight red hair with quick motions of one hand. She wore it long and layered. She rubbed a smudge of dirt off her pale, creamy cheek.

Blue eyes stared back at her. She straightened the blue shirt she had on over a yellow tank top.

Janie was short and very thin. She usually wore a lot of layers. It was the look she liked, but her friends Faith and Eve teased her about it, saying she was just trying to look bigger.

"Boys don't notice you because they can't see you," Faith joked.

Janie could hear Faith's teasing voice in her mind. "You have the figure of a model and dress like a bag lady."

Faith had natural good looks. She was blond and fresh looking, bubbly, an all-American cheerleader type. She never got tired of giving Janie tips on clothes and makeup.

But Janie never wore makeup. And she really didn't want to look like a faded version of Faith. She wanted to look like her own person. She just wasn't sure who that person was.

Where *are* Faith and Eve anyway? Janie asked herself, glancing down the empty hall. She slammed her locker shut. Maybe they're already at Mr. Hernandez's office, waiting for me. Maybe they've started counting the money without me.

She began jogging toward the principal's office at the front of the building. Two teachers walked by, buttoning their raincoats, heading to the parking lot. A rumble of cheers floated up from cheerleader practice downstairs in the gym.

I hope we can count the money quickly, Janie thought. I've got so much homework tonight.

She and her two friends had been in charge of the committee for the school dance. And now they had to count up the receipts and hand the money over to Mr. Hernandez, the new principal.

There was a lot of money to count. The dance had been a real success. A *financial* success, not a *personal* success, Janie thought with some bitterness.

Eve and Faith both had had dates. Faith showed up with Paul Gordon, of course. They'd been going together for weeks. And Eve came to the dance with her boyfriend, Ian Smith.

Janie sighed as she turned the corner and the principal's office came into view. Of the three, only Janie didn't have a boyfriend.

She had gone to the dance anyway. She really had to, since she was one of those in charge. She danced with a few guys. But she didn't really have a good time. She kept watching Faith and Eve with their boyfriends and had to fight back feelings of jealousy and loneliness.

That was Saturday night. Now it was the following Monday. The first day of the rest of my life, Janie thought. Whatever that means.

She passed the printed sign on the wall— PETER HERNANDEZ, PRINCIPAL—pulled open the door, and burst into the outer office. "Sorry I'm late, guys—"

Janie stopped short when she realized the office was empty.

Where *were* Eve and Faith?

She took a few steps toward the inner office. The door was slightly ajar and the lights were on. "Anyone here?"

No reply.

I'll bet Faith is hanging out with Paul, Janie thought. She's probably making him late for basketball practice.

4

But where's Eve? She can't be with Ian. Ian has an after-school job.

Janie glanced at the big clock on the wall. Nearly a quarter to three. She pulled both hands through her long red hair, then shook her head to smooth it out.

Suddenly the door to the hallway swung open, and Eve hurried in. Eve had dark, dramatic looks. Her long, sleek hair shone almost blue-black under the ceiling light. Her olive eyes flashed excitedly.

"Did you hear the news?" she asked Janie breathlessly. "Deena Martinson broke up with Gary Brandt!"

"Huh?" Janie's mouth dropped open. "They were at the dance together Saturday night. Where'd you hear that?"

"I was just talking with Deena," Eve said, pushing her black hair over the shoulders of her lime-green sweater. "She's upset, but not too bad. She said they're still friends."

Janie nodded thoughtfully. "How come you always know everything before anyone else?"

"It's easy to know things before *you* do," Eve teased. "You never know anything!"

Janie forced a halfhearted laugh. "Well, we can't wait for Faith," she said, moving to the round table against the wall. "Let's get started. Where's the money?"

"Huh?" Eve's dark eyes grew wide with surprise.

"The money," Janie repeated impatiently. "Where is it?"

"I thought *you* had it!" Eve cried.

Janie felt her throat tighten. She had a sudden heavy feeling in the pit of her stomach.

"Come on, Eve," she said, trying to stay calm. "You were supposed to pick the money up from Mrs. Fritz last period."

The light in Eve's eyes faded. Her expression grew solemn. "Faith picked up the money for me this morning," she told Janie. "She put it in her locker. But when it wasn't there after school, she figured *you* took it."

Janie gasped. "But I didn't!" she cried shrilly. "I didn't!"

"Oh, no," Eve moaned, shaking her head. "That means—that means it's been *stolen!*"

chapter

2

Janie felt her throat tighten even more. She swallowed hard, trying to fight down a sick feeling.

"Eve," she cried. "We—we're responsible. It's over a thousand dollars. If—if—" The room was spinning. She couldn't think clearly.

Eve tugged at her sleeve. "Come on. Let's go find Faith. Quick."

The two girls hurried down the empty hall. The shouts of the cheerleaders floated up from the gym. Several teachers were huddled in front of a water fountain, laughing.

Janie didn't feel like laughing. She felt like crying.

If the money really was stolen, how would they ever pay it back? And would *they* be accused of stealing it?

No. No way. That couldn't happen, she assured herself.

They found Faith at her locker. She was brushing her blond hair.

"Faith—the money!" Janie cried in a shrill, frightened voice. "Did you find it? Do you have it?"

"Of course," Faith replied casually. She pulled a green canvas bag from her locker. "It's right here."

Faith turned to Eve, and her expression changed. "Oh, Eve—you promised you wouldn't pull that stupid joke on Janie!" she exclaimed.

Eve burst out laughing, her olive eyes sparkling.

"That was too mean!" Faith cried. "We decided not to do it."

"I—I couldn't resist," Eve declared through her laughter. She grabbed both of Janie's slender shoulders and hung on. "I'm sorry. I'm really sorry. But— the look on your face. It was worth it for the look on your face!" She started laughing all over again, hugging Janie and laughing at the same time.

Faith shook her head disapprovingly, but she also started to laugh.

"Some friends," Janie grumbled. Angrily she pulled away from Eve. "You're both *awful*. I can't believe you'd be so mean."

"It was just a joke," Eve said, wiping the tears of laughter from her eyes.

"Ha-ha," Janie replied bitterly.

"You really shouldn't have," Faith told Eve, tucking her hairbrush into the little compartment of her backpack. "You know what a worrier Janie is."

"I'm sorry, Janie," Eve said again, forcing her dark features into a serious expression. "Really."

"Let's just go count the money," Janie said impatiently, picking up the canvas bag. "The sooner we turn it over to Mr. Hernandez, the better."

She started back toward the office, Faith and Eve following close behind.

Janie had just turned the corner when she saw the new boy again.

First she saw his dark, troubled eyes. Then she saw the twisted expression on his pale face.

She gasped when she saw the puddle of bright blood on the floor at his feet.

"Please—help me," he called to her.

And then she saw the blood dripping down his arm.

chapter

3

With a cry of alarm Janie rushed forward. Her two friends quickly followed.

The boy was breathing hard. His features revealed that he was in pain.

Blood spread over the white sleeve of his shirt.

"What happened?" Eve cried.

"It—it's not as bad as it looks," the boy said, holding his sleeve. "Really."

"But the blood—" Faith started to say.

Janie hung back, holding the money sack in both hands at her waist, like a shield.

"If you could help me find the nurse's office—" he said. "I'm new here. I don't know where it is."

"I'll take you," Faith declared, grabbing his uninjured arm.

"I'll go, too," Eve said quickly. "Her office is up those stairs. She usually stays late. What happened?"

"A stupid accident," he said, shaking his head, his brown hair falling over his forehead. He glanced at Janie. "I was trying to help a girl. Outside. Her bike got stuck in the fence. You know. Behind the parking lot."

He grimaced in pain.

Janie glanced down at the puddle of blood on the floor.

"When I pulled her bike free," he continued, "the wire cut right through my arm. Just sliced it."

"Let's see if the nurse is still there," Faith urged, holding on to the boy's arm. "What's your name?"

"Ross Gabriel," he said.

Faith and Eve were leading Ross away. "I—I'd better take the money to the office," Janie called after them.

Her two friends were talking to Ross and didn't reply.

"Meet me there, okay?" Janie shouted.

They disappeared around the corner.

Stepping around the bloodstain, Janie headed glumly toward the office, the heavy canvas bag under one arm.

"It's not fair," she muttered to herself. "I saw him first."

Janie had dumped the money onto the round table in the outer office and was sorting the bills when Faith and Eve returned. "Did you find the nurse?" she asked, glancing up from the piles of money.

Faith nodded, a smile on her face. "Yeah. We saved Ross's life. He owes us big now."

"I think I'm in love!" Eve gushed.

"He's real cute," Faith quickly agreed, taking a seat at the table. "Do you think he ever smiles?"

"Who cares?" Eve replied, picking up a stack of ones and flicking them through her fingers. "He's terrific. Where'd he come from?"

Faith shrugged. "I like his eyes. It's like they're staring right through you. He kept looking at me like—"

"You know, I saw him first!" Janie blurted out, surprised by the anger in her voice.

Faith's eyes widened in surprise. "Janie, you liked him? You didn't say a single word to him."

"Why didn't you come to the nurse's with us?" Eve demanded, taking a seat at the table.

"I—I don't know," Janie stammered. She could feel her face growing hot.

"Oooh, you're blushing!" Eve teased, pointing at Janie.

"You've got to stop being so shy around boys," Faith instructed her as she toyed casually with a stack of fives. "Boys can't *guess* that you like them."

"Listen to the expert," Eve commented, rolling her eyes.

Faith tossed her blond hair off her shoulders. "I might just walk up to Ross and say, 'Let's get a Coke after school.' Or maybe ask him to a movie Saturday night."

Eve dropped the money she'd been fiddling with.

"Huh? You'd ask Ross out? Aren't you forgetting about Paul?"

A devilish grin was Faith's reply.

"Paul's such a jock. I really don't know what you see in him anyway," Eve said, avoiding Faith's eyes.

"You mean besides the fact that he's tall and cute and smart, and drives the coolest car in Shadyside, *and* made All-Conference last year?" Faith demanded defensively.

Janie could have added to that list. She had to confess she had a secret crush on Paul.

"Admit it, Faith. Paul is his own biggest fan," Eve said, still avoiding her friend's eyes. "He's so stuck-up. Frankly, it makes me sick to see you trail after him like a lovesick puppy."

Faith let out an angry cry. Then she took a deep breath. "I'm not going to let you get me mad, Eve," she said softly. "You're too pitiful."

"Huh? Me? Pitiful?" Eve cried.

"You're just jealous of Paul and me," Faith accused her friend. *"You're* the lovesick puppy. I watched you throw yourself at Ian at the dance Saturday night. You danced so close to him, I thought we'd need a crowbar to pry you apart!"

Eve gasped.

Janie laughed. "It's a good thing we're best friends," she said. "Otherwise, people might think we hated each other!"

"Ian may not be a jock like Paul," Eve continued breathlessly, ignoring Janie's attempt to lighten things up. "But I have a lot of respect for Ian. Did you know he's working *two* jobs after school to try to save money for college? All Paul has to do is throw a ball and recruiters are camping out in his front yard to offer him scholarships. It's not fair."

"Can't Ian's parents help him out?" Janie asked.

"They could if they wanted to, but Ian's dad is such a jerk," Eve replied bitterly. "He thinks if Ian works himself to death to raise money for college, it'll improve his character."

She sighed. "Maybe it will—if he *lives* through it! But I never get to see him anymore except in the hall between classes or in the lunchroom."

Janie glanced nervously up at the wall clock. "We've got to stop yakking and get to work. I promised Hernandez we'd have the money counted and stacked and banded and ready for him when he gets here."

Eve pointed her thumb at the door to the inner office. "Hernandez isn't in there?"

"Not yet."

"So relax," Eve replied. She swept her hands over the table of money. "I didn't know there was this much. How much do you think it is?"

"Well, if you count the money from the concessions . . ." Janie did some quick calculations in her head. "There must be at least twelve hundred dollars. Maybe more."

"Twelve hundred dollars!" Eve's eyes grew wide.

Janie stared at her friend. She knew that both of Eve's parents were out of work. Even when they were working, the Mullers didn't make much money. The hole in the knee of Eve's faded jeans wasn't a fashion statement.

Faith narrowed her eyes, her expression serious. "Hey, guys—let's split up the money and make a run for it," she whispered.

Janie shot a suspicious glance at Faith. Faith's full pink cheeks darkened to red.

Was Faith serious?

No. Janie knew that Faith's parents were loaded. And they spoiled Faith rotten. Faith had everything she ever wanted.

Except maybe for Ross, Janie thought.

Janie started to stack five-dollar bills. The hallway door opened. Janie glanced up, expecting to see Mr. Hernandez. But it wasn't the principal.

Ian and Paul walked in together. Their eyes immediately shot to the table and the mound of money.

"Money!" Ian cried, rubbing his hands together greedily and making lip-smacking sounds.

"Wow! We're rich!" Paul cried. He dropped his basketball gear to the floor, grabbed a handful of bills, and started stuffing them into the pocket of his sweats. "My car needs a new transmission. This should cover it!"

"No way! It's all mine!" Ian cried. He started shoving dollar bills down the front of his T-shirt. "This is my scholarship! Thanks, girls!"

"Give that back!" Eve cried. She pounced on Ian, reached into his T-shirt, and started pulling out dollar bills.

Laughing loudly, Ian tried to squirm away. "Hey, come on! Cut it out! You're tickling me!"

Faith and Janie chased Paul around the table. "Give it back, Paul! Give it!"

15

They had him backed up against the wall when he spotted the stack of bills Janie had just banded together. Janie dived at him.

But Paul was too fast. He plucked the money from the table. "Ian! Go deep for the bomb!" he shouted gleefully.

Ian tore away from Eve's grasp, still laughing, and ran across the office toward the door to Mr. Hernandez's inner office.

Paul whipped the stack of money like a football over Eve's outstretched hands.

As he tossed it, the door to the inner office suddenly swung open.

Ian leapt for the money. But the pass was a little too high.

Mr. Hernandez stuck his balding head out through his doorway—and the stack of bills hit him hard on the forehead.

Thock.

Janie gasped. The others froze.

Mr. Hernandez turned bright red as his hand went up to his head.

Then his eyes narrowed as they swept from one face to the next.

"You're all suspended for the rest of the year," he said.

chapter
4

Janie's breath caught in her throat.

She could feel the blood pulsing at her temples.

Immediately she thought of her parents. How upset they'd be. How disappointed in her.

Her eyes locked on Ian. Poor Ian. He had been working so hard. Working two jobs to earn the money to go to Yale next fall.

And now all his plans were ruined.

It's not fair! The words formed in her mind, but she didn't say them.

Then she noticed that Mr. Hernandez was grinning. "Scared you," he said, chuckling, his big stomach bouncing up and down.

Janie and her friends didn't react.

"Okay, okay. People say I have a sick sense of

humor," Mr. Hernandez said, still smiling. "I'm sorry. Principals have to have *some* fun, you know?"

"Ha-ha. Good joke!" Paul was the first to break the silence.

The others forced halfhearted laughter.

This is a day for mean jokes, Janie thought wistfully. Ross flashed into her mind for some reason. She wondered if he was okay. She wondered if he was still in the building.

"No way I could suspend you people," the principal said, his eyes on Janie. "You three girls just organized the most successful dance in the history of Shadyside High."

"That's great!" Eve cried.

"Wow. We're a hit!" Faith declared. She slapped Janie a high five.

Mr. Hernandez's expression darkened as he turned to Paul and Ian. "And what are you two doing here?"

"Uh . . . I was just on my way to basketball practice," Paul said, scratching his thick, curly blond hair. His cheeks became bright pink.

"And why aren't you there now?" Mr. Hernandez demanded.

"Mrs. Fritz asked me to give this to one of the girls," Paul said. He reached into his pocket. Several dollar bills came tumbling out.

He turned both pockets of his sweats inside out, and more bills flitted to the ground. "Ah . . . hmmm . . . where is it?" Finally he found what he was looking for—a small silver key. He tossed the key to Eve.

Janie recognized it. It was the key to the filing

cabinet where the dance committee kept its receipts and other stuff.

Mr. Hernandez fixed Ian firmly in his sights. "And what's your story?"

"I thought I could . . . ah . . . help them." He pulled his T-shirt free of his jeans, and money spilled out.

"Perhaps you could be more useful by leaving," Mr. Hernandez said dryly.

"Bye," Ian said, giving everyone a quick wave. He turned to Eve. "I'll . . . uh . . . wait for you."

Ian disappeared out the door. Paul quickly followed.

"I'm sorry about all the craziness, Mr. Hernandez," Eve said sheepishly. "Ian was supposed to give me a ride to the Division Street Mall after I finished counting the money. But then Paul showed up—"

"It was my fault, Mr. Hernandez," Faith interrupted. "I forgot the key when I picked up the receipts from Mrs. Fritz—"

Mr. Hernandez lowered his gaze to the money scattered on the floor. "I take it you haven't finished yet."

The girls shook their heads.

"Well, hurry up so we can get out of here." The principal sighed.

He started to disappear into the inner office, then poked his head back out. "By the way, girls, anything left on the floor, I keep!"

Ten minutes later Janie and her friends had finished. The money lay stacked on the table in neat little piles. The coins, now in rolls, were piled next to the stacks.

"And the grand total is one thousand two hundred and forty-one dollars and sixty-five cents," Janie announced. She jotted the amount down on a slip of paper. "I can't believe how great we did! It was having a live band, you know. That was so much better than just a deejay and records."

"That money sure could pay off a lot of bills at my house," Eve said with a sigh.

"Or it could pay for one totally decent shopping spree at Dalby's Department Store!" Faith exclaimed, her blue eyes lighting up.

"Keep your paws off!" Janie teased, shoving Faith's hands away. She stuffed the money back into the canvas bag, then dropped in the slip of paper with the amount written on it.

Eve opened the file cabinet drawer and put the canvas bag inside.

Janie knocked lightly on Mr. Hernandez's door.

"Come in."

The three girls entered the office. Mr. Hernandez was at his desk, on the phone, clearly annoyed. Rolling his eyes in a helpless gesture, he motioned to the girls to take seats. "Mr. Jefferson . . . Mr. Jefferson, if you'd just listen to me . . ." he said into the phone.

Eve leaned over to Janie and whispered, "I have a feeling Ian is still waiting for me in the hall. I'd better go tell him not to wait. I don't want him to be late for work."

Janie nodded. Eve got up from her chair and silently left the room.

She returned a few minutes later. The principal was still on the phone, still pleading for Mr. Jefferson to give him a chance to talk.

Faith glanced at her watch. She leaned over to Janie. "I'd better call home and let them know I'm going to be late." Janie nodded, and Faith crept out of the room.

Janie's eyes searched the office for something of interest to help the time pass more quickly. She spotted a photograph of three young men in soccer uniforms, almost totally covered in mud, with their arms on one another's shoulders. The huge grins on their faces indicated they had just won a big game.

With a start Janie realized that the one in the middle was Mr. Hernandez. He was pretty good-looking way back when he had hair, she thought.

Faith quietly returned and sat down next to Janie.

Glancing at her watch, Janie noted with surprise that Faith had been gone for over five minutes.

With a weary sigh Mr. Hernandez finally hung up the phone. He rubbed his bald head as he turned to Janie and her friends. "So? What was the grand total?"

"One thousand two hundred and . . ." Struggling to remember, Janie turned to Faith and Eve. "How much was it again?"

They both shrugged.

"You wrote it down," Faith said.

"I'm sorry, Mr. Hernandez," Janie said, jumping

up from her chair. "I wrote the amount down on a slip of paper and put it in the bag. Be right back."

Janie quickly made her way out of the office, closing the door gently behind her.

She was surprised to find Paul in the outer office.

He flashed her an embarrassed grin and held up his basketball shoes. "Forgot these. Can't practice without them."

He stuffed the sneakers into his gym bag and slung it over his shoulder. "Tell Faith I'll call her later," he said, heading out the door.

Janie pulled open the drawer to the file cabinet.

She had started to reach inside to pull out the canvas bag when she realized the drawer was empty.

"Whoa," she murmured out loud. "Wrong drawer, I guess."

She pulled out the next drawer. It was filled with files and papers.

The third drawer was stuffed with old math workbooks.

Janie pulled out the original drawer—the right one—and stood frozen, gaping into it in disbelief.

Empty.

Totally empty.

She grew cold all over. Her knees were trembling.

"Mr. Hernandez!" she managed to choke out just above a whisper. She took a deep breath and tried again. "Mr. Hernandez!" she cried in a shrill, frightened voice. "Please—come quick! It's gone! The money is gone!"

This time it really was gone.

chapter
5

Up in her room after dinner that night, Janie stared at her social studies text until it became a white blur.

I can't study, she thought miserably. I can't concentrate on anything. My mind just keeps going back to this afternoon. I can't stop thinking about the stolen money.

With an unhappy sigh she slammed the book shut and jumped to her feet. Grabbing her down jacket from where she had tossed it on the floor, she hurried downstairs.

"I'm going out!" she shouted to her parents.

She ran out the door before they could ask where she was going and why she was going out on a school night.

She drove to Faith's house in North Hills. Faith greeted her at the door in baggy jeans and an oversize sweater, her blond hair disheveled, surprise on her face. "Janie—what's up?"

"I just had to talk to somebody," Janie replied, following Faith across the polished floor of the large living room filled with antiques, to the dark-paneled den.

Paul was standing by the fireplace, tending the fire with a brass poker. He glanced up in surprise as Janie entered. The firelight made his round cheeks and curly blond hair glow.

"Oh. Hi. I didn't know you were here," Janie said awkwardly.

Paul seemed uneasy too, which was unusual for him. "Faith and I were just . . . talking about school," he said, glancing at Faith.

They sat down on the long leather couch that faced the fire. The bright flames bent and crackled. The room smelled sweet.

"I can't stop thinking about this afternoon, about the stolen money," Janie said, clasping her hands in her lap.

"At least Hernandez doesn't suspect *us,*" Faith replied, darting a nervous glance at Paul. "I mean, that's a relief, huh?"

"But who else could have known the money bag was in the file drawer?" Janie demanded. "I've been asking myself that over and over."

"Hernandez probably suspects Ian and me," Paul said, and then he let out a high-pitched, nervous laugh. "I mean, Ian was out in the hall the whole time, waiting for Eve. And I was in the office. You know. Picking up my basketball shoes."

"I don't know *what* Hernandez thinks," Janie said, biting her lower lip. "I don't know *what* to think about anything. I'm just so upset."

Janie suddenly wished she hadn't come to Faith's. Paul and Faith were acting weird, she thought. They kept casting nervous glances at each other. They seemed so uncomfortable.

"I keep feeling guilty," Janie admitted, staring into the fire. "It's stupid, I know. But I feel guilty. You know what it reminds me of, Faith?"

Faith frowned at her, the fire sending flickering shadows over her face. "What?"

"It reminds me of the time you, me, and Eve broke into that boarded-up old house on Fear Street. Remember?"

"Yeah. It was supposed to be haunted," Faith replied, smoothing her hand over the leather couch arm.

"Remember? The police came in and got us before we were halfway up those creaking stairs," Janie continued. "We were so surprised and frightened. I remember I was actually a little glad we'd been caught. I mean, if there were ghosts in that old house, I really didn't want to know about it."

Faith and Paul let out halfhearted laughs.

"You dared us to go in," Janie recalled. "Eve and I didn't want to do it. But you dared us, Faith. And I guess we were too embarrassed not to take the dare."

"We really got into trouble," Faith said, pushing her hair behind her shoulders.

"I was grounded for a month," Janie added. "The police made us feel like real criminals." She sighed. "That's how I felt today. That same guilty feeling— even though I *know* none of us could have done it."

There was an awkward silence. All three of them stared into the fire. A loud pop made them jump. Paul laughed.

"Let's change the subject," Faith said, getting up to put on another log. "Paul says he knows who Ross is. You know, that new boy we helped this afternoon."

"You know him?" Janie asked a little too eagerly.

"Well, I don't really know him, and I didn't know his name," Paul replied. "He's in my calculus class. But I remember him from last fall when we played New Brighton. First football game of the season."

"He's from New Brighton?" Janie asked. "I wonder why he transferred in the middle of the year."

Paul shrugged. "He was a running back. He *killed* us. It was that real rainy night, remember? The field was soft and muddy, like pig slop."

"Very colorful," Faith interrupted sarcastically.

"This guy Ross ran about eighty yards in the mud for a touchdown," Paul continued, ignoring her. "Our guy fell down, and Ross just kept going. Only score of the game." He made a disgusted face, his blue eyes shining in the light from the fire. "Big hero," he muttered.

"I think he's cute," Faith said, poking the fire.

"He's a jerk," Paul said sharply.

26

"Just because he ran for a touchdown against the Tigers?" Janie demanded.

"No. Because he has an attitude," Paul told her. "After he scored the touchdown he ran past our bench, high-stepping and pumping his fist. What a hot dog. And he has a real attitude in math class, too. Like he knows everything. Like he's too smart for the rest of us. He's real stuck-up."

"Maybe he's just shy," Janie said.

"Maybe he's a jerk," Paul insisted.

"I still think he's cute," Faith said, grinning.

Paul scowled at Faith. "You have no taste."

They all laughed.

Paul left a little after ten. Janie knew she should go home, too, but something held her back.

She wanted to talk with Faith about the stolen money, see if Faith had any theories. She wanted to ask why Faith and Paul had acted so strangely, so tense all evening. But she didn't think she could.

Yawning, Faith dropped another log on the fire. "Fires always make me sleepy," she said. She slumped back onto the couch. "So are you going to ask Ross out, or am I?" she asked, her blue eyes glowing playfully.

"Huh? Ask him out?" The question caught Janie by surprise. "Well, how can *you* ask him out, Faith? You and Paul—"

"Paul won't have to know," Faith replied, grinning.

"Well, maybe . . ." Janie felt her face growing hot.

"I *know* you're interested in him," Faith teased.

27

"Hey—how about a little bet? You know. Which of us can go out with Ross first?"

"A bet? You mean for money?"

Faith laughed. "Okay. For money. Ten dollars, say. It'll be a little race. The first to go out with Ross takes the money."

Before Janie could reply, the cordless phone beside the couch rang. Faith picked it up.

"Oh, hi, Eve. You want in on our bet?"

Janie listened to Faith explain the bet to Eve. "Ian is always working. He won't know," Faith assured Eve. "Yeah. Yeah. Janie, too."

They discussed it more. Then Faith turned to Janie. "Eve is in. See you tomorrow, Eve." She hung up the phone. "A date with Ross and twenty dollars. What do you say?"

Janie sighed. She knew she was probably too shy to ask Ross out. Faith wouldn't have any problem just going up to him and inviting him to a movie or something. Neither would Eve.

"I'll lose," Janie said softly. "But okay, Faith. I'm in."

A short while later Janie picked up her down jacket, and Faith walked her to the front door. "See you tomorrow," Janie said. And then the words flew out of her mouth: "Why were you and Paul so weird tonight?"

"Huh?" Faith reacted with surprise.

"You both acted sort of—nervous," Janie said. "Was there a problem or something?"

Faith hesitated. "Well—kind of," she said reluctantly, her blue eyes locked on Janie's.

"I—uh . . ." Janie felt embarrassed. "What kind of problem?" she asked, lowering her eyes.

Faith hesitated again. "Well, Janie, it's just that— uh . . . Paul and I know that it was *you* who stole the dance money."

chapter

6

"*H*uh?" Janie cried, her mouth dropping open.

Faith's eyes burned accusingly into Janie's.

"You—you think that *I*—" Janie stammered in disbelief.

Faith burst out laughing. "April fool," she murmured. "I tried, but I couldn't keep a straight face."

Janie let out an angry roar. "Faith—it isn't April yet, and you're not funny!" she screamed. "Can't you take *anything* seriously?"

Faith's grin faded. "I'm going to take our bet about Ross seriously," she said.

As chemistry class began the next afternoon, Janie opened her lab book and started to set up her test tubes. But her mind wasn't on the lab assignment. It was on Ross Gabriel.

She had been thinking about Ross all day, asking herself again and again why she had been so foolish as to bet against Faith and Eve.

There's no way I can compete against either of them, Janie thought miserably.

"Janie," Mr. Mancuso's voice startled her from her thoughts. She glanced up—and was sure she must be hallucinating.

Next to Mr. Mancuso stood Ross Gabriel, his brown hair over his forehead, his dark eyes locked on her.

"Would you please work with Ross until Pam is better?" the chemistry teacher asked. Janie's usual lab partner, Pam Dalby, was out with the flu. Mr. Mancuso walked to the front of the room to demonstrate the experiment.

"Hi again," Ross said, dropping casually onto the high stool beside her. "You're Janie, right?"

Janie's heart was pounding so hard, she wondered if Ross could hear it. "Yeah. Hi," she managed to croak out. "How's your arm?"

"No problem. We'll ace this experiment," he told her, reaching across her to rearrange the test tubes. "I've done it before. At my old school. In seventh grade, I think. This is all Mickey Mouse stuff."

"Yeah, I know," Janie quickly agreed. She actually thought the assignment was pretty hard, but there was no way she could admit it.

"Watch out for that one. That's ammonia," she warned him, pointing to a clear test tube. "I sniffed a test tube of ammonia once by mistake. My nose burned for a week!"

She expected him to laugh, but his expression remained solemn. "Yeah. You've got to be careful," he said, studying the test tubes. "Of course, I drink that stuff for breakfast!"

Janie laughed. His dark eyes flashed, but still he didn't smile.

"I guess we should start," Janie said, turning to the test tubes. "Is this the magnesium ferride?"

"Whatever," Ross replied. His attention was on the front of the room, where Mr. Mancuso was leaning over a table, helping a group get started.

Ross turned back to Janie and placed a hand over hers, stopping her from picking up a test tube. "Want to see something really *bad?*" he whispered, bringing his lips close to her ear, so close she could feel his warm breath on her face.

She shivered. "Something bad?"

He raised a finger to his mouth to signal that she should be quiet. He glanced up again to make sure the teacher still had his back turned. Then he quickly poured a green liquid into a clear liquid. "Watch," he instructed Janie.

The liquids rolled together. White steam rose up from the green mixture.

"What is it?" Janie whispered.

"It's a stink bomb," Ross replied, staring down at the test tube. The green liquid fizzed over the top. The wet steam rose up. "Take a sniff."

Janie reluctantly inhaled. She made a disgusted face. "Yuck!"

The sour odor began to float over the classroom.

Kids began to groan and complain. A few heads turned back questioningly toward Janie and Ross.

"Oooh, what stinks?" someone cried.

"Ricky—is that *you?*" someone called to Ricky Schorr, the class clown who was always blamed for everything.

"No way!" Ricky cried.

Kids were coughing and gagging.

Janie slid off the stool and backed away from the table, her eyes watering.

Mr. Mancuso finally caught on that something was wrong. He raised his face and sniffed. "Oh." He let out a sick gasp.

"Mr. Mancuso, it's over here," Ross called. "I think Janie and I did something wrong."

"Huh? Me?" Janie cried. "I didn't—"

Mr. Mancuso hurried to Janie's lab table. "Janie and I got the steps wrong, I think," Ross said. "It—it smells like rotten eggs!" He winked at Janie.

Mr. Mancuso's eyes narrowed as he stared down at the bubbling green mixture. He was holding his breath, trying not to inhale the disgusting, sour aroma. "I'll take care of it," he told Ross.

The teacher picked up a test tube holder, lifted the green tube from the rack, and hurried from the room with it.

As soon as he was gone the room erupted in laughter and wild cheers. "Way to go, Ross!" Ricky Schorr cried.

"Let's party!" someone yelled.

"Open the windows—please!" someone else begged.

Ross turned to Janie. "Sorry," he said. "I just wasn't in the mood for that dumb assignment today."

Janie laughed. The air in the room was starting to clear. "Where did you learn to make that?" she asked, climbing back beside him.

"My mom bought me a chemistry set when I was eight," he told her. "It was the first thing I ever made."

Janie snickered. "You did a great job, Ross. You'll probably get an A."

"I like to mess people up," Ross said. She waited for him to smile, but he didn't.

What a weird thing to say, Janie thought.

I like to mess people up.

She glanced up at the clock. She didn't want the class to end. She wanted to sit there beside him and talk for hours.

She thought suddenly of the bet.

Can I do it? Can I ask him out?

This was the perfect chance.

The bell rang. She collected her books and followed him out into the hall.

He stopped outside the door and turned back to Janie as if he were expecting her to say something to him.

She smiled, struggling to think of something.

Do it now! she thought. Ask him out for Saturday night.

"Maybe I'll teach you some more useful things

tomorrow," he told her, brushing his hair off his forehead.

He's so great-looking, Janie thought. He's so great-looking, and he knows it.

Ask him. Ask him.

"Uh . . . Ross . . ." she started to say, clearing her throat. She clasped her backpack tightly in front her. "Uh—Saturday night . . ."

Janie stopped when she saw Ross's expression change.

His eyes, staring over Janie's shoulder, grew wide. His face went pale.

"Ross?" she cried, bewildered.

He didn't seem to hear her.

His mouth dropped open in shock. And his handsome features twisted in horror.

chapter

7

S tartled, Janie spun around and followed Ross's gaze.

Across the crowded hall she saw a very tall girl with long, curly white-blond hair. The girl was staring hard at Ross.

Who *is* that? Janie wondered. I've never seen her before.

"Ross, what's wrong?" Janie demanded. "You look like you've seen a ghost!"

But to Janie's surprise, Ross had disappeared.

She searched for Ross after school but didn't find him.

She had thought about the girl with the white-blond hair the rest of the afternoon. The girl was tall and beautiful, with that spectacular curly hair cascading down her back.

Why hadn't Janie noticed her before?

Was she new to Shadyside High?

Janie pulled on her jacket and slammed her locker shut. She began walking slowly to the front exit when she saw Eve hurrying toward her.

"Guess what," Eve cried, her dark eyes flashing and a broad smile on her face. "Guess what—I win! I have a date with Ross Friday night!"

Friday night Janie lay on her bed, staring up at the ceiling, listening to a Beatles song on the oldies radio station. The phone rang. She reached toward the bed table, turned down the clock-radio, and yanked the receiver off the cradle. "Hello?"

"Tonight's Eve's big night." It was Faith.

"Tell me something I don't know," Janie groaned. "Eve borrowed my blue blazer."

"And she's wearing those sexy red denims she saves for special occasions." Faith was silent for a moment. Janie could almost picture her shaking her head. Faith really hated to lose bets.

"Eve just walked right up to Ross and asked him out," Faith said finally. "I wonder what she said."

"Whatever it was, it worked." Janie sighed. "I admit it—I am *so jealous!*"

"Hey—me, too," Faith said.

"At least you have Paul," Janie told her.

"Know what? I should tell Ian," Faith said nastily. "I should call him up and tell him where Eve is. He'll be furious!"

"No, you shouldn't," Janie said sharply. "You'd better not. You know how jealous Ian gets. Give the poor guy a break. He's working every night this weekend."

Faith hummed mischievously.

"This whole stupid bet was your idea," Janie snapped. "So why do you want to cause trouble for Eve?"

"Trouble is my middle name," Faith replied, snickering. Then she added, "Hey, Janie, I'm only kidding. I wouldn't call Ian."

"I can never tell when you're kidding," Janie admitted.

"That's why you're the perfect victim," Faith said.

"Thanks, pal," Janie replied dryly.

Faith sighed. "I've got my own problems."

"Huh? What problems?" Janie sat up on the bed and transferred the phone to her other ear.

"Oh . . . things aren't great around here," Faith answered reluctantly. "Wait. Let me close my door." She went away for a few seconds, then returned. "Things aren't great with my parents, I don't think," she said in a low voice. "They're almost never in the house at the same time anymore. When they *are* home, they keep closing their bedroom door and having long, heavy discussions."

"You mean—" Janie started.

"I think maybe they're going to split. I don't know." Faith sighed. "And then that creep Paul—"

"What about Paul?" Janie asked.

"Do you know what that creep wanted to talk to me about yesterday at lunch?"

"When did he become a creep?" Janie demanded, unable to conceal her surprise.

"When he asked me for three hundred dollars so that he could buy a new transmission for his car. Can you believe that?"

Janie thought about it for a moment. "Yeah, actually I can."

"I was beginning to think he really liked me," Faith said unhappily. "But he goes out with me just because I'm rich."

"Eve *said* he was a loser," Janie commented.

"For once Eve was right," Faith said bitterly.

"So, you want to go to a movie or something?" Janie asked, trying to change the subject.

"Not really. I think I'm just going to stay in my room and think hateful thoughts all night."

Janie laughed. "At least you've still got your sense of humor."

"I wonder how Eve and Ross are getting along," Faith said wistfully.

"Yeah. Me, too," Janie replied. "I can't wait to hear about it. I'll bet Eve will have quite a story to tell. . . ."

chapter

8

After the movie Ross drove his tiny blue Civic to the edge of the Fear Street woods and parked.

He reached across the seat, pulled Eve to him, and kissed her. His lips felt dry and hot against hers.

Eve eagerly returned the kiss. She ran her hands through his tousled hair, then wrapped them around his shoulders.

They stopped to take a breath.

Ross started to kiss her again, then suddenly broke it off. He leaned back against the seat with a sigh. "Sorry," he said.

"Why?" Eve asked. Her heart was pounding.

He's terrific! she thought.

Ian's face kept popping into her mind. She kept forcing the picture away.

"I usually don't put a move on a girl the first date." He shrugged. His eyes locked on hers. "I usually wait until the second date!"

"Then I guess it's up to me," Eve said, pulling Ross to her. She pressed her lips to his and kissed him long and hard. Her hand became entangled in her blue scarf. She tugged it off and let it drop onto the seat.

"It's getting all steamed up in here," Ross said when the kiss finally ended. "Want to go for a walk? In the woods?"

"Huh? These are the Fear Street woods," Eve protested.

"So?"

"I forgot that you're new here," she said, squeezing his hand. "You don't know the horrible stories about these woods."

"And I don't want to know. My house is on Fear Street. Come on. A short walk will cool us off. What could happen? You're not afraid—are you?" It was more of a challenge than a question.

Ross climbed out and walked around to the passenger side. Eve still hadn't made a move to get out of the car. He opened the door and held out his hand. Eve hesitated, then placed her hand in his and stepped outside.

Ross led the way into the woods.

The wind kicked up, swirling around them in gusts.

Eve felt a chill. She shivered, draped the blue scarf around her neck, and pulled up the collar of Janie's blue blazer.

"Where are we going?" she asked with a shudder.

"Not far," Ross replied softly.

She felt his arm wrap around her shoulder.

When Janie opened her eyes Saturday morning the sun was already streaming in the bedroom window. She rubbed the sleep from her eyes and stretched.

She could feel a draft of cool air coming through the closed window. It's the end of March already, she thought. I wish spring would hurry up.

She snuggled deep under the warm comforter. Maybe I won't get up yet, she thought. What time is it anyway?

She glanced at the clock-radio. Only eight-fifteen.

She yawned. Something had been troubling her, keeping her from falling asleep the night before. What was it?

Oh, right, she remembered. Eve's date with Ross.

I'll have to call Eve and get the whole story.

A surprising question floated into her still-half-awake mind: if Eve starts going with Ross, should I try for Ian?

Janie pictured Ian. He was nearly as short and skinny as she was. He had wiry dark brown hair, cut very short. And he had serious, steely gray eyes behind his rimless glasses.

He's a great guy, Janie thought, turning onto her side. And he's really smart.

But Ian just isn't my type.

Ross is my type. . . .

She hugged the pillow to her cheek and must have dozed off again. The phone ringing on the bed table made her sit straight up.

She reached for it, blinking herself awake. "Hello?"

"Hello, Janie?" It was Ian. "Is Eve there?" he asked breathlessly. "Is she at your house?"

Janie felt a stab of dread. "Uh, no. Why?"

"She's missing!" Ian cried. "She never returned home last night!"

chapter
9

*J*anie nearly dropped the phone. The receiver suddenly felt like a heavy weight in her hand. She squeezed her eyes shut and felt the pain at the base of her skull slowly inch its way upward.

"Janie!" Ian's shrill voice broke into her thoughts. "You still there?"

She brought the receiver back to her ear. "Yes," she said in a shaky voice.

"Eve didn't sleep over at your house?" Ian demanded.

"No. Did you call her parents?"

"Yeah. They're frantic, Janie. They called the police."

Janie's throat tightened. She felt a wave of nausea sweep over her.

Ian's voice was strained now. "Janie—did Eve go out with someone last night? Some guy? I went over to her house after work, but her little brother said she'd gone out. He wouldn't say where or anything."

"I'll give Mrs. Muller a call," Janie said, fighting back the waves of nausea.

Eve has got to be okay, she thought. She's *got* to be.

"What's going on, Janie?" Ian demanded. "Eve was out with some guy, wasn't she?"

"I—I don't know, Ian." Janie hated to lie. But she didn't want to break her promise to Eve either. "That's not important now," she told Ian. "What's important is finding Eve."

"Janie, can I come over? I'm really worried."

"I don't think so, Ian. I—" She really didn't want to see him now.

"Janie? Please?" He sounded so frightened. Like a little boy.

"Okay, Ian," Janie relented. "I'll be here."

"You're a real friend," Ian said. "I'll be right over." The line went dead.

Janie sat on the edge of her bed. She fought off the dizziness by closing her eyes.

What could have happened to Eve?

What?

Janie forced herself to her feet. She had to wash up and get dressed. Ian would be there any minute. She made her way across the hall to the bathroom and splashed cold water on her face. She felt as if she were moving in slow motion, as if she weighed a thousand pounds.

She slipped into jeans and a hooded sweatshirt, tugged on her sneakers, and went downstairs to wait for Ian.

"Mom? Dad?"

A note on the refrigerator told Janie they'd gone shopping.

"Maybe Faith has heard something," Janie said out loud, feeling her fear choke her throat. She punched in Faith's number. The line was busy.

With an exasperated groan she hung up and punched in Eve's number. Her fingers were trembling so badly, she had to try it three times before she got the number right.

Be home, Eve, she thought. Please be home.

Maybe I'm getting all worked up over nothing, Janie told herself, listening to the phone ring. Maybe Eve is home by now. Maybe she had such a great time with Ross, they stayed out all night.

Please be home. Please . . .

Marky, Eve's little brother, finally answered after the fifth ring. "Marky? It's Janie Simpson. Is your mom there?"

"Hold on. I'll go get her, Janie." She heard sobbing in the background. Not a good sign.

Janie shuddered, listening to the muffled sobs. She heard Marky's voice. Footsteps.

Finally Mrs. Muller came on the line. "Janie, is Eve with you? Have they found her? Did you hear anything?" The frantic pace of her questions revealed her panic.

"No, Mrs. Muller," Janie replied in a trembling

voice. "I—I thought she might have come home by now."

"No. She isn't here," Eve's mother sobbed. "Her father. The police. They're all looking for her. They— they—" She broke into loud sobs.

"Mrs. Muller—" Janie wanted to get off the line. She didn't want to upset the poor woman any more.

"They're all searching for her," Mrs. Muller managed to say through her tears. "Searching for Eve and that boy she was with."

"Huh?" Janie cried. "Ross? Is Ross missing, too?"

"Yes," Eve's mother replied. "I'm afraid the boy is missing, too."

chapter

10

*I*an arrived a few seconds after Janie got off the phone with Mrs. Muller. He stood at the front door in wrinkled chinos and a stained sweatshirt, his eyes red-rimmed and bloodshot.

Janie offered a grim hello and held the storm door open for him. But he didn't come inside.

"Can we drive around a bit?" he asked in a weary voice, motioning to his yellow Ford Escort. "I don't feel like just sitting."

Janie nodded. "I guess. Let me leave my parents a note."

She ran to the kitchen, scribbled a note, and stuck it on the refrigerator door with a magnet. Then she grabbed her down jacket and ran out the front door.

It was an unusually cool day for early spring. The trees on the front lawn shivered in the swirling wind.

Ian was sitting in his little yellow car with the motor running. He threw the car into gear and started pulling away from the curb even before Janie had her door shut.

"Janie, what's going on?" Ian asked frantically.

"I wish I knew, Ian."

"You know something," he accused her, turning onto Canyon Drive and speeding through a stop sign. "I know you do. You and Eve and Faith always tell each other everything." He stared hard at her, as if trying to read her thoughts.

"Did you come over just to give me a hard time?" Janie wailed. "If so, you can turn around and drop me back home. I'm scared to death about Eve, Ian. Scared to death. I don't want to be questioned by you."

Her angry outburst startled him. He adjusted his glasses and shifted uncomfortably in his seat, turning his gray eyes straight ahead to the windshield.

"Sorry," he said quietly. "I—I'm real scared, too."

They rode on in silence. Ian drove aimlessly around town. They drove past Eve's house in Old Village. No cars out front. No sign of life.

They drove past Shadyside High, dark and empty on a Saturday morning. On Old Mill Road the tall trees arched their bare branches over the road.

Janie had a strong impulse to tell Ian about Ross. About Eve and the bet. But why should she make him feel even worse?

Glancing out the window, she saw they were driving by the Fear Street woods now.

"Hey!" Janie cried out as Ian slammed on the brakes.

Her body jolted forward. She raised her hands just in time to keep her head from smashing into the windshield as the car screeched to a halt.

"Stupid dog!" Ian cried. He turned to Janie, swallowing hard. "Did you see it? Ran right in front of the car. I almost hit it."

"No. I—I guess I wasn't watching," Janie said shakily.

The car had stalled out. Ian made no effort to restart it. "Are you okay?" he asked her.

Janie started to reply but stopped.

What *was* that in the woods?

Something on the ground in front of the trees.

Something bright blue.

"Oh!" She pushed open the car door and leapt out.

"Janie—hey! Where are you going?" Ian called out to her.

Leaving the car door open, she started running toward the spot of blue in the woods.

"Janie—wait up!" Ian was right behind her.

"What *is* that?" she cried. "See it, Ian? The bright blue thing?"

First it was a blur. But as she ran closer the whole scene came into sharp focus.

She saw the blazer first. The bright blue blazer. *Her* bright blue blazer.

Then she saw Eve's lifeless body.

Then she started to scream.

chapter

11

*E*ve's face was turned sideways, half buried in three inches of mud. The top of her skull had been bashed in, cracked like an eggshell. A thick circle of dried blood was caked and matted in her dark hair.

Flies crawled over her body. Janie watched in horror as one fly slowly creeped across Eve's face. It crawled over her eye and into her open mouth.

With a loud gasp Janie turned away and shut her eyes. But the gruesome sight stayed with her.

"Eve? Eve?" Ian's tortured cry cut through the air. He fell to his knees beside the body. He took Eve's pale, limp hand in his and started rubbing it, as if rubbing the hand might bring her back to life.

"Eve? Eve?"

Janie slumped down into a pile of cool, damp leaves

and lowered her head between her legs. She thought she might faint.

Breathe. Just breathe, she told herself.

She raised her head slowly, struggling to breathe normally. The trees spun wildly all around her.

The wind seemed to surround her, carrying the sour aroma of the corpse. She tried to hold her breath, but started to gag.

Janie resisted the impulse to look again. She had already seen enough for a lifetime of nightmares.

"Eve? Eve?" Janie heard Ian's repeated cry, a chant of his horror and disbelief. "Eve?"

We've got to get help. Got to get away from here, Janie realized.

She stumbled to her feet.

Ian continued his eerie chant. He was still frantically rubbing Eve's lifeless hand.

"Ian!" Janie's voice echoed through the woods. She grabbed Ian by the neck of his sweatshirt and yanked him up and away from the body. "Ian, let's go," she pleaded, shaking him. "We've got to call the police. Ian—*please!*"

A fly buzzed near Janie's ear—its sound seemed to swell and block out everything else. Was it one fly or a hundred? She closed her eyes, but she still saw them. She still heard them buzzing. Flies. They descended like black death over her once-beautiful friend.

The radio in the police cruiser crackled loudly. The two police officers had inspected Eve's body. Now they returned to their cruiser to call for more help.

Janie stood at the edge of the road, watching them.

She had led Ian to his car and deposited him there while she ran to a house on Fear Street to call the police. They had arrived five minutes later, and she directed them to the body.

Where is Ross? she wondered, closing her eyes.

We found poor Eve. But where is Ross?

So far there was no trace of him.

Was he dead, too? Was his body in the woods?

Suddenly remembering Ian, Janie turned and spotted him sitting by himself in the yellow Escort, slumped forward, his head lowered to the steering wheel.

Janie tapped on the window of the police cruiser. The window slid down. "Excuse me, sir? I think my friend may need me," Janie said, pointing to Ian's car. "Do you mind if I sit in the car with him?"

The officer glanced over at Ian, then back to Janie. He nodded grimly. "No problem. We'll get you kids home as soon as possible, okay?"

Janie hurried over to the car and slid into the passenger seat. "Ian?" she said in a soft voice. "They said we can go home soon."

Ian slowly raised his head. He covered his face with his hands.

He doesn't want me to see that he was crying, Janie realized.

"Maybe you should let me drive," Janie said. "I don't mind."

"It was the money," Ian said in a choked voice. He wiped the tears from his face with the sleeve of his sweatshirt.

"Huh?" Janie wasn't sure she had heard right. "What money?"

Did Ian know about the bet? Did he know the three girls had bet ten dollars each?

"It was the money," Ian murmured, avoiding Janie's eyes.

"Ian—what money?"

"I know why Eve was killed," he said, his gray eyes narrowing. "It was because of the money. Whoever did this killed Eve for the money."

Janie stared hard at Ian's tearstained face. "Ian, what are you talking about?"

Ian turned to her, choking back a sob. "Oh, Janie. It was Eve who stole the dance money!"

chapter
12

*J*anie rested a hand on Ian's shoulder. "Ian, I'm afraid you're not making any sense," she said gently. "Eve is the most honest person I know. She would never—"

Janie realized she was still talking about Eve as if she were alive. Fresh tears sprang to her eyes.

Ian turned to Janie. His eyes burned deeply into hers. "Janie, who did Eve go out with last night? Don't lie to me! I have to know."

Janie swallowed hard. There was no need to keep her promise to Eve now. Besides, the police already knew about Ross. They were searching for him, too.

"It was Ross," she told Ian. "Ross Gabriel. It wasn't like a real date, Ian. It was just a stupid bet."

"Huh?" Ian's watery eyes narrowed in confusion. "A bet? What kind of bet?"

"The three of us—Eve, Faith, and me—made a bet," Janie said reluctantly, lowering her eyes. "It was a silly bet. The first one to go out with Ross would win. That's the only reason Eve went out with him—" Janie stopped.

The blood had drained from Ian's face. His entire body began to tremble. With anger, Janie realized.

I should have waited, Janie told herself. I should have waited until Ian was calmer.

Ian turned the ignition key with a trembling hand. "Get out of the car, Janie," he said in a hard, cold voice.

"Huh?" Janie turned to face him, startled by the fury in his voice.

"Just get out of the car."

"Ian, what are you going to do?" Janie demanded.

"Get out!" Ian screamed.

"No way," Janie told him. "You've got to get yourself together, Ian." She quickly reached over, shut the engine off, and yanked the keys out of the ignition.

"I can't let you do something crazy," she said. "Can't you see how upset and out of control you are?"

Ian grabbed for the keys, but she pushed him away. "Give me the keys, Janie," he demanded in an icy voice.

Janie heard the low wail of a siren, not far away.

"Let's get you home safely, okay?" Janie said in a low and deliberate voice.

"Give me those keys," Ian repeated through clenched teeth.

The siren grew louder.

56

"Give me the keys!"

"No!"

Without warning Ian grabbed Janie by the sleeve of her sweatshirt and pulled her toward him. Janie held Ian off with one hand and frantically rolled down the window with the other.

She tossed Ian's car keys as far as she could. They landed in the brown matted weeds by the side of the road.

With an angry cry, Ian shoved open the door and jumped out of the car.

Her heart pounding, Janie rolled the window back up and locked both doors. By now the siren had become so loud, she thought it must be inside her head.

She glanced out the back window to see a police cruiser screech to a halt behind Ian's car, its red lights flashing. An ambulance pulled up beside it, blocking the street.

The rear doors of the Emergency Service Unit flew open, and white-coated paramedics jumped out, dragging a stretcher behind them.

A police officer directed the paramedics. They ran into the Fear Street woods, hauling the stretcher behind them.

There's no reason for them to rush, Janie thought sadly. Eve is dead, and no paramedic can bring her back to life.

A third squad car pulled up, siren blaring, lights flashing. And then another. Soon dark-uniformed police officers were swarming through the woods.

Swarming like flies, Janie thought bitterly.

Like flies over a dead body.

Ian was still searching the dead brown weeds for his keys when the paramedics carried Eve's body out of the woods.

The police had found no sign of Ross.

Had Ross been murdered, too? Janie wondered with a shudder. Is he also lying dead in these woods?

chapter

13

The police station looked like something out of a TV cop show. There was a gruff gray-haired sergeant behind the front desk. Phones rang constantly on battered gray metal desks. Computer keyboards clacked away. In the back of the squad room Janie saw two young officers shooting rubber bands at each other.

She glanced at Ian, who was walking beside her. His dark hair was matted to his forehead. Behind his glasses his eyes were still bloodshot and sad. He looked ghostly pale under the fluorescent ceiling lights. They had been at the station for over an hour.

"I'm sorry you had to come in this afternoon," Lieutenant Frazier said, guiding them to the waiting room in front. Lieutenant Frazier was a young man with a soft voice and soothing manner. "I know you're both still terribly shaken by what you discovered this morning."

Janie nodded, fighting back tears.

She had been able to answer all the lieutenant's questions without crying. Why did she feel like sobbing and screaming now?

"I wouldn't have asked you to come in," the lieutenant said softly, a hand on each of their shoulders, "but you both knew the victim so well. I know that what you told me about Eve will help us find her killer."

Killer.

The word tore through Janie's mind like a sharp knife.

She sucked in a deep breath and held it.

I'm not going to cry, she thought. I'm not going to cry here. I won't cry until I get home.

"Your parents are waiting out front?" Lieutenant Frazier asked.

Janie and Ian both nodded.

Suddenly the door to the squad room swung open, and Ross appeared. Two solemn-faced officers moved close behind him.

Janie felt her heart skip a beat.

He's alive, she thought. Ross is okay!

It took a while for Ross to recognize Janie and Ian. He seemed lost in his own thoughts, his expression tense and troubled.

"Janie, hi," he called softly when he finally noticed her. "Ian—"

"Ross—you're okay?" Janie cried.

"I—I don't believe this is happening," he said, shaking his head hard, as if trying to shake it all away. "How can Eve be dead?"

Ian moaned as if in pain.

The two officers tried to make Ross keep walking. But he stopped in front of Janie, his dark eyes peering down into hers.

"I had to go back to New Brighton early this morning," Ross told her. "With my parents. I just got back a few minutes ago. The police—they were waiting at my house. They told me . . . about Eve. I—I—" His voice cracked. He lowered his head.

Janie rested a hand on his quivering shoulder.

"I just can't believe it," Ross repeated emotionally. "After our date I took Eve home. It was a little after eleven. I watched her run up the driveway. She was home, Janie. She was home safe and sound. I—"

"Please keep walking," one of the officers told Ross. "We need to talk to you, son. Back there." He pointed to one of the small rooms against the far wall.

His head still lowered, Ross obediently began walking past Janie and Ian. "You believe me—don't you?" he called back to Janie.

Janie hesitated. She glanced at Ian.

Before she could reply, Ross disappeared into the small questioning room.

"Thanks again. Your parents are waiting out here,"

Lieutenant Frazier said. He held open the squad room door for them.

"Do you believe Ross's story?" Ian asked as they stepped through the doorway.

Janie shrugged.

"I don't," Ian said coldly.

Sunday afternoon dark storm clouds hovered low, threatening rain. The air was wet and cold, bending the still-bare trees as Janie drove to Pete's Pizza at the mall to meet Faith.

They sat across from each other in a red vinyl booth near the front, struggling unsuccessfully to make conversation.

The doors to the sixplex movie theater across from the restaurant had opened, and a noisy crowd was spilling out. The restaurant quickly filled with laughter and loud voices.

A large pepperoni pizza lay untouched on the table between Janie and Faith. Faith played with her plastic knife and fork. Janie stared out the glass wall into the brightly lit corridor.

Finally she broke the silence. "Five more minutes."

"Until what?" Faith asked.

"Five more minutes and I will have gone an entire hour without crying," Janie said.

Faith uttered a mirthless laugh. "You and me both."

"Is Paul meeting you here?" Janie asked.

Faith shrugged. "Maybe," She sighed.

A cruel silence fell over the table again.

"I still don't believe Eve stole that money," Faith said, frowning. "I don't care what Ian says."

"Why would he lie about it?" Janie demanded, resting her chin in her hands.

Faith chewed her lower lip. "I know Eve always worried about money. But did the police search her house? Or her locker?"

"I don't think Ian told anyone she took the money. Except me. And you're the only one I've told."

"Maybe we should keep it that way," Faith said.

"Yeah." Janie nodded.

Faith shook her head. "It just doesn't make sense. Eve has never been in any kind of trouble in her life."

"I know," Janie murmured, feeling the urge to cry again.

"I mean, we were her best friends," Faith continued heatedly. "If she even *thought* about stealing the dance money, we would have known. Sooner or later. No way could she keep something like that from us."

"Ian thinks Ross killed Eve for the dance money," Janie said, staring out through the glass wall.

"Huh? That's *horrible!* What a thought!" Faith cried, truly shocked. She stared across the table at Janie. "What do *you* think?"

"I—I don't know what to think," Janie stammered.

"About what?" a boy's voice interrupted.

Janie raised her eyes to see Ross standing beside her.

Without waiting for an invitation, Ross slid in next to Janie. The sleeve of his leather jacket brushed against her. She edged over to the wall.

Glancing across the table, Janie saw that Faith wasn't doing a very good job of concealing her horror. She was staring accusingly at Ross, her features tight with anger.

"How are you two doing?" Ross asked quietly.

"Not too good," Faith said coldly.

A frosty quiet fell over the table. Janie found it hard to focus on Ross. Faith was staring at him with open disdain.

Janie struggled to think of something to say.

This was so awkward, so embarrassing.

Ross tapped the tabletop with a plastic fork.

Somebody—say something! Janie thought. The silence was suffocating.

But what do you say to a boy who may have murdered your best friend?

Finally Ross broke the silence. He leaned across the table, and his eyes burned into Faith's.

"Maybe I'll kill *you* next," he told her.

*F*aith gasped.

Ross's expression hardened. He continued leaning across the table. "That's what you're thinking—isn't it?" he accused Faith. "You think I killed Eve. You really think I'm a killer, don't you? Some kind of psycho!"

"No, we don't—" Janie started to say.

Faith was gripping the table edge with both hands, her blue eyes wide with fright. "What do the police think?" she asked Ross coldly.

"They believed me," Ross shouted. "But I can see what you two think! Well, I had no reason to kill your friend. No reason at all!"

He was practically screaming now. Heads turned. A waitress stopped in the aisle, watching him warily.

"Give me one good reason!" Ross demanded, glaring across the table at Faith. "One good reason why I'd kill Eve! Come on—I'm waiting!"

"You—you're crazy!" Faith cried. "Everyone is staring at us!"

"I don't care!" Ross hollered, slamming both fists on the tabletop. He let out an exasperated groan and started to pull himself out of the booth.

But Janie grabbed the sleeve of his leather jacket. "I don't think you did it," she told him.

He stared at her uncertainly.

"I really don't," she said. "Faith and I are just so upset and confused, Ross. We don't know—"

"Hey—there's Paul and Ian," Faith interrupted, waving at them through the glass. "I've got to go." She quickly slid out of the booth, not bothering to hide her eagerness to get away. "Are you coming, Janie?" she asked.

"Uh . . . in a minute," Janie replied, her eyes on Ross.

Faith hurried away. Janie watched her greet the two boys outside the restaurant. Ian and Paul stared suspiciously at Ross and Janie.

Janie turned back to Ross.

"You've got to believe me," Ross pleaded, grabbing Janie's hand. His hand, she was surprised to discover, was even colder than hers. "I didn't kill Eve. I had no reason to kill Eve. Do you believe that? *Do* you?"

"Yes," Janie replied quickly.

But she realized she didn't know what she believed. Something horrible had happened. And she felt shattered. In a million pieces, like a jigsaw puzzle. The pieces were all jumbled up. And some of them were missing.

Why was she thinking about puzzles? Why were her thoughts so crazy, so scattered?

What did she believe about Ross? What?

"Ross, why did you go out with Eve?" she blurted out.

He narrowed his eyes in confusion. "Didn't she tell you?"

"Huh? Tell me what?" Janie demanded.

"Didn't Eve tell you?" Ross repeated. "I went out with her for the money."

chapter
15

*J*anie gasped. "The money?" she cried. "You mean—the *dance* money?"

Ross acted confused. "No. I—"

A waitress interrupted. "Is something wrong with the pizza?" She pointed at the untouched pizza growing cold on its metal plate.

"No. It's okay," Janie told her, her mind spinning. "We're just . . . talking."

The waitress frowned and headed away, wiping her hands on her white apron.

"I went out with Eve for the bet money," Ross told Janie. "You, Faith, and Eve made a bet, right?"

"Oh, right," Janie said, feeling her face grow hot. *"That* money." She swallowed hard. "How do *you* know about that?"

"Eve told me," Ross replied. "She told me about

the bet. She said she really wanted to win it. She said we could split the twenty dollars she'd win. It was just a goof. You know. We had a good laugh about it."

"Oh," Janie replied lamely.

A good laugh, she thought. But now Eve is dead.

Lost in her sad thoughts, she suddenly realized that Ross was still talking. "I can't believe this is happening," he was saying. "Especially after what went down back in New Brighton."

"What?" Janie asked, shaking her thoughts away.

"Nothing," Ross replied bitterly.

"What did you say happened in New Brighton?" she asked.

"Nothing," he snapped. "Just thinking out loud."

Faith, Ian, and Paul were waiting for her out in the corridor of the mall. Faith flashed Janie a disapproving look.

"So? Did he kill her?" Paul asked.

Janie let out an angry groan. "How can you talk about it so . . . so casually?"

Paul shrugged. He ran one hand through his thick blond hair. "Sorry, Janie. I didn't mean anything. I was just surprised you'd stay in there with him."

"What did Ross tell the police?" Ian demanded shrilly. "Why did they let him go?"

"We didn't talk about it," Janie replied curtly.

"I'd stay away from him," Paul told her, snapping up his maroon and gray Shadyside jacket. "He's trouble. Really."

"You don't know anything, Paul," Janie said sharply. "Stop pretending to be so tough and wise."

Paul blushed.

"Why are you defending him?" Ian demanded. "He killed Eve. We all know it. I don't care what he told the police. We all know he took Eve to the woods and killed her. So why are you defending him, Janie?"

"I'm going home now," Janie said. "There's no point in our standing around discussing it."

"Yeah. Let's go," Faith said glumly. She took Paul's arm.

"Want a lift?" Paul asked Janie.

"No. I drove," she said, reaching into her jacket pocket for the key. "Hey, Paul—you got your car back?"

He nodded.

"I thought you needed a new transmission," Janie said.

"I got it," Paul told her.

"Where'd you get the money?" Ian asked.

Paul grinned. "What can I tell you? An early birthday present from a secret admirer." He and Faith walked on ahead.

Janie lingered, thinking hard.

How *did* Paul get the money? she wondered. Did Faith break down and give it to him? Faith had sworn she wouldn't.

So how did Paul get the money?

Monday night after dinner Janie was startled to find Ross at her front door. "Ross—what is it?" she cried, staring into his troubled face.

"It's my French homework," he told her, frowning. "I just can't get it. I heard you're good in French. I thought maybe you could help me. You know. Be my tutor tonight."

"Well, okay," Janie replied. She led him into the den.

How odd, she thought, to just show up at someone's house. There isn't anything shy about him.

She realized she was pleased, though.

He likes me, she thought.

She felt a chill down her back. If only I could throw away my doubts about him. If only I could know for sure that he's been telling the truth about Eve.

Janie realized she was very attracted to Ross, even with her doubts.

Sitting side by side on the couch, they studied French together. After about an hour Ross shut his book. "Well, I think I've got it now. You're a great tutor."

He touched Janie's shoulder lightly. Then he gently ran his fingers down her arm and took her hand in his. "Now let's go get something to eat. I'm starving," he said softly.

"Oh, Ross, I can't. It's a school night."

"Sure you can. It's only eight-fifteen. I promise to have you home by ten. So," he said as if the question were settled, "where should we go?"

Janie didn't want to risk running into Faith or Paul or Ian. They would only give her a hard time about being with Ross. So she suggested a little coffee shop in the Old Village.

"It's a neat place. And it's cheap," she told him. She hurried up to her room to get her down jacket.

Janie slid open her closet door, looking for something to liven up her basic jeans and long-sleeved T-shirt outfit. She found a wide black leather belt with a big brass buckle and wrapped it around her waist.

She still needed some color. She searched her closet again. Where was it? Where was that blue blazer . . .

She gasped as she remembered. She had lent it to Eve. Eve had been killed in it.

Janie dropped down on the edge of her bed, suddenly overcome with guilt. Was it wrong to be going out with Ross so soon after Eve's death?

She took a deep breath to let the feeling pass. Then she went back to her closet and pulled out a bright blue scarf to wrap around her neck. Still thinking about Eve, she made her way down to the den.

Ross was just sitting there, staring blankly at the wall. He didn't seem to see her come in.

What is he thinking about so hard? she wondered.

She watched him for a moment. Then she interrupted his thoughts. "Well . . . shall we go?"

Ross stood up and pulled on his leather bomber jacket. He motioned toward the door. *"Après toi."*

They were about a mile from Janie's house when Ross's blue Civic sputtered, made a strange coughing sound, and died.

"What's the matter?" Janie asked shrilly. She glanced out of the passenger window. She could see only dark woods. No houses, no stores, no streetlights.

They coasted to the side of the road and stopped.

Ross flicked the gas indicator with his finger, and the needle, which had been sticking straight up, sank down to *E.*

"Out of gas," Ross moaned.

He turned to her, his dark eyes glowing.

Glowing with excitement, Janie realized.

She shrank back against the car door.

No, she thought. No. This isn't happening.

Faith, Paul, and Ian warned me. They warned me not to go with Ross.

Cold panic rolled through her body.

They were out in the middle of nowhere, she realized.

There was no one to help her.

No one.

chapter

16

"*I*'m really sorry," Ross said softly, his eyes locked on hers. His face, hidden in shadow, moved closer. "I'm sorry, Janie."

What does he mean? Janie wondered, frozen in terror. Why does he keep apologizing?

Is he apologizing for what he's going to do to me?

"We'll have to walk to a gas station," Ross said. He turned away from her and pushed open his door. A burst of cold night air invaded the car. "There's got to be one nearby. We're not far from the Old Village. You coming?"

Walk with him? Walk with him through the woods?

The thought made Janie tremble.

But she didn't want to be left alone in the car either.

"You must think I'm a total jerk," Ross said. He

had climbed out of the car and was leaning in to talk to her. "I really thought I had half a tank." He shook his head. "At least it's not raining or anything. Come on, Janie. Let's go."

She hesitated. Her breathing slowly returned to normal.

He isn't going to hurt me, she told herself. He really ran out of gas.

I'm frightening myself. I'm shaking like a leaf. I got myself so scared, so scared of Ross. And it's all in my mind.

She felt embarrassed. And confused.

If I don't trust Ross, why did I come out with him? she asked herself.

"You coming?" he demanded impatiently. His breath steamed up in front of him. He jammed his hands in his jacket pockets.

"There's a Texaco station up ahead that stays open late," Janie suddenly remembered it. "I think it's just over the next hill."

"Great!" Ross exclaimed. "Scoot over. You steer and I'll push. I hope it's still open."

Janie scooted behind the wheel. Ross has no idea that he just terrified me, she thought. I think he'd be pretty shocked if I told him.

Shocked and hurt.

I've got to start trusting him, she decided. I really do like him. And I think he likes me. I have to start trusting him.

Janie watched Ross in the rearview mirror. He finished pumping gas, dug into the pockets of his baggy jeans—and came up empty. He patted the pockets of his leather jacket. Still no luck.

In the harsh glare of the gas station lights, Janie watched Ross mutter a curse. Shaking his head, his dark hair blowing wildly in the gusting night wind, he came around to her side of the car.

She rolled her window down.

"This isn't exactly my night," Ross muttered, very embarrassed. "I must have left my wallet at home. At least I hope it's there. Can I borrow five bucks?"

"No problem," Janie said, fishing a five out of her bag.

Ross took the money and ran into the station to pay.

For some reason Janie suddenly thought of Eve and the bet money. She and Ross had planned to split their winnings.

Janie sighed. Will I *ever* stop thinking about Eve?

A few seconds later Ross slid behind the wheel, buckled up, and started the car. "Sorry," he said, "but I'd better stop home for a sec to see if I left my wallet there. I don't want to get arrested—" Ross caught himself. "I mean, I don't want to get arrested for driving without a license." Leaning over the wheel, he pulled out of the gas station.

It wasn't until they passed the cemetery that Janie realized where they were. "You live on Fear Street?" she asked.

"Yeah," Ross said, turning toward her and seeing her troubled expression. "Why do I always get that same reaction when I tell someone where I live?" Ross asked, perplexed.

"There's just . . . a lot of . . . stories about this

street," she told him, watching the old, dark houses roll by.

"What kind of stories?"

"Stories about murders and strange creatures and ghosts and stuff," Janie replied, staring out the window.

"Give me a break," Ross muttered. "I stopped believing in ghosts years ago."

It suddenly grew darker as the car rolled past the Fear Street woods. Janie closed her eyes. Eve was murdered right around here, she thought.

To her surprise, Ross stopped the car. Janie stared out the window into the woods.

This is it, she realized. This is where Ian and I found Eve's body.

"Ross—why are you stopping here?" she demanded in a frightened voice.

"That's my house," he answered casually. He pointed across the street to a small, box-shaped house. There were no lights on, inside or out.

"But—but—" Janie stammered. "Right across the street from where Eve—"

"I know!" Ross said sharply. "Don't think the police didn't ask me a thousand questions because of it." He muttered something under his breath. Then he said, "Be right back," and he jumped out, closing the door behind him.

Janie watched him disappear into the darkness.

Now she was alone. Alone on Fear Street.

Parked right across from where Eve had been murdered.

Impulsively, she reached over and locked her door.

Then all the other doors. She stared toward the dark house, hoping Ross wouldn't take long.

Suddenly Janie saw movement at the front window. The curtains were pulled back slightly, revealing a thin crack of light. Someone was peering out.

At her.

Then the curtain was drawn closed. The house settled into darkness again. Janie shifted nervously in the seat.

Where was Ross? Why wasn't he back yet?

Hearing a clattering sound, she gasped and turned away from the house. She stared out the passenger window, her heart pounding.

What had made that sound?

She couldn't see anything. It was so dark. So unnaturally dark.

Was someone out there?

Behind her, the driver's door handle rattled.

Someone was trying to break into the car.

Janie opened her mouth to scream, but no sound came out.

chapter

17

*T*he door handle rattled again.

"Janie—let me in!"

Ross's voice.

Janie leaned toward the driver's window. "Oh. Ross! Sorry!"

She lifted the lock. He pulled open the door. "Did I scare you? I thought I left the door unlocked." He lowered himself into the seat and handed her a five-dollar bill. "I found my wallet. Now where to?"

Janie glanced at her watch, struggling to read it in the dark. "It's getting late. Maybe we should just grab some hamburgers at the White Castle."

"Sounds good," Ross agreed, pulling the car from the curb. "I'll drop you home by ten. Then I want to get home and go over my French assignment one more time."

He made a left turn on Old Mill Road. Janie slid closer to him, smiling, grateful to be leaving Fear Street.

A few minutes before ten Ross pulled his car up Janie's driveway and cut the engine and lights. Janie had started to say good night when Ross slid his arms around her shoulders, pulled her close, and kissed her.

She tried to resist, but his kiss became more insistent.

She kissed him back. Hard. Harder. She had wanted to kiss him all night.

He suddenly seemed so needy, so hungry for her kiss.

When the kiss ended, they were both breathing hard.

"Friday night," he said breathlessly. "Want to go to a movie or something?"

She nodded yes and mouthed the word, feeling almost as if she were in a trance.

Ross reached over her to open the passenger door, and suddenly they were kissing again, their arms wrapped tightly around each other.

This is amazing! Janie thought.

Finally she stumbled out of the car and ran to the front door of her house, still tasting Ross's lips on hers.

She closed the door behind her. The house was nearly dark. Her parents, she saw, had gone to bed early.

The light had been left on in the den. Janie made

her way to turn it off—and saw the textbook on the floor. Ross's French book. He had forgotten it.

I have to return it, she told herself. Ross said he wanted to study more tonight.

She grabbed the car keys and hurried back outside.

A pounding rain had started to fall. The wind gusted as if trying to push her back in the house.

She gripped the French textbook under her arm and hurried to her car. The idea of driving back to Fear Street on this dreary night made her shudder.

Why am I doing this? she asked herself.

To return Ross's book? Or to see him again? Maybe for another kiss? Or several kisses?

Feeling giddy and light-headed, she backed the car down the drive and started for Ross's house.

She could still feel Ross's arms around her, holding her so tightly. She could still feel the warmth of his lips pressing against hers so needily.

She sped through the rain, through the blur left by the clicking windshield wipers. The rain slowed a little as she turned onto Fear Street and his house came into view.

She pulled halfway up the gravel driveway and, leaving the engine running, jumped out.

Ducking her head against the rain, she ran up to the front porch. The house hovered in darkness. She turned around, searching for Ross's car, but didn't see it.

Shivering from the cold, she pushed the doorbell. She could hear it ringing inside.

She waited. Silence.

The wind blew the rain against the house.

Janie pressed the bell again, a little longer this time.

"Come on, Ross. Where *are* you?" she said out loud.

Was he asleep already? Was everyone inside asleep?

Maybe I'd better leave, she thought, sighing, disappointed. She started to step off the low porch when she heard the door lock snap.

The front door slowly creaked open. A very old woman, her white hair tied tightly behind her head, squinted out at Janie.

"Hi," Janie said, forcing a smile. "I—I'm sorry to bother you. I brought this for Ross." She held out the textbook.

The old woman squinted harder. "Who?" she croaked.

"It's for Ross," Janie repeated. "Ross Gabriel?"

The old woman shook her head. "Ross Gabriel? There's no one named Ross Gabriel here."

She slammed the door in Janie's face.

chapter

18

Janie went to school late the next day. She hadn't slept much at all.

She'd kept thinking about the house on Fear Street. Ross's house. And the old woman inside it who said that no one named Ross Gabriel lived there.

I don't like these mysteries, Janie decided as she shifted uncomfortably in her bed throughout the night. There are too many mysteries in my life now. Too many frightening mysteries.

I'm going to find out the truth about Ross, she decided.

She realized how much she was attracted to him, how much she was starting to care about him.

Am I falling in love? she asked herself sleepily, staring up at her bedroom ceiling.

Well, before I fall in love, I'd better learn the truth about Ross. The whole truth.

I can't be in love with him *and* suspicious and afraid of him at the same time.

In school she searched the hallways for Ross between every class. But he was nowhere to be seen.

At lunchtime she checked the attendance list in the office. Ross was listed as absent.

Janie hurried to the lunchroom. Faith was sitting by herself at their regular table with a glum look on her face and a pile of cookies stacked in front of her.

Janie dropped down across from her. "Where are Ian and Paul?"

Faith shrugged, frowning. She offered Janie a cookie. "Where were you last night? I called a little after nine."

"I . . . uh . . . was with Ross," Janie admitted reluctantly.

Faith's blue eyes widened in surprise. "Janie—you're not really going to tell me that you and Ross—"

"Everyone's wrong about him!" Janie blurted out in a shrill voice.

Faith rolled her eyes.

"No, really!" Janie insisted. "You're not being fair, Faith! No one is."

Janie couldn't hold herself in any longer. She hadn't been able to talk to Faith about Ross because Faith and the others were so sure that Ross had killed Eve.

But she *had* to talk to someone, and Faith was still her best friend.

Leaning over the table, her heart pounding loudly

in her chest, Janie revealed her feelings to Faith. She told her about the night before, about how much she was starting to care for Ross, and how she found herself frightened of him at the same time.

"I think you *should* be frightened," Faith interrupted, her eyes burning into Janie's.

"Huh? What are you saying?" Janie demanded.

"You don't know the real Ross," Faith replied with surprising bitterness.

Janie didn't like the way Faith said his name. She made it sound like a curse. "What are you talking about?" she demanded.

"Just some things I heard," Faith replied mysteriously.

Janie swallowed hard. She leaned closer to her friend. "Faith—what did you hear?"

"Just some rumors."

Janie felt a stab of dread. "What *rumors?*"

Faith's eyes narrowed. "Janie, listen to me. Don't go out with him again, okay? I heard some things. Maybe they're true, maybe not. I'm going to check them out. But in the meantime . . ."

"Faith, you're driving me crazy!" Janie screamed, feeling herself lose control. "You've *got* to tell me what you've heard."

Faith crinkled up the cookie wrapper. She frowned, chewing thoughtfully on her lower lip. "I have to talk to this girl first. Jordan Blye."

"Who?" Janie demanded.

"Her name is Jordan Blye. You've probably seen her. She's very tall and has long white-blond hair."

Janie gasped. She remembered the girl. She remembered the fear and horror on Ross's face when he had seen the girl in the hall.

"What *about* her?" Janie cried. "Who is she, Faith?"

"Jordan just transferred here from New Brighton High," Faith revealed.

"Ross's old school," Janie murmured.

"She knows some things about him," Faith continued. "She told Deena Martinson that—"

"Hey, what's up?" A boy's voice interrupted.

Janie spun around to see Paul behind her chair, an excited smile on his face.

"Paul, where were you?" Faith asked.

"Did you hear about Ross?" Paul asked, ignoring her question.

"Huh? Ross? What about him?" Janie cried.

Paul's pleased grin grew wider. "Wow, you two are really out of it," he said, shaking his head. "The whole school is talking about it. Ross isn't in school today because the police arrested him this morning."

Janie gasped. "Arrested him? For what?"

"For murder," Paul said, grinning.

chapter

19

*J*anie became cold all over. Faith, the table, the crowded lunchroom all seemed to shimmer away. She felt as if she were alone, alone in cold, dark space.

Murder. Murder. Murder.

The ugly word repeated in her ears.

"Janie—are you okay?" Faith's voice broke into her thoughts.

She found herself back in the lunchroom, back at the table, surrounded by loud voices, familiar faces.

And when she glanced at the doorway, she saw Ross.

"Hey—he's here!" she cried to Faith and Paul.

Did he see her?

No. He didn't seem to. She watched him stride slowly to a table against the far wall and sit down by himself. He had his hands shoved into the pockets of his leather jacket. He stuck his feet up on the ledge and stared out a window as if he were the only person in the cafeteria.

"Paul—you're a liar!" Janie accused him angrily.

Paul's round cheeks reddened. "I just told you what I heard."

Janie's chair scraped loudly against the floor as she scooted it back and jumped up.

"Janie—come back!" she heard Faith calling to her.

But Janie was already halfway across the lunchroom. She strode quickly over to Ross. He sat in sullen silence, gazing out the window. He didn't see her until she placed a hand on his shoulder.

"Hey!" He jumped, startled from his thoughts. He pushed a chair out for her with his shoe.

Janie realized that a lot of kids were staring at her. Let them stare, she thought. I don't care about their stupid rumors and ugly gossip.

She sat down across from Ross.

"You're not afraid to be seen with me?" he asked bitterly.

"Where were you this morning?" Janie asked. "Where were you last night? I drove back to your house."

"Huh?" His glum expression turned to surprise.

"You left your French book at my house. I drove to your house to return it," Janie told him. "But something weird happened."

He didn't reply. He waited for her to continue.

"An old woman answered the door," Janie said. "She said you didn't live there. She said she didn't know anyone named Ross Gabriel."

Ross uttered a long sigh but still didn't say anything.

Janie locked her eyes on his, searching for answers in them but not finding any.

Finally he lowered his feet from the window ledge and leaned toward her. "Janie," he said softly, so softly she could barely hear him over the voices and laughter at the other tables, "Janie, I'm going to tell you the truth."

chapter

20

Janie felt a cold chill down her back. Glancing across the lunchroom, she could see Faith and Paul staring at her.

"The old woman is my grandmother," Ross confided. "Her mind isn't quite right anymore. Sometimes she gets confused. She calls me by my father's name. And sometimes she confuses my father with her younger brother who died twenty years ago." He sighed. "It isn't easy having her live with us."

"I—I see," Janie said, feeling relieved.

"That's the truth," Ross said. "Do you believe me?" It wasn't a question. It was a challenge. "No one in this town seems to believe a word I say," he continued bitterly, not waiting for her reply. "How about you, Janie? Do you believe me? Or do you think I'm a liar, too?"

Janie could feel her throat tighten. She felt angry and hurt at the same time. This wasn't the Ross she had seen the night before. This was a sullen, angry Ross. A very different Ross.

"What's happened?" she asked in a trembling voice. "Where were you this morning? Paul said you were arrested."

"What's Paul's problem?" Ross demanded, shooting a furious glance across the room toward Paul and Faith.

"Everyone's talking about you," Janie told him.

He turned away from her and gazed out the window at the gray winter sky.

"So where were you?" Janie demanded.

"At the police station," he murmured, avoiding her eyes.

"Do you want to tell me about it?" she asked with real concern.

"What's to tell?" he snapped. "More questions about Eve. I guess your friend Ian told the police that Eve stole the twelve hundred dollars from that dance."

"He did?" Janie couldn't conceal her surprise.

"The police told me they searched Eve's house and all her belongings and couldn't find a penny. They even tried to check her parents' bank account. But— get this—they barely have any money!"

"That's terrible," Janie murmured.

"So naturally they came to me," Ross continued with a bitter sneer. "They wanted to know what I knew about the money. Of course I didn't know a thing. But I knew what they were getting at. They think I took it. They think I—" Ross shook his head sadly. "What do *you* think, Janie? Do you think I'm a thief and a . . ."

Murderer.

Janie finished the sentence for him.

A thief and a murderer.

"No. Of course not," she answered quickly.

Am I really so sure? she asked herself.

Am I really so sure what I think?

"Of course I don't think that," Janie repeated as if trying to convince herself.

Ross allowed himself a bitter smile. "Thanks," he said under his breath. He sighed. "It's all starting to get to me, Janie. Did you see the way everyone in the lunchroom stared at me when I walked in?"

"I know—" Janie started.

"All the rumors. Everyone talking about me. Accusing me," Ross said angrily. "Your friends. Faith and Paul and that skinny guy—Ian—I can see the hatred on their faces. I—"

"Eve was very popular," Janie said softly. "But don't worry about my friends," she told him. "When the police find Eve's murderer, things will change."

"Yeah. Right." Ross sneered. "*If* they find the murderer." He shook his head, avoiding her gaze. "Sometimes I feel like trouble follows me everywhere I go."

"What do you mean?" Janie asked.

He didn't answer. He appeared lost in his glum thoughts.

Suddenly his expression brightened. "Oh. I almost

forgot!" he exclaimed, reaching into his jacket pocket. "I've got something for you."

He pulled out something blue and held it out to her.

"No!" Janie screamed, jumping up. Her chair toppled noisily to the floor.

"No!"

It was Eve's scarf. Janie recognized it immediately. Eve's favorite scarf.

She must have been wearing it with the blazer the night she was murdered.

chapter

21

"Janie—what's wrong?" he cried, holding the blue scarf out to her.

"Are you *sick?*" she screamed.

Heads turned to gape at them. She heard cries of surprise around the room.

But she didn't care. She ran blindly for the door.

"Janie! Janie!" she could hear Ross calling after her.

But she kept running. Up the stairs and out the back door. Into the gray cold.

He's sick, she thought. He's really sick.

One minute he tells me how upset he is that everyone thinks he's a murderer. The next minute he waves the dead girl's scarf in my face.

He's crazy, she decided, gasping in mouthfuls of the cold air, her heart pounding.

He's crazy and dangerous.

I've got to stay away from him. I've got to.

Janie avoided him the rest of the afternoon. He tried to talk to her in chem lab, but she moved to a table at the front of the room.

She saw him hurrying toward her locker after school. She slammed it shut and escaped through the crowded halls.

Out in the student parking lot she searched for Faith. Faith, where are you? she thought, watching the cars back up and pull away. I need a ride home. I need to get away from here—fast.

She spotted Faith near the fence. Paul was standing beside her. Both of them were talking at the same time, gesturing wildly with their hands.

Janie started toward them. "Hey, Faith—"

She stopped when she realized they were in the middle of a screaming fight.

As Janie watched from behind a parked car, Paul yelled something at Faith. Then he jumped into his car, fired up the engine with a deafening roar, and squealed away.

Faith, red-faced, her shoulders heaving up and down, turned and started running from the parking lot.

What's going on? Janie wondered. She took a few steps toward her friend, then stopped.

Faith doesn't need me interfering now, Janie thought. I'll call her later, when she's calmed down.

I'll call her tonight. I'll tell her she was right about

Ross. I'll tell her about the scarf. I'll tell her how crazy Ross is.

I'll tell her everything. And then she can tell me about Paul.

Janie looked forward to confiding in her old friend.

As she began walking home she had no way of knowing that she would never see Faith again.

chapter
22

Ross tried to call her after dinner. But Janie made her mother tell him she wasn't home.

"Who *is* that boy?" her mother asked, staring suspiciously at Janie. "He sounded very angry when I told him you weren't here."

"Just a guy from school," Janie told her. "Do you need anything at the mall? I have to get out for a short while."

The mall seemed empty and depressing. Maybe it's just my mood, Janie thought.

After she picked up the few items she needed, she stopped at the Doughnut Hole to see Ian. She hadn't talked with him for a while. She wondered if he was feeling any better.

She found him behind the counter, wiping down the coffee machine with a wet towel. He turned, surprised to see her.

His glasses caught the pink light from the neon sign in the window. He looked pale and very tired.

"How's it going?" he asked, squeezing the towel between his hands. He forced a smile. "Want a doughnut? We're having a special today on jelly filled."

"No, thanks," Janie said, smiling back. "I just wondered how you were doing."

He shrugged his slender shoulders. He looked like a little boy in the too big red and white apron they made him wear. "Better, I guess. I still don't sleep too well."

"Tell me about it," Janie said dryly.

"When I do sleep, I have nightmares," Ian told her. "Really bad ones."

"Could I have some more coffee?" a man in a blue work uniform interrupted from down the counter. He was waving his plastic cup at Ian.

Ian picked up the coffeepot and hurried down the counter.

"How much are the crullers?" a teenage girl with blond hair piled high on her head asked. "Not those. Those." She pointed.

Ian bent down to the glass display case to check the price. The girl asked for two crullers. She pointed to the two she wanted.

Ian took care of another customer. Then he returned to Janie, a weary frown on his face. "What a night," he said. "I worked a shift at Sporting World right after school. Then I came here at six. Know what I had for dinner? Two chocolate doughnuts."

"Very healthy," Janie said, rolling her eyes.

Ian glanced up at the clock. "Only half an hour to go," he said, picking up the wet towel. "Want to go get a hamburger or something when I get off?"

Janie suddenly remembered she had planned to call Faith.

"No, I can't," she told Ian. "I've got to call Faith. I saw her and Paul having a screaming fight in the parking lot after school."

"So what else is new?" Ian remarked. He swept a hand back through his spiky brown hair. "Think they're going to break up?"

"I don't know," Janie replied. She realized she'd been so caught up in her own problems, she hadn't thought much about Faith and Paul.

"See you in school," she told Ian.

"Not if I see you first!" he joked without enthusiasm.

As soon as she got home, Janie hurried to her bedroom. She yanked the antenna up on her cordless telephone and pushed the button that automatically dialed Faith's number.

Faith picked up on the first ring. "Where have you been?" she asked in an exasperated tone. "I've been calling you all night!"

"I was at the mall," Janie told her. "I stopped to see Ian."

"Oh," Faith said. "How's he doing?"

"A little better, I think," Janie replied. "He really misses Eve, of course. But he's working so hard, he doesn't have much time to sit around and feel sorry for himself."

"I guess that's good," Faith said thoughtfully. She changed the subject abruptly. "Listen, Janie, I talked to that girl who went to Ross's school. You know. The one with the white-blond hair. Jordan Blye."

"You did?" Janie leaned forward on her bed.

"She told me some really frightening things," Faith confided.

Janie felt a cold stab of dread in her stomach. I don't want to hear this, she thought. But I have to.

"Frightening things? About Ross?" she asked.

"I'm afraid so," Faith said in a low voice. "Janie, this is going to upset you. But she told me that Ross—"

They were interrupted by a clicking on the line.

"Hold on a sec. That's my call waiting," Faith said.

She clicked off. The line went silent for nearly a minute.

Then Faith got back on the line. "Listen, Janie, can you come over? You've really got to hear this about Ross, and it's better to hear it in person. It'll be better if we're together."

"Faith—why are you keeping me in suspense like this?" Janie protested. "Can't you tell me now on the phone?"

"Come on over," Faith begged. "Please? I'm all alone here. My dad's at some cocktail party and my mom's still in Switzerland. And it's the housekeeper's night off."

"Well . . . okay," Janie agreed. "Then you can tell me about your fight with Paul, too."

There was a moment of silence on the other end of the line. "How'd you know about that?" Faith asked.

"I was in the parking lot. I saw you," Janie admitted.

"What a day." Faith sighed. "Hurry over, okay?"

Janie drove to North Hills, the wealthy section of Shadyside, and pulled onto Faith's long, circular driveway. As she made her way up the flagstone walk she was surprised that the front door was slightly ajar.

"Weird," Janie said to herself.

She nudged the door open. "Faith?"

No answer.

"Faith? Your door is open!"

Still no answer.

Warily Janie pushed the door open enough to enter the house. "Faith? Are you upstairs?"

No reply.

Janie made her way across the living room with its expensive antique furniture.

"Faith? Are you in the den? It's me."

The sweet, piny aroma of a wood fire floated out from the den. Janie hurried toward it, eager to find her friend.

She stopped in the doorway. On the far wall a fire was blazing away in the wide fireplace.

"Faith?"

Janie let out a shriek of horror when she saw her friend.

Faith lay sprawled on her back, her blue eyes staring lifelessly at the ceiling. Blood had seeped over a dark, gaping wound on the side of her head and ran in rivulets over her blond hair.

The brass poker from the fireplace lay at her side on the blood-soaked white carpet.

chapter

23

*J*anie tried to scream again, but no sound came out.

She pressed her hands against the sides of her face, her mouth frozen wide in horror.

Faith found out something about Ross—and now she's dead, Janie thought.

What did she learn about Ross? Janie wondered. And why did it cost her her life?

Her entire body trembled. The room began to sway and tilt.

She walked toward the leather couch and dropped down onto it, burying her face in her hands.

"Faith, Faith." The name escaped her lips.

What was that sound?

She raised her head and listened.

A door opening somewhere? A footstep?

"Who's there?" Her voice came out tiny and weak.

Was the murderer still in the house?

"Who's there? Is somebody there?"

No reply.

Another creaking sound.

Swallowing hard, Janie fought off her dizziness and lifted the cordless phone from the coffee table.

With a trembling finger she punched in 911.

"Hello—please! My friend—she's been murdered!"

The woman's voice on the other end remained calm. "What is the address, please? We'll have someone there in five minutes."

Janie struggled to remember Faith's address. Her mind was a blank. Finally she remembered it and stammered it into the phone.

"Oh!"

Were those footsteps? In the hall outside the den?

Dizziness swept over her.

I'm going to die. I know it.

The room started to spin. "I think the murderer's still in the house," she said into the phone in a hoarse whisper. "Please—help me."

The room tilted at weird angles.

I'm going to pass out, she thought.

And then I'll be dead.

"Get out of there immediately," the voice instructed her calmly and deliberately. "Just put the phone down and leave the house. Get as far away as you can. The officers are on their way right now."

"Hurry. Yes. I should hurry," Janie repeated. She knew she wasn't thinking clearly.

She wasn't sure she could stand up.

The room was spinning. Spinning and tilting. The fire was roaring. Roaring inside her head.

"Just get out of the house now," the voice instructed her firmly.

Janie let the phone fall to the carpet.

She took a deep breath, clutching the arm of the couch.

Stand up. Stand up. *You've got to stand up!*

She pushed herself up, ignoring the trembling of her knees.

One step. Another step.

To the den doorway.

The footsteps were coming closer.

Run, she thought.

I have to run.

But I can't.

The fire crackled loudly behind her in the fireplace.

Move! *Move!*

I can't! I'll run right into him!

Into the bloodstained hands of the murderer.

Think clearly, she told herself, leaning on the door frame. Think clearly, Janie.

But how?

I'll close the den door. And lock it.

Yes! I'll lock the door.

I'll be safe in the den. I'll be safe here.

She reached for the doorknob.

A figure loomed in front of her.

Too late.

Janie threw her hands in front of her face, backed away, tripped over her own feet, and fell to the floor.

As the figure stepped into the den, she gaped in astonishment.

"What are *you* doing here?" she cried.

chapter

24

"**J**anie—what's wrong?" Ian cried.

He moved quickly to help her to her feet.

"Ian—it's you," Janie moaned.

"Janie—what are you doing?" Ian demanded.

Then he saw Faith.

He froze, not moving, not blinking—as if the scene of horror had clicked a switch inside him, shutting him down.

"Ohhh," A strange cry escaped his lips. He dropped to his knees on the white carpet. His glasses fell off, but he made no attempt to pick them up.

"I—I just talked to her on the phone," he told Janie.

"Me, too," Janie said softly, dropping back onto the couch.

"She said she wanted to tell me something about

Ross," Ian said. "So I—I hurried over. The door was open. I—I—" His words ended in a muffled sob.

Ian moved across the carpet, past the bloodstained poker. He leaned over Faith to listen for a heartbeat.

"Ian, she's dead!" Janie cried.

Ian grabbed for his glasses, then stood up shakily. "We have to call the police," he said.

"I called them already—"

"We have to call them," he repeated, staring at her but not focusing.

"Ian, listen to me," Janie said slowly, deliberately. "I already called them."

"Why did Ross kill her, too?" Ian demanded.

"I don't know," Janie said, feeling hot tears roll down her cheeks.

"We have to call the police," Ian said.

"Ian, please. Sit down, I called them. I already called them."

"But we have to call the police," Ian said, his entire body trembling.

Janie uttered a sigh of relief as she heard the sirens growing louder, coming closer.

The funeral was held a few days later at Shadyside Memorial. School had been suspended that morning so friends and classmates of Faith's could attend.

Sitting near the back of the chapel, Janie gazed at all the flowers, so bright and colorful, so out of place on that sorrowful day.

In the front she saw Faith's mother, who had flown in from Switzerland for the funeral, holding hands with Faith's father, silent and close in their grief.

Paul sat a few rows in front of Janie. She saw him fighting back tears.

He really cared about her, Janie thought, wiping her eyes with a wadded-up tissue.

Ian sat in the same row as Paul, his face a sick yellow color, dark circles under his eyes.

Faith's friends were there, and there were many, silently paying their last respects.

Ross was not there.

Janie hadn't seen Ross since the afternoon he had plucked Eve's scarf from the pocket of his jacket and held it up to her like some cruel trophy.

The police were looking for him, Janie had heard.

So were his parents.

No one had seen Ross.

The final bell rang, signaling the end of the school-day. Janie pulled open her locker and began stuffing books into her backpack.

She turned to see Paul walking hurriedly in her direction, his basketball gear slung over his shoulder, dodging kids in the crammed corridor as if they were would-be point guards.

He slowed down when he saw Janie, hesitated, then stopped.

They hadn't spoken since Faith's funeral three days before. They had never really been good friends.

Paul mumbled hi.

She asked him how it was going.

"Okay, I guess," he replied awkwardly.

They stared at each other uncomfortably, unable to think of anything to say.

"I've got to go," Paul said, swinging his basketball uniform to his other shoulder.

"Me, too," Janie said. "See you."

Janie watched him head down the hall toward the gym. She suddenly remembered watching Paul and Faith arguing in the parking lot.

She had never found out what the argument was about.

It doesn't matter now, she thought bitterly.

She hoisted her backpack onto her shoulder and slammed the locker shut. Starting toward the door, her mind still on Paul, she bumped right into Jordan Blye.

"Oh!"

"Sorry!"

"Hi. I don't think we've met. I'm Janie Simpson."

"I know," Jordan said with a slight nod of her head, which made her curly white-blond hair bounce. "You were Faith's best friend, weren't you?"

Janie nodded. "Do you have a moment? I wanted to talk to you."

"It's about Ross, isn't it?" Jordan asked bluntly.

"Yes, it is."

A group of basketball players rushed past them on their way to practice. They pushed open the double gym doors, allowing the sound of bouncing balls to escape into the hallway.

"How about a short walk in the park?" Janie suggested, leading the way to the back exit. Shadyside Park stretched behind the school building, leading down through the woods to the Conononka River. "It's not too cold today. It's almost springlike."

"I can't wait till spring," Jordan said, "It's been such a long, terrible winter."

It was colder outside than Janie had thought. A gusting wind swirled around them as they walked. Jordan pulled up the hood on her down coat.

They walked past the teachers' parking lot, past the soccer field, past the baseball diamond, making small talk about school and their teachers.

Janie suddenly stopped and glanced behind her.

"What is it?" Jordan asked, nervously glancing over her shoulder.

"Just a feeling I had," Janie said. "Like we were being followed."

They hurried along a path into the woods. Above their heads the tree branches were still bare and brittle, as fragile and vulnerable as Janie felt.

Once again she glanced behind her. She couldn't shake the feeling of being followed.

But the park was empty.

"Sorry I'm so jumpy," Janie said. "It's just that—"

"You're afraid of Robert, aren't you?" Jordan interrupted.

"Who?" Janie asked, confused. "Robert?"

"Robert. Ross," Jordan said. "I told Faith I went to school with him last year. At New Brighton. Only his name wasn't Ross then. It was Robert. Robert Kingston. We called him Robby."

"Robert Kingston? Huh? I don't get it."

"He changed his name this year," Jordan said.

"Are you sure we're talking about the same guy?"

"I'm sure," Jordan replied. "You don't mix up a guy like Robby."

"Why—why did he change his name?" Janie asked, stopping in the path to face Jordan.

"I don't know for sure," Jordan replied. "I think it probably was because of his old girlfriend in New Brighton."

Puzzled, Janie studied Jordan's face. "Why would he have to change his name just because he broke up with his girlfriend?"

Jordan paused as if considering whether to go on. She took a deep breath. "They didn't break up," she said. "He killed her."

chapter

25

Janie gasped. She felt her breath catch in her throat.

She dropped down onto a low tree stump, letting her backpack fall to the ground.

Jordan stood over her, her expression grim. Her hood fell back on her shoulders, but she made no attempt to pull it up. Now that she had started talking, she needed no encouragement to continue.

"Robby's girlfriend was named Karen Anders. She had been going out with Robby for a few months, I guess. But I heard they broke up. Then Karen was killed. Murdered in the woods a few blocks from New Brighton High."

Janie shook her head, then gazed up at Jordan. "And Ross was arrested?"

"No," Jordan replied. "He was questioned. But he

had an alibi. The police let him go. But everyone in school knew he did it."

"They did?" Janie asked, feeling light-headed from hearing this shocking news.

"Yeah. You know how stories get out," Jordan said, tossing her hair behind her shoulder with a gloved hand. "Everyone knew Robby killed her. He acted really upset. But everyone knew he did it."

Dark storm clouds rolled overhead. The ground darkened. The bare trees shivered in a swirling breeze.

"Wow," Janie exclaimed, shaking her head. "Wow. Wow."

Secretly, she thought: How could I have been so attracted to this creep? How could I have let a *murderer* kiss me?

"The New Brighton police never solved Karen's murder," Jordan continued. "But anyone at school could have told them it was Robby. Robby got in some other trouble after the murder. He was in a stolen car with a bunch of guys. He said he didn't know the car was stolen. But who's going to believe that?"

Jordan made a disgusted face. "He's just trouble," she said. "His parents moved to Shadyside soon after that. To give Robby a new start, I guess. I guess that's why he changed his name to Ross. Gabriel is his mother's maiden name. He wanted a new start."

"Some new start," Janie said bitterly. A sob escaped her lips. "Some new start. He comes down here and murders my two best friends."

A cold drop of rain landed on Janie's forehead. Startled, she jumped as if she had been shot. Raindrops pattered against the ground.

Jordan reached down to place a comforting hand on Janie's shoulder. "He's bad news wherever he goes," she said softly. "But the police will catch him, Janie. Don't worry."

"I *am* worried!" Janie admitted. "I'm *very* worried. What if he comes back, Jordan? What if he comes back for *me?*"

Thunder rumbled overhead as Janie walked home. A jagged line of lightning cracked the charcoal sky.

Janie adjusted her backpack on her shoulders and lowered her head against the falling rain.

So cold. I'm so cold, she thought.

Cold as death.

She crossed Park Drive and started to run. The rain was coming down harder now. A river of rainwater flowed along the curb.

Pale white light rolled over the street in front of her. At first Janie thought it was another streak of lightning. But as the light stretched over her, she realized it came from car headlights.

She stopped running and turned, squinting through the curtain of rain.

And saw a blue car pull up beside her.

A small blue car.

Ross's car!

"No!" she cried out loud, starting to run again.

The window slid down. "Want a ride?" An unfamiliar voice.

She turned to see a young man in a black baseball cap grinning out at her.

"Want a ride?"

Janie breathed a grateful sigh. It isn't Ross. Thank goodness it isn't Ross.

She hesitated. She wanted to get out of the storm. But she didn't know this guy. "No, thanks." She had to shout over the steady roar of rain.

"Come on, honey. I won't bite," the young man called out, grinning.

"I said no thanks," she insisted.

"Really. I won't bite—unless you want me to!" He laughed.

"Get lost!" Janie screamed.

"Go ahead and drown!" he cried angrily. The window rolled up. The blue car sped off, its tires sending up a wave of rainwater.

What a creep, Janie thought. She realized she was trembling. Why are there so many creeps in the world?

She lowered her head and started to run down the street.

She was thinking about a hot bath.

Another crackling flash of lightning, then thunder crashed, making the ground shake.

Rainwater rolled down her face. She couldn't see a thing. The world was a gray blur. A cold, wet blur.

She ran right into him.

He grabbed the sleeve of her coat.

"Ross!" she cried.

His dark eyes burned menacingly into hers. He tightened his grip on her arm.

"Get into my car," he said.

chapter

26

"Ross—what do you want? Let *go* of me!" Janie screamed.

She struggled to pull free, but he tightened his grip. "Get in the car," he repeated through clenched teeth.

Janie saw the blue Civic across the street, the driver's door open, the engine running.

Ross said something else, but a roar of thunder drowned out his words.

"Leave me alone! Go away!" Janie cried, staring in fear at his hard expression.

How could I have ever cared about him? she wondered.

How could I have been fooled by him?

"I just want to talk," he insisted.

"You're hurting me!" she cried.

His eyes were wild. His dark hair was dripping. The rain poured down his forehead.

"Let *go!*" She jerked her arm away and started to run.

Her sneakers slid on the wet pavement.

He grabbed her around the waist. He shoved her into a glass bus shelter.

The rain drummed noisily against the bus shelter roof. He pushed her against the back wall.

"No! Please!" she screamed.

"What is your *problem?*" he demanded, his eyes wild, his features twisted in anger. "I thought I could talk to you!"

"No!" Janie cried, overcome with fear.

"You've been acting crazy ever since I tried to return your scarf!" he shouted over the deafening roar of rain.

"*My* scarf?" Janie screamed. "*My* scarf?"

Is he totally crazy? she wondered.

And then: Is he crazy enough to kill me right here on the street?

I've got to get him talking, she decided. If I can keep him talking, maybe someone will come along. Someone will see him holding me prisoner here. Someone will save me.

"Where have you been?" she demanded.

"Driving around," he said, pressing her shoulders against the bus shelter wall. "Driving around for days. I checked into a motel near New Brighton. When I heard about Faith I just lost it. I had to get away. I had to try to figure out—"

But you killed her! Janie thought.

Unable to hold back her fury, she cried out, "Why did you kill her? Why?"

His dark eyes narrowed. A roar of thunder drowned out his reply.

"Why are you accusing me?" he demanded.

"Oh, Ross—you're such a phony. I know the truth about you," Janie told him. "Your name isn't even Ross!"

She could see the shock on his face. "You—know?" he demanded.

"Ross, I'll help you," she offered.

"Huh?"

"We'll call the police," Janie said. "We'll get you help. You need help, Ross. You need someone to—"

"Shut up!" he screamed. "And stop fighting me!"

"Okay, okay," Janie replied, retreating.

I'm only making him angrier, she realized.

She gazed over his shoulder into the street. Why didn't anyone come by? Wasn't anyone going to help her get away from him?

A flash of lightning lit up the shelter.

"Get in the car," he ordered.

So much anger, Janie thought. It was this anger that made him kill Eve and Faith.

"No, Ross. Please!" she begged.

"Get in the car. I won't hurt you. I just want to talk. I *need* to talk to you, Janie."

"No—I can't! I can't, Ross." Her entire body was trembling. Her heart fluttered in panic.

"Janie—you're really upsetting me. I—"

119

"I'll meet you later!" she blurted out.

I have to get away from him now, she thought. I have to get home.

"You'll meet me?" His eyes studied her face suspiciously.

"Yes. Later," she said. "We can talk later."

I'll get home and call the police, she told herself. I'll tell the police where to find him. There's no way I'm going to meet him. No way.

"Where?" he demanded. "Where will you meet me?"

"Uh . . . at the mall," she said, her mind racing. "The pizza place. You know. How about eight o'clock? I'll meet you there at eight." The words tumbled from her mouth in a voice she didn't recognize.

He let go of her. The anger seemed to fade from his eyes. "Sorry," he muttered. "I didn't hurt you, did I?"

She shook her head.

Is he letting me go? she wondered. Is my trick going to work?

"I—I'm not thinking clearly," he said. "I've been so mixed up."

He's really crazy, Janie realized. Sick and crazy.

"Let me give you a ride home," he offered.

Now he's being his old self, Janie thought, staring hard at him. When the anger goes away he's a different person. It's like he's two people in one. Robert . . . Ross . . . two people in one.

"The rain has nearly stopped. I want to walk home," she told him.

His eyes narrowed suspiciously. "But you'll meet me tonight at eight? Promise?"

"Promise," she said.

She watched him from the bus shelter, her back pressed against the wall, until he slammed his car door and drove away.

I'm safe, she thought.

I got him to leave.

I'm safe—for now.

Breathing hard, her heart still racing, she brushed the wet hair off her forehead and shifted her backpack on her shoulders.

Then she hurried home.

The note on the refrigerator told Janie that her mother had some shopping to do. Then she was picking Mr. Simpson up at the airport. "Should be home around six-thirty. Please start dinner," the note said.

Janie tossed her backpack and wet coat on the kitchen floor. She sighed, disappointed. She had wanted to talk to her mother. She didn't want to be alone now.

Shivering in her wet clothes, she made her way to the kitchen phone on the wall next to the counter.

The police will pick up Ross, she assured herself.

I'll be okay.

She lifted the receiver to her ear.

Silence. No dial tone.

She clicked the phone several times.

Silence.

This happened every time it rained. The lines were down because of the storm.

Janie swallowed hard, trying to keep down the panic that swept over her.

I'm all alone here, she realized.

And the phone is dead.

Totally dead.

At eight-thirty Janie was nervously pacing back and forth in the living room. The curtains were drawn over the front window. All the lights in the house were on.

Where are Mom and Dad? she wondered.

She picked up the phone for the thousandth time. Still dead.

With an unhappy groan, she slammed it back down.

Ross must be at the mall now, she thought. He must have figured out that I'm not coming to meet him.

So where are Mom and Dad?

I need them here. I don't want to be alone.

She wrapped her arms over her chest, trying to warm herself. The hot bath hadn't helped. Neither had the dry clothes or the bulky sweater she had pulled on over her lighter sweater.

She stopped pacing when she heard footsteps on the front porch.

"Finally!" she cried out loud. "You're finally home!" She eagerly pulled open the front door.

Her smile vanished. She gasped. "Ross!"

He glared at her, his face half hidden in the glare of the yellow porch light. "Did you forget our date?" he snarled.

"You can't come in!" Janie cried. "My parents—they're asleep upstairs. You'll wake them!"

She tried to slam the door, but Ross jammed his shoe in the crack.

"Don't worry," he said coldly. "I can be very quiet."

chapter
27

Ross pushed his way into the house and shut the door behind him. Janie backed into the living room.

"So where were you?" he demanded, unzipping his leather jacket as he advanced on her. "When you didn't show up, I got worried."

He studied her face. All the while he scowled angrily.

"Listen, Ross—" Janie started to say. Her eyes darted around the room, searching for something she could use as a weapon.

"No, *you* listen," he said sharply, shoving his hands into his jeans pockets.

Janie glanced at the clock on the mantel. Mom and Dad, where are you? Please hurry!

"I see the look on your face," Ross said heatedly. "I

see how afraid you are. I know what you're thinking. It's what everyone else is thinking. That's why you didn't meet me—isn't it? Isn't it?"

"No!" Janie cried, unable to hold back her terror. "I—I was supposed to get a ride. From Paul. That's right. Paul was supposed to give me a ride to the mall. But he got hung up."

Ross shook his head bitterly. "You're such a bad liar, Janie. You really shouldn't even try."

"I'm not lying!" she insisted.

He took a few steps toward her.

She glanced at the clock again.

Where were her parents? Where?

When she turned back, Ross had pulled the blue scarf from his jacket.

He twisted it tautly around his hand.

Janie shrank back as Ross advanced on her.

"Ross—what are you going to do?" she cried.

chapter

28

Ross took another step toward Janie. Then he angrily tossed the blue scarf at her.

She made no attempt to grab it. Instead she shrank back from it.

"Here's your scarf!" he cried. "I—I don't understand. What did I do wrong? Why did the stupid scarf make you turn against me?"

Is it possible he doesn't know? Janie wondered.

Is it possible he doesn't remember killing Eve and taking her scarf?

"It isn't my scarf?!" she told him in a trembling voice. "The scarf—" She lowered her eyes to the floor and suddenly recognized it.

"It *is* mine!" she cried, raising her hands to her cheeks.

It wasn't Eve's scarf. It was the blue scarf Janie had

worn the night she and Ross had ended up at the White Castle.

"You left it in my car that night," Ross said in a low voice, staring down at the scarf on the floor. "So what did I do wrong?"

Janie's heart pounded. She could feel her face turn red.

"Tell me!" Ross insisted.

He's out of control, Janie realized. I made a mistake about the scarf. But that doesn't mean I'm totally wrong about him.

She stared at him, unable to hide her fright.

"I—I could *kill* you for not trusting me!" Ross cried.

Yes. I *know* you can kill, Janie thought. What am I going to do? How can I save myself?

"I'm not a killer," he said softly, moving closer, backing her against the sofa. "You found out about the girl in New Brighton?"

"Yes," Janie admitted. "I heard—"

"I didn't kill her. I was taking a shortcut through the woods. I found her. That's all. She was already dead." He swept his dark hair back off his forehead with one hand.

Why don't I believe him? Janie asked herself.

Why am I certain that he's a liar?

"The rumors started," Ross said bitterly. "They hounded me. The kids at school—they were vicious. My family and I had to move. And now—and now— it's happened all over again."

What a phony, Janie thought. Does he really believe the lies he's telling me? Is he really that crazy?

"I didn't kill Eve. I didn't kill Faith," Ross said, starting to pace back and forth, taking long, hurried strides. "I didn't kill them. I didn't kill them," he said in a singsong chant.

He's crazy. He's crazy and dangerous, Janie told herself, edging away from the couch.

"Why don't you believe me?" Ross demanded, stopping his pacing to confront her. "Why, Janie?"

She didn't reply. She just stared back at him, thinking hard, trying to figure out how to escape.

"I told the police," Ross confided, standing stiffly, arms tensed as if preparing to grab her. "I told them this afternoon. I didn't kill anyone. Why do they keep picking me up, asking me more questions?"

"You talked to the police this afternoon?" Janie asked.

He nodded. "They won't leave me alone. I told them I was at my cousin's in Waynesbridge when Faith was killed. My cousin backed me up."

He and his cousin cooked up a story to save Ross, Janie figured. The police had to let him go.

Now there was no point in calling them, Janie realized sadly.

"You're frightened of me," Ross accused her suddenly.

Janie didn't know how to reply.

"Look at you. You're terrified of me," Ross said, pointing at her scornfully.

"No! No, I'm not!" she protested.

What is he going to do now? she asked herself. Why is he *doing* this?

"You're totally frightened," Ross said, a strange smile on his face.

"Ross, just get out, okay?" she demanded, trying to keep her voice low and steady. "Just go home."

She could see hurt in his eyes. And then anger.

When he bent down to pick up the blue scarf, she darted away from the couch, ran past him, and headed for the front door.

"Hey!" he called angrily. She could hear him scrambling to catch up.

She tore open the door, shoved the storm door open with her shoulder, and, breathing hard, leapt off the front stoop.

Into the cold night, the ground still wet from the afternoon storm.

Her sneakers pounded against the hard driveway. Her breath burst out in loud, steamy gasps.

Got to get away from him. Got to get away.

She made it halfway down the driveway before he tackled her from behind.

She let out a groan of pain as she hit the wet pavement and Ross fell on top of her.

"You're not getting away," he growled, his breath hot in her ear.

chapter
___
29

"*P*lease—let me go!" Janie begged.

He rolled off her and quickly climbed to his feet. Breathing hard, he stood over her.

"You're not getting away," he repeated, "until you tell me why you don't believe me."

She climbed to her knees. The cold rainwater from the driveway had soaked through the knees of her jeans. Her elbow ached from where she had fallen on it.

"Tell me, Janie," Ross said softly, lowering his voice now. "Please tell me."

He can't decide whether to be angry or sweet, Janie thought. He can't decide whether to yell or beg. He's so mixed up. Robert . . . Ross. Robert . . . Ross.

I know only one thing for sure.

He isn't going to let me go.

He's crazy, and he isn't going to let me go.

The blinding white light made her cry out.

She grabbed the back of her head. For a moment she thought Ross had struck her and she was seeing stars.

But as the light rolled over her she realized it came from headlights.

Car headlights.

Her parents were finally home, finally pulling up the drive.

"Ross—it's my parents!" she told him. "My parents are here!"

To Janie's surprise, Ross had disappeared.

When the alarm rang the next morning, Janie awoke with a heavy feeling of dread. She pulled the covers over her head, trying to drown out the voices of her parents, already moving around downstairs.

She didn't want to go to school this morning. She was afraid Ross would be there, waiting for her.

She realized she was more afraid of him than ever. She had seen him at his worst. She had seen his violent side the night before.

Why had the police let him go? Why couldn't the police see how dangerous Ross was? Why did they always buy his excuses and alibis?

I won't feel safe until Ross is taken away, Janie realized. I *can't* feel safe until he's arrested.

Sure enough, he came after her in the hall at school before homeroom. When Janie saw him coming, she ran into the girls' room and waited for the bell to ring.

Leave me alone, Ross. Please leave me alone, she asked silently.

Later she had to run from the lunchroom when he tried to talk to her. And she cut her chem lab in the afternoon, hiding in the library because she knew Ross would be waiting at the lab table.

After school Janie quickly put her books into her backpack, eager to get out of the building. She slammed her locker door and started down the hall to the front exit.

And there he was.

Ross had just turned the corner. His eyes locked on hers. He was wearing a black sweater over black denims. His dark hair was down over his forehead.

Janie frantically spun around. She was desperate to get away from him.

The halls were emptying out. A few kids stood talking way down at the other end. A girl just past the next classroom was down on the floor, searching the floor of her locker.

"Janie," Ross called. "Wait."

She turned and began hurrying away in the other direction.

"Wait!" Ross called.

She heard him running after her. She started to run, too.

"Janie!" he called angrily, close behind her.

She turned a corner and heard laughing voices.

"Paul!" she cried breathlessly.

Paul and two friends from the basketball team were laughing hard about something. They stopped when they saw Janie's expression.

"Hey, wait!" Ross turned the corner. He stopped short, his eyes growing wide as he saw Paul and the other two boys.

"Leave her alone, man," Paul said, stepping in front of Janie. She was breathing hard, struggling to catch her breath.

Ross's expression hardened. Janie could see his jaw twitch. "I just want to talk to her," Ross said softly.

"Leave her alone," Paul repeated menacingly. He moved quickly toward Ross, his two friends right behind him.

Janie edged back to the wall.

Ross raised his hands high, as if surrendering. "Hey, I don't want any trouble," he said, taking a step back.

"You *are* trouble," Paul shouted. "You know something? I've been wanting to do this for a long time."

"Whoa!" Ross cried out.

Janie gasped as Paul let out an angry cry and his fist shot forward, landing hard in Ross's stomach.

Ross opened his mouth in a silent protest. His eyes bulged. His face turned purple. He grabbed his stomach and collapsed to his knees.

"Hit him again, Paul," one of the boys said.

I can't take this, Janie thought, feeling sick. I just can't take it.

Her backpack fell heavily to the floor. She started to run.

She could hear the excited shouts of the boys behind her. But she didn't look back.

She was running as fast as she could now. Out the

door. Through the parking lot. Through the cold gray blur of another rainy afternoon.

I can't take it. I really can't.

She ran through Shadyside Park behind the school, her sneakers thudding over the hard ground.

She ran until a sharp pain in her side forced her to stop. Gasping for breath, she dropped onto a tree stump by the path. The same tree stump where she had talked to Jordan Blye, where Jordan had revealed to her the horrible truth about Ross.

Burying her head in her hands, Janie began to sob.

Her shoulders heaved up and down as she cried. Cried for Eve. Cried for Faith.

Cried for her own fear.

There's *got* to be a way to prove that Ross is guilty, she thought miserably. There's *got* to be a way to prove that he killed my friends. My best best friends.

There's *got* to be a way to prove to the police that he's the one.

But how? How?

Alone in the silent park, Janie cried for a long while. When she finally stopped and raised her head, the sky had darkened. The trees hovered over her, black against a charcoal sky.

"I've got to get home," she said, sighing wearily.

Then she remembered her backpack. She had dropped it in the middle of the hall. Would it still be there?

Wiping the tearstains from her face with both hands, she hurried back to school. Would the back door still be open?

Yes.

Janie slipped silently into the building and made her way toward the front. No sign of her backpack. It wasn't where she had left it. Maybe someone had taken it to the office.

She turned the corner into the front hall and suddenly heard voices. The door to the principal's office swung open.

Ross stepped out, his head lowered. Mr. Hernandez had a firm hand on his shoulder. The principal had a stern expression on his face as he talked to Ross.

"Oh!" Janie gasped.

Had Ross seen her?

A stab of panic made Janie freeze for a second. Then she dived for the nearest doorway and pulled the door shut.

Total blackness.

This isn't a classroom, Janie realized immediately, her heart pounding. She had leapt into a small closet.

Shutting her eyes in the darkness, she pressed her hands against the closet door and listened for footsteps. A few seconds later she could hear Ross and Mr. Hernandez pass by.

"We cannot tolerate any kind of violence," Mr. Hernandez was saying.

What a joke, Janie thought bitterly. What world do you live in, Mr. Hernandez? Ross has already killed three girls!

Holding her breath, she moved farther back into the closet as they passed.

Something brushed against her cheek.

Something cold.

And dead.

Janie felt damp hair brush against her face.

She clamped a hand over her mouth to keep from screaming.

But she knew she couldn't hold her scream in for long.

There was someone else in this dark closet.

chapter

30

Janie's chest felt ready to burst. She couldn't hold the screams in any longer.

I've got to get out of here, she thought. Got to get out!

Fighting back her panic, she gripped the door handle and pushed.

The door didn't open.

A terrified moan escaped her throat.

The hair brushed against her face again.

She pushed the door. Pushed it again.

"Let me out of here! Somebody—let me out!" She tried to scream, but her fear muffled her cries.

Was the door jammed? Was she locked in?

Locked in with a corpse?

With a desperate cry, she rammed her shoulder against the door—and it swung open.

She tumbled out into the hall.

The mop tumbled out after her.

She gaped at it in shock. A large wet floor mop.

Not a corpse. A floor mop.

"This is what Ross has done to me," she muttered to herself, waiting for her breathing to return to normal. "He has frightened me so much, I am imagining corpses wherever I go."

She was trembling all over.

I'll never be calm again, she thought. Never.

Still breathing hard, she picked up her backpack in the office and hurried home.

The phone rang as soon as Janie walked in the door.

She glanced at the kitchen clock—nearly five.

Where are Mom and Dad? she wondered. Still at work, I guess.

She picked up the kitchen phone. "Hello?"

"Janie, it's me. Ian." He sounded breathless, excited.

"Ian—hi. What's going on?" Janie asked, pulling a can of Coke from the refrigerator.

"Janie—I've found proof," Ian said. "Really. I've found proof."

"Huh?" Janie was confused.

"I'll be right over," Ian said. "I'll take you there. I'll show you. Okay, Janie? Then we can both take it to the police. Okay?"

"Ian, slow down!" Janie cried. "Take *what* to the police?"

"The proof I've found," he replied breathlessly.

"Proof? What proof? What are you talking about, Ian? Why do you sound so weird?"

"Proof that Ross killed Eve and Faith," Ian said.

chapter

31

*I*an's yellow car pulled up her driveway ten minutes later. Janie hastily scribbled a note to her parents telling them she'd be back in a few minutes. Then she hurried out to meet him.

"Ian—what have you found?" she asked eagerly, climbing into the car.

His gray eyes flashed excitedly behind his glasses. He was wearing a bulky navy blue sweater over faded denims. The dark sweater made his face appear even paler than usual.

He flashed Janie a pleased smile. "Wait till we get there," he said softly. "I want you to see for yourself."

"You really have proof?" Janie asked.

He nodded, backing the car down the drive. "I really do. I really, really do."

"Well, where?" Janie asked impatiently. "Come on,

Ian. What did you find? Where is it? Where are we going?"

He raised a finger to his lips, signaling her to be quiet. "I want you to see for yourself," he insisted.

"I don't understand why you have to be so mysterious," Janie complained. "It's not as if we're playing a game, Ian. If you can prove that Ross is a murderer—"

"Don't worry. I have proof," Ian interrupted. He had both hands gripped on the wheel. He leaned forward, as if eager to get where he was going. "We're almost there, Janie."

He turned onto Fear Street.

"We—we're going to Ross's *house?*" Janie cried.

Ian shook his head. "No. Not to his house. Right across from it."

Ross's tiny boxlike house came into view on the left. The Fear Street woods stretched across the street from it.

"You mean—the woods? Where we found Eve?" Janie asked, unable to hide her horror.

Ian nodded, his expression solemn. He pulled the car up onto the dead grass, shifted into Park, and cut the engine and lights.

"This is where we found her," Janie said weakly, all kinds of horrifying pictures flashing through her mind as she stared through the car window at the trees.

"Yes," Ian said, reaching for his door handle.

"What did you find here, Ian?" Janie demanded. "What kind of proof? Did Ross leave something here?"

"You'll see. Follow me," Ian replied mysteriously.

Janie obediently climbed out of the car. It wasn't yet six o'clock, but the sky was as black as midnight. The moon and stars were hidden behind heavy blankets of clouds. The air was cold but still. Nothing in the woods moved.

She followed Ian toward the trees, toward the very spot where they had found Eve's lifeless body. "Ian, where is it? Over here?" she asked, feeling a cold shiver run down her back.

I never wanted to come back here, she thought unhappily. I never wanted to stand in this horrible spot again.

"Ian—please tell me!" she cried. "It's so dark. How can we see anything?"

Ian snapped his fingers. "Oh. Sorry. I left something in the car," he told her, shaking his head. "Don't move."

"D-don't worry!" Janie stammered. "Hurry back, okay?"

He disappeared into the darkness. A few seconds later Janie heard his car trunk slam. Then she saw him walking slowly back to her, a black figure against the dark sky.

"Ian—where's the flashlight?" Janie asked, shivering.

"No flashlight," Ian said softly. "I brought this. The proof."

What was he holding up to show her?

A baseball bat?

"Ian—what's that for?" Janie demanded, bewildered.

"It's the proof," Ian replied flatly. He was standing

a foot in front of her. He gripped the bat in both hands and took a swing, forcing Janie to take a big step back.

"There's dried blood on this bat, Janie," he said softly. "Eve's blood. It's the proof, see? It's the proof of who killed her."

"I—I don't understand," Janie cried, taking another step back. "Who—"

"I did!" Ian exclaimed. "I killed her! Here's the proof!"

chapter

32

"*I*an—what are you saying?" Janie demanded in a trembling voice. "Why are you saying that?"

"It's true," Ian replied, holding up the bat. "Here's the proof."

Even in the darkness Janie could see the strange, dreamy smile on Ian's face. "You—you killed Faith, too?" she stammered.

"I had to," he replied calmly. "You should know, Janie," he said, his tone turning nasty. "You were on the other line with Faith when I called. You were on the phone with her that night. She was telling you about me."

"Huh? No, she wasn't!" Janie exclaimed.

"Yes, she was," Ian insisted softly, taking a step

toward her. "She was telling you everything, wasn't she? About Eve and the dance money? Faith knew about the money, and she was telling you. Right?"

"No. No way," Janie told him, feeling a wave of fear roll over her body. "We weren't talking about you."

"You were, Janie. So I had to hurry over to Faith's before you got there. I had to make sure Faith didn't tell you more. But you already know too much—don't you?"

"Ian, stop!" Janie cried. "Faith and I didn't talk about you or the dance money. I never believed for a minute that Eve stole that money. I—"

"But she did!" Ian cried, raising his voice for the first time. "Do you believe it, Janie? Straight-arrow Eve! The most honest girl in town—she stole the money, Janie. And do you know why? She stole it for *me!* She stole it for me because I needed it to go to college."

"And—and you *killed* her?" Janie shrieked, the horror of his words sinking into her mind. "Why, Ian? Why?"

"Eve was too honest after all," Ian murmured. "She instantly had second thoughts. She said we had to give the money back. She said we had to confess what we did and give it back." He let out an angry sob. "I couldn't do that, Janie. I worked too hard. I couldn't get *another* after-school job. I couldn't give the money back. I didn't know what to do."

He took a step toward Janie, the bat tensed in both hands. "After work I went to Eve's house to talk to her. I had this bat. From Sporting World, where I worked. I was going to give it to Marky, her little brother. But Eve wasn't home. Marky told me she was out on a date. I—I couldn't believe it."

"Whoa. Listen, Ian—" Janie cried.

"Shut up!" he shouted shrilly. "Eve went out that night. With Ross. That wasn't right. I was so hurt. I was devastated. I deserved better than that. I worked too hard. Too hard. I waited. I watched Ross and Eve in his car. I saw them kiss. Ross drove away. I called Eve off the front porch. I still had the bat in my hands. I didn't mean to kill her, Janie. But I was so angry. I felt so . . . betrayed."

Ian let out another agonized sob. "After I killed her I drove her body here to the woods. Right across the street from Ross's house. I wasn't thinking clearly. My brain was all messed up. But I knew I could make everyone think that Ross had done it. I knew my life could return to normal."

"And the next morning you deliberately drove me here so we could find Eve's body together?" Janie demanded in a trembling voice.

Ian nodded. "So—Eve died. And Faith, too," he said, running a hand through his spiky hair.

He raised the bat in both hands and pulled it back. "And now you, too, Janie," he said softly. "I'm sorry. I'm really sorry. But I've worked so hard, so hard. I'm going to college in the fall. I've earned it."

"Ian—no! Please!" Janie begged.

"I've earned it, Janie," he said, preparing to swing the bat. "I can't let you ruin it for me."

"But Ian—" Janie murmured, backing away. "You're not going to kill me. You're not! Ross is standing right behind you." She pointed desperately over Ian's shoulder.

Ian let out a sarcastic groan. "Really, Janie. You can do better than that."

"Turn around, Ian," Janie insisted. "Ross is right behind you."

"Do you think I'm stupid?" Ian cried angrily.

"Drop the bat, Ian," Ross said. Even in the darkness Janie could see the tension on Ross's face.

"You!" Ian cried in shock, turning his head.

With an angry shout he pulled the bat back, then swung it with all his might at Ross's head.

Janie shut her eyes.

She heard a sickening crack as the bat hit its target.

She heard Ross's startled groan of pain.

When she opened her eyes, Ross lay sprawled in the dirt, and Ian was advancing toward her, the bat gripped firmly in both hands.

chapter

33

*I*an pulled the bat behind his shoulder, preparing to swing.

Janie took a step back, nearly stumbling over a half-buried tree root. Behind Ian she could see Ross sprawled lifelessly on his back.

"Ian—you killed *all* my friends!" Janie shrieked. "All of them!"

Ian swung the bat.

Driven by a fury she didn't know she could feel, Janie ducked under it—then leapt at Ian.

With an animal roar, she grabbed his shoulders, spun him around, and shoved him to the ground.

This is for Eve, she thought. This is for Faith. This is for Ross.

She grabbed the bat and dropped down onto Ian.

As Ian struggled to get up she kept him pinned down, the bat pressed against his throat.

"I—I can't breathe!" he gasped.

She pushed it down with all her raging strength. Pushed it. Pushed it and held it, choking him, keeping him down, down in the dirt.

For Eve. For Faith. For Ross.

To her surprise, she heard a loud groan of pain.

Still holding Ian down, she saw Ross slowly lift himself up.

"Ross—you're alive!" Janie cried happily.

"Am I?" he asked, sounding dazed. He pulled himself to his feet, rubbing his shoulder with one hand.

"Help me," Janie pleaded. "I can't hold him much longer."

Ross lumbered over and sat on Ian's chest.

Ian groaned helplessly, pinned to the ground.

Janie leaned her head against Ross's shoulder. "I—I heard a crack. I thought Ian smashed your head. I thought—"

"He choked up too much on the bat," Ross said. "Got my shoulder instead." He lowered his gaze to Ian. "Good follow-through, but you've got a choppy swing. You don't play much baseball, do you?"

Ian let out an angry growl in reply.

"Ross, how did you know we were here?" Janie asked.

"I'd been driving around, trying to get my head together," he told her. "I was just getting home when I saw you and Ian go into the woods. I had to find out what was going on. So I followed you."

"I—I'm so glad," Janie told him.

Ross smiled, the first time she'd ever seen him smile. He had a nice smile, she decided.

"You've been really good at running away from me," he said. "Let's see how fast you can run to my house and call the police."

"Okay." Janie jumped up, tossing the bat to the ground. Then she started running toward the street. Halfway there, she stopped and turned back. "Hey, Ross—I won't run away again!" she called.

Then she hurried across Fear Street to call the police and bring all the horror to an end.

About the Author

"Where do you get your ideas?"

That's the question that R. L. Stine is asked most often. "I don't know where my ideas come from," he says. "But I do know that I have a lot more scary stories in my mind that I can't wait to write."

So far, he has written nearly three dozen mysteries and thrillers for young people, all of them bestsellers.

Bob grew up in Columbus, Ohio. Today he lives in an apartment near Central Park in New York City with his wife, Jane, and thirteen-year-old son, Matt.

THE NIGHTMARES
NEVER END . . .
WHEN YOU VISIT

Next: *THE DARE*
(Coming February 1994)

It starts as a joke. Johanna Wise's gorgeous new boyfriend, Dennis Arthur, challenges her to a few easy little dares, just to see if she'll do them. She says she'll do *anything* to keep him. But he keeps raising the stakes.

One dare leads to another, until finally Dennis dares her to kill their teacher, Mr. Northwood. Soon the whole school is taking bets on Johanna. Will she do it? Or will she chicken out—and pay the price?